GORBALS DIEHARDS

To the Incredible Gorbals Diehards –
they came, they saw, they conquered.

GORBALS DIEHARDS
A WILD SIXTIES CHILDHOOD

COLIN MACFARLANE

MAINSTREAM
PUBLISHING

EDINBURGH AND LONDON

First published in Great Britain in 2010 by
MAINSTREAM PUBLISHING COMPANY
(EDINBURGH) LTD
7 Albany Street
Edinburgh EH1 3UG

ISBN 9781845965655

This book is a work of non-fiction based on the life, experiences
and recollections of the author. In some instances, names of
people, places, dates, sequences or the detail of events have been
changed for artistic purposes and to protect the privacy of others.
The author has stated to the publishers that, except in such
respects, the contents of this book are true

All picture section images courtesy of Glasgow City Council
planning and development department except where
otherwise stated

The author has made every effort to clear all copyright permissions,
but where this has not been possible and amendments are required,
the publisher will be pleased to make any necessary arrangements at
the earliest opportunity

A catalogue record for this book is available
from the British Library

Typeset in Didot

Printed in Great Britain by
CPI Mackays of Chatham, Chatham, ME5 8TD

1 3 5 7 9 10 8 6 4 2

CONTENTS

PREFACE

I was fortunate enough to experience the last decaying days of the Gorbals in the 1960s. So, in a sense, I am a witness to history. They really were incredible times to live through, with scarcely a boring moment. My friends and I had magnificent escapades that were sometimes a wee bit hairy. This meant that we all had to grow up very quickly and we felt like worldly-wise adults well before our time. Growing up in the old Gorbals was an education in itself and, because it was a melting pot, we encountered people from all over the world, with their own languages and cultures, who had chosen the area to be their home.

As Alex, Chris, Albert, Rab and I sauntered through the back courts and streets, we treated them as a sort of adventure playground and we were afraid of almost nothing – even though we encountered some of the most dangerous sorts of people you can imagine, including violent drunks and razor-gang members. However, we also met numerous very nice Gorbals people who worked hard to survive in what was considered to be one of the roughest and most poverty-ridden places in Britain. Our adventures on the streets were part of the process of growing up and we loved almost every minute of it. Whatever absurd events unfolded, we always kept our sense of humour and, as you will read in this book, laughter was our biggest friend.

The old Gorbals no longer exists but the memories of my childhood and the wild escapades of our gang, the Incredible

Gorbals Diehards, live on in this book. Although the Gorbals is often portrayed in the media as a mean place, I can honestly say I had a happy, and highly eventful, upbringing. In fact, when I look back, I often think that it was like being in an old black-and-white movie, with a host of individuals who were stars in their own right. In recounting the Diehards' exploits, I wanted to create as broad and vivid a picture of the area at the time as possible and, in order to achieve this I have allowed myself a degree of artistic licence; for example, some of the characters in these pages are based on more than one real person. In some ways, because I am writing about my life more than 40 years ago, it has been like writing a history book, with all the great Glasgow characters I knew then coming to life once again.

My thanks go to Ron Smith of Glasgow City Council's planning and development department, who was gracious enough to provide most of the old Gorbals photographs for this book; Norrie McNamee, who has a unique knowledge of the area; Bill Campbell, boss of Mainstream, and his team, including Graeme Blaikie, editor Claire Rose and designer Kate McLelland; the staff of the Mitchell Library; Mick Murray in Clydebank; the people of the Cardiff Marriott, including IT consultant and adviser Norman Faulkner, Dic and Margaret Cook, general manager Derek Harvey, front-office manager Vidyadhar Patole and concierge Lee Evans.

Thanks also go to the present MacFarlane clan, including Catherine, Philippa and James, who laugh at all my daft stories and jokes.

Colin MacFarlane

CHAPTER ONE

✳

LITTLE STAR

Twinkle, twinkle, little star,
How I wonder what you are!
Up above the world so high,
Like a diamond in the sky!
Twinkle, twinkle, little star,
How I wonder what you are!

Downtown Gorbals, 1966

I was lying in bed feeling exhausted after another gruelling day as a Gorbals street boy. But, strangely, I just could not get to sleep. It must have been something to do with the weather. For a change, Glasgow had been warm, almost Mediterranean, and my Scottish body was not made for such sweltering weather. I felt the muggy atmosphere had clouded my brain, dulled my senses, and at one point I started to imagine that I had been drugged by a mysterious potion administered secretly by an adversary. But I soon dismissed these adolescent thoughts, putting my odd state of mind down to the unusual weather.

The window of my bedroom in our tenement in Crown Street was wide open to let the air in, as earlier in the evening I had been finding it hard to breathe. But leaving the window open had its disadvantages. The reek of the middens and the outside toilets wafted through the air, and I felt as though I was trying to get to sleep in the middle of a sewer. It was a Friday night, and the smell was worse at the weekend. I assumed this was because of the greater consumption of alcohol, which would have drunken men urinating all over the place and the toilets overflowing with waste. Another negative aspect of the open window was that I could hear all the foul-mouthed shouting coming from down on the street.

After the oppressively hot day, a brief thunderstorm had sent rain cascading over the mucky streets, and the majority of the drunks had staggered straight home after the pub to avoid the downpour, but there were still a few drifting around like intoxicated nomads cursing for all the world to hear.

'Ya f***in' dirty bastard, ye! Ah'll kick ye in the baws so hard, ye'll need tae start pissin' through a tube, ya bampot, ye!'

'Aye, you and whose army?' came the reply. 'You couldnae punch yir way oot a wet paper bag! Ye're jist a wee bachle wi a big mooth!'

I was used to that kind of talk, but it was a bit on the annoying side considering I was earnestly trying to get some shut-eye. As the drunks drifted off, I heard a beautiful little voice floating through the air:

> When the blazing sun is gone,
> When there's nothing he shines upon,
> Then you show your little light,
> Twinkle, twinkle, all the night.
> Twinkle, twinkle, little star,
> How I wonder what you are!

I was intrigued, so I rose from my bed, walked towards the open window and looked out onto Crown Street. The rain had given the streets an almost polished look. In the tenements opposite, every window had a tale to tell. It was just past ten and the lights were still on in most of the flats. Through one window, children were getting ready for bed with their grimy string vests on; another revealed a bearded fellow glugging from a bottle of cheap El Dorado wine; a third showed a depressed-looking elderly woman staring onto the street as if her life had been washed down the drain; and yet another exposed a couple having an aggressive bawling match. I could hear their shouts clearly. 'Ye've been pishin' yir money against the wa',' the woman was shouting. 'How am Ah supposed tae feed the weans when Ah'm married tae a nae-use drunkard like you? Ma maw wis right – ye're no worth a nod in the desert, ya swine, ye.' It was pandemonium – but if the Gorbals was to have an alternative name, that would be it.

Looking down at the corner of Crown Street and Rutherglen Road, I saw the source of the beautiful voice. A small girl aged around ten and wearing a cheap-looking, soiled, floral dress was standing there. She had blonde curly hair and a pretty face. She was wearing a pair of green wellington boots, although it was the height of summer. In the Gorbals, this was a sign of real poverty. Children whose families could not afford proper shoes wore wellingtons all year round. I often imagined they even went to bed in them.

The girl carried on singing:

> In the dark blue sky so deep,
> Through my curtains often peep,
> For you never close your eyes,
> Till the morning sun does rise.
> Twinkle, twinkle, little star,
> How I wonder what you are!

I laughed to myself: the Gorbals Shirley Temple! As she was singing in her delightful tones, a shabby, intoxicated guy staggered over to her. He had been urinating against a nearby wall but the beauty of the girl's voice had made him zip up his fly, wander over and exclaim in a wine-sodden fashion, 'Ye've got a wonder . . . a wonder . . . ye've got a wonderful wee v-v-voice oan ye. Lang may yir lum reek, ma wee doll.' He then pressed what looked like a silver shilling into her little hand. She grasped the money tightly, and I saw that she had other coins in her hand. The drunk had not been the only one to appreciate her talent.

She carried on singing. Perhaps the man's compliment had increased her confidence, but her voice just sounded better and better. A group of women who were passing by stopped to listen. They looked as if they'd been out all evening on a hen night. One of them, a fat lady with a coarse voice, exclaimed, 'Oh, ye've got the voice o' a wee angel, hasn't she, girls?' They all chorused their agreement and proceeded towards the girl to press more coins on her.

'Thanks, ladies!' the Gorbals Shirley Temple replied. 'Ah'll put it towards gettin' maself a pair o' shoes so Ah won't have tae wear these wellies any mair.'

'Oh, poor wee soul!' the fat lady exclaimed, before she and her half-cut friends headed off towards Rutherglen Road and their beds. A few yards away, two scruffy-looking mongrels were humping in a corner, and two closes along a drunk man wearing a plastic Beatle wig was leading an equally drunk woman into a dark close, presumably to emulate what the dogs were up to.

As the little girl began to count the money in her hands, apparently oblivious to the fact that two rats were scurrying past her on their way to one of the filthy, rubbish-strewn back courts, a large fat-faced man appeared at a window in the tenement above her. He bellowed, 'Hey, get yir arse up tae bed noo, otherwise Ah'll gie ye a hidin'!'

The girl looked up at her father in the window and replied, 'But, Daddy, Ah want tae stay oot a bit longer tae sing. Ah've made ten shillin's awready.'

'How much?' Fat Face enquired.

'Ten shillin's,' the wee angel replied.

'Ah'll be doon noo,' Fat Face shouted back.

I had seen Fat Face quite a few times before and I didn't like him at all. The first time was when I was standing behind him late one night in a queue to buy the next day's *Daily Record*, which a vendor sold at the Bank Close in Crown Street. There had been a disgusting odour coming from him, as if he was a stranger to a bar of soap. He was steaming drunk as well and reeked of cheap wine. After Fat Face had gone, one of the guys hanging about on the street corner said to me, 'See that big fat bastard? He's nae good tae man nor beast. He drinks any money he gets, mostly fae sellin' scrap, and when he's drunk he beats up his wife and weans. They always look as though they need a good feed and a wash tae boot. It's time that piece o' shit got his comeuppance. People take an instant dislike tae him. It saves time.' Not long afterwards, I'd seen Fat Face's wife, frail and unkempt with two black eyes and trembling hands, asking for 'tick' (credit) in the local grocer's shop.

The girl had just finished counting her coins when Fat Face appeared on the street. 'Right, lassie, Ah've told ye, up the stair noo and gie me that money.'

'But, Daddy,' the little girl replied, 'it's ma money. It's fur ma new shoes.'

'F*** the shoes. Ye've got a nice pair o' wellies Ah got ye. Gie's the cash noo or ye'll be feelin' the back o' ma hand.'

'No, Daddy, please. It's ma money. Ah sang fur it,' she pleaded, with tears running down her cheeks.

'Any money ye get is mine, cos Ah'm the wan who clothes and feeds ye. Ah'm the stupid bastard who puts a roof over yir heid. Gie's the ten bob noo!' he shouted at her.

'No! Daddy, it's mine. Ah sang ma heart oot fur it!'

'Heart!' Fat Face shouted. 'Heart! Ah'll show ye heart!'

At this, he lifted his right hand and smashed the little girl across the face. She went flying, dropping the money on the pavement. Her nose began to run with blood as she lay in a heap on the corner. Fat Face picked up the money, then he lifted his bloodied daughter up, placed her over his shoulder like a small bag of coal and carried her into the dark close, shouting, 'F*** the shoes! That money is mine tae do whit a want wi, ya stupid wee besom!'

At first, I thought he had murdered her, but then I could hear the little girl whimpering. *A bloodied child in a bloody awful situation*. My first instinct when he'd hit her had been to shout from the window, but I realised there was nothing I could do to stop him. I stumbled back to bed in shock and mumbled to myself, 'Ah'm gonnae get that fat bastard even if it kills me.' And then, at last, I fell soundly asleep. At least with your eyes shut you can block out reality.

CHAPTER TWO

✳

THE BOYS

'Ah, vengeance will be mine!' I thought the next day as the sun cascaded down on the decaying tenements. It was another bright summer's morning, and I had a real feeling of optimism as I strolled out of my close and sauntered along Crown Street, where I bumped into my pals.

They were all around the same age as me, ten, and we had grown up playing on the Gorbals streets together. There was Chris, who had red hair and great patter and was utterly fearless. His parents were from hard-working Irish stock. They were the sort of people who, while they were not big drinkers, lived life to the full. There was wee Alex, a good-looking kid, thin with an almost Mediterranean look about him. He never really knew who his father was and lived in Thistle Street with his mother and sister. There was Rab from Hospital Street, the product of a wild family who had a reputation for being avid cheap-wine consumers. Their drinking sessions could last all day long. And there was Albert, probably my best pal, just ahead of Chris. Albert was out of his flat and on the streets early every day because he couldn't tolerate his home environment. In the poverty stakes, Albert and Alex were probably about equal.

Then there was me. My father was a chef and my mother a barmaid. They were in work most of the time. We lived in a not bad flat in a tenement in Crown Street. We weren't exactly well off, but we weren't as poor as many families who lived nearby.

We even had an inside toilet, a small claustrophobic cubicle, which was considered a luxury.

The boys and I thought of ourselves as a little gang, and the combination of our patter and personalities made us feel stronger than we would have done apart, almost invincible sometimes. The Gorbals was supposed to be one of the toughest places in Britain to live, but when our little mob got together we treated it like our very own adventure playground.

We had a gathering in a Thistle Street back court and I relayed to them what I'd seen the night before – Fat Face thumping his daughter. The boys looked alarmed. We all sat in a circle like conniving thieves, discussing the predicament.

'Then the big bampot slapped her right in the mooth,' I told them. 'He took the money and carried her over his back up the stairs while her nose wis bleedin'.'

Chris told us, 'Aye, Ah know the fat bastard ye're talkin' about. Ah wis standin' behind him in Cha Papa's fish-and-chip shop last week. And instead o' the smell o' fish, chips and vinegar goin' up ma nose, aw's Ah could smell wis three things.'

'Whit wis that?' I asked.

'Pish, shite and beer comin' fae that guy. He wis honkin'. He smelled like a rat had crawled up his fat arse and died. The big smelly bastard has had it comin' tae him fur a long time. Let's do him.'

Alex added, 'Ah heard he wis beatin' his missus up. Last week, Ah saw her in the dairy shop in Rutherglen Road. She had two black eyes, a bigger state than Texas. She told the woman behind the counter that she'd fell. Battered tae f***, mair like. She looked like she wis at the end o' her tether, as ma maw would say.'

Rab chipped in. 'That wee woman is goin' through a hell o' a time wi her man. She looks as if she's been a few rounds with Muhammad Ali. There's nae excuse fur that big lump o' lard givin' her black eyes.'

Albert tried to lighten things up. He was always quick with a joke. 'Whit d'ye say tae a Gorbals woman wi two black eyes?'

'Ah don't know,' I replied, expecting a genuine answer.

'You don't have tae say anythin',' Albert answered. 'She's been told twice awready!'

We all laughed, but we knew the situation was serious. Albert continued, 'Naw, jokin' aside, we're gonnae have tae do somethin' about that big balloon.'

Chris agreed. 'Let's burst him good and proper.'

It was then that we formulated a plan. We knew that Fat Face staggered out of the Wheatsheaf bar in Crown Street at about eight most nights. Presumably tonight, having squandered his daughter's ten shillings, he would be 'well fu" and would be easy to deal with. First, we would go over to his close and smash the bottom landing lights so that it would be in complete darkness when the drunken bully entered. Then, armed with sticks, we would beat Fat Face senseless and leave him in a pool of blood.

That afternoon we went through the back courts nearby, in Thistle Street, Crown Street, Rutherglen Road, Hospital Street and Florence Street, and gathered up the sturdiest planks of wood we could find in preparation for our assault. Alex, never one to think things through too carefully, had picked up a thick plank with a large, sharp nail sticking out of it. 'That reekin' nae-good swine is gonnae get this through the heid!' he exclaimed.

He looked half-mad as he waved the plank wildly about and it had me concerned. 'Naw, Alex,' I said, 'take the nail oot. We want tae beat the guy up, no do him in. We don't want tae end up on a murder charge. If you're gonnae wallop intae him wi it, go fur the baws, no the heid. Ye can still do a lot o' damage that way.'

Chris agreed. 'Ah don't want tae be locked up fur years fur murderin' a stinkin' nae-user. Take the nail oot and we'll gie him a good old-fashioned doin', wan that he'll never forget. In fact, wan that we'll never forget!'

It was agreed, then, that the attack would take place in the blacked-out close around 8 p.m. We had just finished hiding our weapons in a Thistle Street midden when three older boys approached us. They looked like Irish Gypsy types, all aged around 15 or 16. They were much taller and bigger than us. 'Hey, youse!' one of them shouted in a menacing tone. 'Are youse the so-called Gorbals tough guys we've been hearin' about?'

They might have been bigger than us, but we weren't prepared to back down immediately. 'Maybe we are and maybe we urnae,' I replied.

Chris was always the gamest one in such situations. He shouted back, 'Whit the f*** has it got tae do wi you, ya thick Irish bastard?' He was fearless, but at times like this I wished that he could have been somewhat more diplomatic. Calling the boy an 'Irish bastard' was a bit ironic, as Chris himself was the son of Irish immigrants. But he had been born and brought up in the Gorbals and considered himself a Gorbalian first, Irish second and Scottish third.

The boys ran towards Chris and one of them managed to send him hurtling to the ground. They then began kicking into him, shouting all the time. The kicks and punches were raining down on Chris and I honestly thought that he was going to be kicked to death. Amazingly, though, he managed to get to his feet, still defiant, and he ran off, shouting, 'The next time we see you tinkers, you'll be the wans gettin' a doin'.'

'Hey,' I called to them, 'that wis way out of order. There wis nae need fur that.'

The tallest of the boys just sneered and replied, 'You eejits should remember we're from Dublin and we're tougher than you. We could eat you for dinner. We're the new top guys in town, so don't mess with us.' He and the others walked off, giving us menacing looks and laughing like a pack of hyenas.

Alex, Albert and Rab shook their heads in disbelief. Rab said, 'They're that load o' gadgies who've moved intae Thistle Street. A bunch o' low-life hobos.'

'Aye,' said Alex, 'Ah heard they've been breakin' intae auld people's hooses and connin' them oot their money.'

Albert joined in, 'Ah've seen the faither, he's a right nae-user, a waste o' space. He's always oan the cadge fur a drink. Hangin' is too good fur they bastards.'

Chris appeared back on the scene, bruised but laughing loudly. 'That bunch o' vagrants thought they would have me cryin', but they'll never do that. Boys, it looks like we'll have tae put them oan oor hit list.'

'Yeah, ye're absolutely right,' I replied. 'But first of aw we've got that fat-faced liberty-taker tae attend tae.'

That night, we waited for Fat Face to come out of the pub. Sure enough, his stolen ten shillings had done the trick. He was steaming drunk when he staggered past us as a nearby clock chimed eight times. A short time earlier, we had rescued our planks from their hiding place and we were geared up for the attack. But as Fat Face tottered towards his close, I heard 'clip-clop, clip-clop, clip-clop'. It was the sound of the metal segs on a policeman's boots. As Fat Face entered his darkened close, two policemen were marching steadily towards us: 'clip-clop, clip-clop, clip-clop'. It was a threatening sound to us. It evoked images of handcuffs, being beaten over the head with a truncheon and lying in a dank police cell, of being banged up for a long time in approved school or Barlinnie prison.

The two officers reminded me of Laurel and Hardy. The stout officer was the first to speak to us. He had the air of an arrogant oaf. 'Hello, boys,' Hardy bellowed in a real 'teuchter' (Highland) accent. 'Has there been anything happening that we should know about?'

Laurel chimed in, 'Aye, you wee guys must know what's going on. Sure, you're playing out on the streets day and night. Ye must see a lot of things that we might be interested in.' That might be so, but 'tell the polis nothing' was a Gorbals mantra.

Laurel had a lower-middle-class Glaswegian accent but his fellow officer's twang sounded completely incongruous on the Gorbals streets. Hardy had told me before that he was from Gairloch, a quaint little fishing village on the west coast of Scotland. His family were all either fishermen or farmers. What the hell he was doing in the Gorbals baffled me. Mind you what the hell I was doing in the Gorbals also baffled me.

Hardy was out of breath after all his clip-clopping. 'Come on, boys, a wee word in my ear and we could make things a lot easier for you. For example, a wee bit o' the right information and we'll no longer book you for playing football in the street. You scratch our backs and we'll scratch yours!'

His back looked a bit too large for us to scratch; besides, we had a golden rule: never be a grass, never give the police any information they can use. We always used the mushroom technique on policemen; that is, keep them in the dark and feed them shite.

Putting on a serious face, Alex said, 'Well, officer, ma uncle broke intae . . .' He tailed off.

'Broke into what?' enquired Hardy.

Alex smiled. 'He broke intae a pound last week. He's always been a miserable so-and-so!' We all laughed apart from Laurel and Hardy. If looks could kill!

Chris was next to do a bit of mushroom growing. 'Officer, Ah'm disgusted. A clergyman wis walkin' through Gorbals Cross this mornin' and wan o' they hooligan gang members threw a bottle o' Domestos over him!'

'Oh, aye?' said Hardy, clearly interested. 'Who was the hooligan that threw the bleach and who was the holy fella?'

Chris replied, 'Ah don't know, officer, but Ah think ye should do him fur bleach o' the priest.' Perhaps Chris had gone too far. We all laughed but the officers were stern; their faces looked like they'd been carved out of Aberdeen granite.

Suddenly, Hardy announced, 'I'm burstin' for a pish.' He looked at the younger officer and said, 'Cover for me.' Laurel nodded in agreement. Hardy then went into a close and urinated loudly into the back court. I was sure that Niagara Falls would have been quieter. After he'd finished, he zipped up his fly and came towards us. 'Great pish,' he announced. I thought it was ironic, as I had seen him on previous occasions arresting harmless drunken men for doing the very same thing.

He then raised his unwashed hands and rubbed them through Alex's dark hair. It was the officer's way of showing us that we had been too cheeky and not shown them the required amount of respect. Alex just stood there, but I could see the anger on his face. His beautiful black hair had been polluted by a policeman's pish.

'Be good now, boys,' shouted Hardy as he clip-clopped off with the benign-looking Laurel.

'A couple o' clowns in uniform,' I muttered.

Alex's face had turned a bright, angry red and it was getting redder by the second. 'Ah'm gonnae shoot that bastard!' he announced. 'Shoot him right in his f***in' ugly face.'

'But, Alex,' I said, 'ye cannae shoot a polis!'

'Who cannae?' Alex replied. 'Ah'll show you . . . Ah'll show you all.'

He stomped off in a temper. But the thing was, I didn't disbelieve Alex. I was convinced he was really going to shoot the copper.

CHAPTER THREE

✳

SUMMERTIME

A few days later, there was a heavy banging on the door. It was shortly before nine in the morning and I had just got up. I glanced out of the window and noticed that the sun had graciously decided to visit the Gorbals yet again. On the radio, someone was singing the song 'Summertime' from *Porgy and Bess*. I opened the door and it was the boys, all grinning like the proverbial cats that had got the cream.

'We've got it!' Alex said excitedly.

'Got whit?' I asked.

'We've got an airgun,' Chris said in a jubilant tone.

'Aye, it's a cracker!' Rab said.

'Should sort that big polis oot nae bother,' Alex chuckled. 'Let's go doon the stairs and Ah'll show ye it.'

As we trooped down the stairs, I noticed that some of the landing windows had been smashed, which made the stench of the Gorbals summertime even stronger. The smell in the air was terrible. It was caused not only by the overflowing outside toilets but also by the filthy, brimming middens in the back courts. The middens contained everything imaginable, from the usual household waste to the rotten corpses of rats, and even dead cats and dogs. I began to sing, 'Summertime and the Gorbals is filthy. Rats are jumping and the rubbish is high . . .'

When we got to the first-floor landing, we found a man rolled up into a ball and sleeping soundly, oblivious to our presence and the stench that surrounded him.

'Bloody hell! It's a lobby dosser!' I exclaimed.

'Aye,' said Chris, 'we passed him oan the way up. We didnae want tae wake him.'

'The poor bastard looks like he needs a good kip,' said Alex.

'Even dossers need their beauty sleep,' Rab observed.

Lobby dossers were a common sight in the Gorbals. These homeless men, mostly alcoholics, had hit skid row and the only place they could have a half-decent sleep indoors was the lobby of a tenement. The man was a typical dosser, clad in what could only be described as rags. He was wearing a tattered army greatcoat. Presumably that was what was supposed to keep him warm through the night.

'Wake up, Jimmy!' I shouted. I didn't know his name, but at that time in Glasgow you could address any male stranger as 'Jimmy'. It was a precursor to the modern 'mate'.

'Aye, Jimmy, wake up before the polis do you!' Alex shouted. He wasn't joking. The police and magistrates were coming down hard on lobby dossers, sentencing them to heavy fines and even imprisonment. But I imagined that a cell in Barlinnie was surely preferable to sleeping in the lobby of a slum tenement in the Gorbals.

The dosser's eyes opened and he rubbed the sleep away. He growled and rose to his feet. 'Where the f*** am Ah?' he asked.

'Crown Street, the Gorbals,' I told him.

'Crown Street? How the hell did Ah end up here? Wait a minute, it's aw comin' back. Ah met a few o' the boys and we chipped in fur a carry-oot – bottles o' El Dorado and Lanliq, plus cans o' Tennents.'

'How did ye afford a carry-oot like that?' Albert enquired.

'Did ye have a win oan the horses?' asked Rab.

'Ah found an auld necklace in wan o' the middens and Ah went away tae pawn it. They gave me a couple o' bob fur it.' His eyes brightened up. 'And whit does any good Glesga man do when he's got money? He has a bevvy, of course! Ah bumped into a few cronies and we had a wee party in the back court nearby. That's about aw Ah can remember. If booze is the answer, Ah think Ah've forgot the question!' he said.

Then he pulled a wine bottle out of his greatcoat. There was still some 'electric soup' left and he took a glug. 'Ah, that's better!' he exclaimed. 'Ah'll be oan ma way, then, before the bizzies catch up wi me.' Reeking of wine, he gave a magnificent smile, flashing his rotting teeth, before making off down the stairs.

Alex laughed and said to Rab, 'That's how you're gonnae end up – a lobby dosser jist like that poor idiot!'

Rab became indignant at this insult, perhaps fearing there might be some truth in the comment. 'Aye, that'll be right! Ah'll never be a lobby dosser. Ah'm too fly a guy tae end up like that. When Ah get older, Ah'm gonnae have a big hoose – a mansion – in somewhere like Pollokshields, and Ah'll have servants, even ma ain butler. Mair like you'll be a lobby dosser, Alex.'

We all guffawed. Albert said, 'The only big hoose you're gonnae end up in is Barlinnie. But Ah suppose the wardens'll be like servants when they lock ye up every night.'

The banter continued as we headed through the close into the back court. As we made towards the overflowing midden, several rats darted out and scurried off. 'It's a pity we cannae eat rats,' Chris said.

'Why's that?' I asked him.

'Because if rats were OK tae eat, then naebody in the Gorbals would go hungry. There's enough here tae feed the starvin' millions in Africa.'

Alex entered the midden, waving his arms to brush away all the flies that were surrounding him. 'It must be great bein' a fly,' he shouted. 'Ye can zoom about the place and eat any auld shite!' He pulled several bricks out from the back of the midden and exclaimed, 'Here it is!'

He emerged clutching a Webley pellet rifle. It looked impressive. As Alex stood there holding it, he reminded me of a cowboy movie I'd recently seen in the George, the local cinema. This, of course, was not the Wild West, although some people did think the Gorbals was just about as lawless. There was a small rat sitting on a wall nearby, seemingly unperturbed by our presence. 'Watch this!' Alex told us. He took aim and fired. The rat was hit in the head and it went flying over the wall. The shot had killed it outright.

'Right, that's wan rat doon. The next wan who's gonnae get it is that big polis who put his pishy hands in ma hair!' Alex declared. I was a bit worried about all this. Killing a rodent was one thing, but what if he did the same to the policeman? Nobody could shoot a policeman, even with an air gun, and hope to go undetected and unpunished.

The boys had the same thought. Albert spoke up: 'But, Alex, ye cannae shoot a polis and get away wi it.'

'Aye, Alex,' Chris said, 'ye could end up killin' him and they'll lock ye up and throw the key in the Clyde!'

'If Ah wis you, Ah would stick tae shootin' rats and tin cans. The polis are way oot o' yir league. Who do ye think ye are? John Wayne?' Rab enquired.

'Ah'm gamer than that bampot cowboy. That polis is gonnae pay fur whit he did. As John Wayne would say, this toon ain't big enough fur the both o' us! Noo it's time fur a bit o' target practice!' Alex shouted, waving the rifle wildly in the air.

He raided the overflowing midden, found several empty cans and bottles and propped them up on a nearby wall. He took aim and fired. I was impressed with his marksmanship. He knocked down each bottle and each can with just one shot. He never missed a single one.

'Alex, shootin' cans and bottles is aw very well, but how are ye gonnae get away wi shootin' a polis?' asked Albert.

'Simple,' Alex said. 'See that brick wa' over there?'

'Aye.'

'There's a wee brick missin' and the hole looks doon oan Cleland Street. Those two polis usually parade doon there about three in the afternoon. Ah'll position maself behind the wa' wi the rifle until they come ploddin' along, then Ah'll fire.'

We agreed it was an incredible idea. We discussed our battle plan. Me and the rest of the boys would stand at a corner in Cleland Street and when we saw the policemen coming I would start whistling, as a signal to Alex that they were on their way.

We stood and waited for them to come. Three o'clock came and went, and still no sign of the policemen. When it came to half past, Chris said, 'Ach, this is a waste o' time, let's away and do somethin' else.'

The other boys agreed. 'Ah don't think they're comin',' said Rab. 'Alex'll have to wreak his vengeance another day.'

'Aye,' added Albert, 'maybe it's jist as well. Shootin' a polis is no somethin' ye do lightly.'

As he said that, I heard the familiar clip-clopping heading in our direction. I could see Laurel and Hardy coming down the street. Alex had positioned himself behind the wall. We could just barely see the tip of the rifle protruding from the small hole. I began to whistle loudly and quite out of tune, and I was sure Alex could hear me. Laurel and Hardy had wide grins on their faces as they made towards us. In a strange way, we kept them amused with our cheek and must sometimes have brightened up their day. 'Even clowns need someone to make them laugh,' I thought.

Breathing heavily, Hardy slapped me on the back and said in his usual tone, 'What's been happening, young man?' It was mushroom time again.

'Officer, the big fella's cracked up,' I said.

'Who's cracked up?' Hardy asked.

'Humpty Dumpty!' I replied. The boys and I laughed and even the two policemen seemed to find it funny. A brass neck can work wonders.

Albert was next. 'Officer, Big Nose has been in a bit o' bother.'

Hardy looked puzzled. 'Big Nose? Who the hell is that?'

'Pinocchio!' Albert answered.

The cheeky patter continued, then suddenly, right out of the blue, Hardy's right cheek exploded. He screamed, 'Aaaaaarghh! I've been shot!' and fell to the ground clutching his face.

Laurel was at first too shocked to do anything but then shouted into his walkie-talkie, 'Call for immediate reinforcements, a police officer has been shot!' The noise and commotion in the street had all the neighbours looking out of their windows.

Hardy got to his feet and spat out a mouthful of blood onto the street. The blood lay on the pavement and I could clearly see a pellet. Hardy covered the small hole in his cheek with a handkerchief and shouted, 'Don't go near that blood! It's got a pellet in it that forensics can have a look at. It's evidence.' A few moments later, the street was swarming with police cars. Hardy was taken away in an ambulance with Laurel escorting him to the hospital.

Two CID men approached us. 'Who did it, boys? You must know.'

'Ah hivnae got a clue, officer,' I said. 'It could have been anybody, cos Ah don't think that big polis is that popular roon here. He's arrested too many people fur daft things.'

'I know what you mean,' the CID guy replied, 'but the law is the law, and the Gorbals is the Gorbals. All he's trying to do is make people a bit more law-abiding, but clearly from what's happened today he's not succeeding.'

'Aye,' Rab said, 'Ah don't envy you guys. It must be like bein' Wyatt Earp in Tombstone.'

While the CID were questioning passers-by, Alex appeared at the street corner. The police were wasting their time because no one in the Gorbals would give the cops any information. Nobody wanted to be branded a grass.

I whispered to Alex, 'Good shootin'! Whit did ye do wi the gun?'

Alex grinned. 'Ah hid it back in the midden.'

'But whit about the fingerprints?' I asked.

'Don't be daft! Ah wis wearin' an auld pair o' gloves. There's nothin' they can pin oan us. In fact, they've got mair chance o' catchin' Hitler!'

As we walked away from the scene towards Crown Street, the boys and I could not stop laughing at the incredible scenario. It was a day we would never forget. One of us had shot a policeman, and now it was time to shoot off.

CHAPTER FOUR

✳

GETTING EVEN

'Get oot ma lobby, ya dosser! Get oot or Ah'll hit ye over the heid wi this. Ah'll beat ye tae a pulp if Ah ever see ye here again!'

I had just walked down the tenement stairs to find Mrs McDougall, a large stout woman, waving a frying pan at our favourite lobby dosser. She was shouting at Jimmy and he looked hungover and frightened.

'Awright, missus!' Jimmy shouted back. 'Ah wisnae daein' any harm. Ah wis jist havin' a kip, that's aw!'

'Well, if Ah see ye in ma lobby again, Ah'll batter ye. This is a respectable close and we don't want filthy lobby dossers like you sleepin' here. Away and get yirself a hoose like normal people,' Mrs McDougall shouted.

'Ah get the message. Ah'll no be back again. Yir lobby's stinkin' anyway!'

'Aye,' Mrs McDougall replied, 'and it wis you reekin' o' wine and pish that made it stinkin'. Ye're lucky ye didnae get this fryin' pan over yir heid, ye dirty bastard, ye.'

The scene struck me as more comical than sad. I met Jimmy at the close mouth, and the sun was still shining. 'Lovely day!' Jimmy said.

'Aye,' I replied, 'but no a good day tae have yir heid bashed in wi a fryin' pan.'

'No, son, ye're right,' he replied. 'Ah don't think Ah'll be kippin' there again. Ach, there are other places tae sleep anyway, and the weather isnae that bad.'

'Where are ye aff tae noo?' I enquired.

'Ah've got a pal who Ah said Ah'd meet at Gorbals Cross aroon ten this mornin'. He says he might have a couple o' quid comin' his way and if he does, we'll be havin' a wee party.'

He made off around the corner into Rutherglen Road. He looked like man on a mission. Mind you, all alcoholics look like that when they're on the hunt for a drink.

I met up with the boys. Alex, Chris, Albert, Rab and I walked along Gorbals Street towards the Cross. Standing outside of the bookie's was a man we called Peter the Punt. Unlike most racehorse fanatics, he regularly made half-decent amounts of money through betting, and he sometimes gave us a bung from his winnings. Peter, an ex-con, loved the horses and hated the police in equal measure.

'How's it goin', Peter?' we called out.

His eyes lit up when he saw us, but he just shrugged his shoulders and said, 'Ach, ye know how it is. Ah'm still waitin' fur the big win that'll change ma life. But Ah cannae seem tae pick a good horse fur love or money jist noo. Ma luck will turn wan o' these days.' He looked us up and down and laughed. 'You guys are no the size o' tuppence, and a wee bird tells me ye had somethin' tae do wi the big copper gettin' a pellet through the mooth!'

I wasn't surprised that he knew. The Gorbals had a grapevine that the police would never tap into, and Peter always knew what was going on.

Alex laughed. 'Peter, Ah'm sayin' nothin' until Ah see ma lawyer!'

There was more laugher and banter, and then Peter declared, 'Ah've got a new name fur you young scallywags!'

'Whit's that?' Chris asked.

'The Gorbals Diehards!' Peter replied.

'The Gorbals Diehards? That's no bad!' I said.

'No, even better,' Peter said, 'after shootin' that polis – it wis a phenomenal thing tae do – yir name should be the *Incredible* Gorbals Diehards! There's nae mistakin' it, you lads crack me up – you're incredible!' He then headed back into the bookie's, laughing loudly.

Me and the boys liked our new nickname. In fact, we were elated. We were now fated to be known locally as the Incredible Gorbals Diehards! We felt like comic-book superheroes. There was Superman, Spiderman, the Hulk, and now the Incredible Gorbals Diehards. No doubt about it, our new moniker sounded great. But what the hell did 'diehard' mean? 'There's only wan thing fur it,' I told the boys. 'We'll have tae go tae the library and find oot.'

We climbed the steps to the Gorbals public library and entered to find a stern-looking librarian behind the counter. His face fell when he saw us bunch of scruffs coming in. He must have sensed trouble. I decided to speak first. 'Sorry tae bother ye, mister, but we want tae find oot whit the word "diehard" means.'

He stroked his beard and gave us an inquisitive look. 'Are you being serious?' he asked.

'Aye, deadly serious,' I told him. 'Look, we don't want tae cause ye any bother, but it would be great if ye could find somethin' oot fur us.'

A look of relief came over his face, then he grinned and went to fetch a large dictionary for us. He laid the book on a table and flicked through the pages until he came to 'diehard'.

'There it is there,' he said, pointing his stubby finger at the place.

'**diehard** *adj. (always before noun)* supporting something in a very determined way and refusing to change. *noun* commonly used to describe any person who will not be swayed from a belief.'

'That's us tae a tee, boys,' I said. 'We stand up fur whit we think is right and naebody's gonnae change that.'

'Aye,' Chris said, 'we believe in ourselves and nae hard man, polis or drunk in the Gorbals is gonnae stop us!'

The librarian disappeared off to the shelves and came back with a volume of an encyclopedia. 'According to this,' he said, 'the phrase "die hard" was first used in 1811, during the Peninsular War. In the midst of battle, Lieutenant-Colonel William Inglis of the 57th West Middlesex Regiment of Foot was seriously wounded, but he refused to give up and shouted to his troops as they came under French attack, "Die hard, 57th, die hard!" As a result, "The Diehards" became the regimental nickname.'

'Great, mister!' I said. 'It looks like the Diehards were the sort o' brave guys who never gave up.'

'Who are you chaps and why do you want to know about it?' the librarian asked with a look of curiosity on his face.

'Oh,' I replied, 'we're the Incredible Gorbals Diehards!'

'Aye,' Alex added, 'and wan o' these days people might be readin' about our exploits in a book in this very library!' The librarian looked dumbfounded as we left, but there was a sparkle in his eyes.

We were all in a buoyant mood as we headed home, and we had almost reached Gorbals Cross when Chris exclaimed, 'Oh, no! Look who it is.' The wild Irish boys and their father were coming towards us. They were carrying two bundles and obviously in a hurry. I couldn't see what it was they were carrying, but I suspected that they had burgled yet another house. The father, a lanky man with thick, wavy black hair, was shouting at them, 'Hurry up, boys, for f***'s sake, before the polis spot us. Get movin', pronto, or you'll be gettin' my boot up your arses!'

When dealing with such people, there are times to be cautious and times to be brave. I could see that they were under pressure and decided that this was one of the latter.

'Hey, bampots, whit have ye got in those parcels? Have ye screwed another hoose?' I shouted. They looked taken aback by such insolence.

Chris shouted, 'Put that gear back where ye found it, ya bunch o' nae-good bloody tinkers.'

The father looked at us, his face filled with exasperation. 'Piss off, boys, can't you see we're busy? Be good, lads, and leave us be, otherwise you'll wish you were never born once Ah finish wi ye!'

'Hey, big fella, we're no scared o' you. You couldnae beat an egg, ya Dublin imbecile, ye!' Alex taunted him.

At this, the father ran over and tried to thump Alex, but he was too speedy for the big man and quickly outmanoeuvred him.

Rab was next to join in. 'Why don't ye get a job instead o' robbin' workin' people, ya big balloon?'

Albert shouted loudly, 'Get the f*** oot the Gorbals! Ye're no wanted here, so beat it! Scram!'

When he heard that, the father stopped and pulled out a large knife. 'Any more cheek from you eejits and you'll be getting this! So get out our road or I'll gut you like chickens.'

We didn't fancy being gutted like chickens, and we knew it was never a good idea to argue with someone who had a knife, especially an angry Gypsy with a knife, so we let them go on their way with their stolen booty. We weren't about to forget the incident, though.

Later, we found ourselves back in Cleland Street, where the shooting had taken place. The CID were still hanging around the place several days after the incident, still trying to get information, anything that would help them to capture the culprit. On seeing us, they were quick to approach. The taller of two officers said, 'Boys, you were here when the PC was wounded – have you heard anything? Do you know who did it?'

We all replied no and the officer looked disappointed at the lack of cooperation. He knew that we knew, and knowledge is power. He had one more go. 'Look, boys, my balls are on the line. The Chief Constable wants an arrest and heads will roll if we don't get one. I don't fancy being put on traffic duty for the rest of my career. So if you give us a wee bit of useful information I'll make sure you'll never regret it. It'll be remembered by us far into the future and if you ever land in trouble, it'll be taken into consideration.'

It wasn't a bad offer – quite good, in fact. 'OK, officer,' I said, 'Ah may have a bit o' useful information fur ye. Let's go intae that close away oot the road.' The boys were aghast, gazing at me as if I was a Judas. If looks could kill!

The policeman followed me into the close. 'What have you got?' he asked.

'Look,' I said, 'Ah'm nae grass, but Ah don't agree wi whit happened tae the officer. Ah know who shot him.'

'Good man!' said the cop, smiling broadly. 'Who was it?'

'Well,' I said, 'it wis . . .' I felt myself hesitating. I had never been an informant before.

'Come on, who was it?' the CID man urged.

'It wis . . . it wis . . . ach, Ah don't know if Ah can tell ye,' I said nervously.

'Look, I know you don't want to be thought of as a grass, but nobody will know you told me. It'll be confidential. Top secret! Who shot the policeman?'

'OK, officer,' I said, trepidation in my voice, 'it wis . . . it wis that bunch o' Irish tinkers who live in Thistle Street.'

His face drained of blood and took on a pale, chalky look. 'What? Those dirty bastards! Thanks for the info. This will not be forgotten, son!' He patted me gently on the shoulder, walked over to the other CID men and uniformed police officers and began excitedly telling them what he'd found out. They all jumped into their cars and panda wagons and sped up Thistle Street.

'Whit the f*** did ye tell that big CID guy?' Alex asked.

'Oh,' I replied laughing, 'Ah said it wis the tinkers who did the shootin'. Mushroom-growin' at its best!'

Chris laughed. 'That wis some move, man. You wurnae at the back o' the queue when they were handin' oot the brains, were ye?'

We ran up Thistle Street to witness the action. About ten policemen were banging on the door. 'Open up! Police!' they were shouting. But nobody was about to open the door for the police. 'F*** it!' one of the CID men shouted. 'Let's kick the door in.' They began putting their boots to the door and after a few minutes it flew open.

The father appeared, shouting, 'Piss off, you pigs, and get away from my house!' He threw a punch at one CID officer, sending the policeman flying down the close, then he kicked a uniformed officer between the legs. He could scrap! But the force of the policemen's truncheons battered him to the ground, still shouting. 'F*** the polis! You bastards'll never beat me!' But they did, and after several more minutes of violent struggle he was handcuffed and thrown into a Black Maria.

The rest of the police ran into the house and the boys were handcuffed and put in the van with their father. I heard one policeman shouting, 'F***in' hell, boys, it's like an Aladdin's cave in here!' They then began to take all the stolen stuff – including TVs, radios, jewellery and even women's handbags, into another van.

'No sign o' the gun yet,' commented one of the policemen.

'Aye,' his colleague answered, 'they're shrewd people, these tinkers. They've probably hidden the gun in one o' the back courts. But gun or no gun, we've got enough gear here to make sure they'll all be behind bars for a long time.'

CHAPTER FIVE

✳

THE GARDEN PARTY

'Aye, ye know whit they say,' one bunnet-headed patter merchant was saying to another as the boys and I walked past the Bank Corner on Crown Street.

'Whit's that?'

'When wan door closes, another wan slams shut in yir face!'

They laughed loudly as we went on our way, heading down Crown Street and through my close to the back court, where we found Jimmy the lobby dosser with some of his comrades having a Gorbals garden party. Now this was quite unlike the sort of thing you might imagine being hosted by the Queen or some other luminary. It was a gathering of down-and-outs who had chipped in enough money to buy themselves a 'carry-oot' consisting of strong wine and cans of beer. Jimmy was sitting with two other ragged fellows. One of them was so drunk he was unconscious and the other had an eyepatch. He was down at heel, but he had the look of an old seaman about him.

'Come and join us, boys, and gie's yir patter!' Jimmy shouted over to us. We were a bit apprehensive but went over as invited guests to this makeshift party. We were astonished at how much drink they'd got hold of. There were at least ten bottles of cheap wine and a dozen cans of beer waiting to be consumed.

Albert put on a posh accent and joked, 'How different from the life of our dear Queen!'

'Where the hell did ye get the money fur aw this bevvy?' Rab asked.

'Did ye rob a bank?' Albert enquired.

Jimmy took a glug from a large bottle of Four Crown wine and replied, 'Naw, don't be daft. The only bank Ah've ever robbed is a piggy bank. We pooled together a few coppers, stuck them oan a rank outsider and it romped hame. Here, boys, have a wee drink and help us celebrate!' He passed the wine round and I took a small slug. The boys did the same. We'd seen adverts for such cheap wine declaring things like, 'Demand Growing Daily!' or, more ominously, 'Sip with Caution'. We were streetwise enough to know that it was dangerous stuff. Some people called it 'wreck-the-hoose juice'. From what we had seen on the streets, we knew that ultimately it could turn people unstable and violent. Jimmy and his pals were certainly not sipping with caution, but we did.

Jimmy pointed to his comatose friend and told us, 'See that man there? He could have been a champion boxer, champion o' the world, but there wis wan opponent he couldnae beat: the bottle. Ah call him "The Mountie" because whenever there's a carry-oot he always gets his can!' He then waved his bottle towards the fellow with the eyepatch. 'And this here is Sinbad. He wis a sailor fur mair than 35 years and he's been aw over the world!'

Sinbad, who must have been in his late 60s, nodded his head and replied, 'Aye, boys, Ah wis a ship's cook fur aw that time and Ah've been everywhere ye can think of. You name it, Ah've been there, and a bird in every port! But Ah've decided ma last port o' call is gonnae be Glesga.'

It turned out that Sinbad, like Jimmy, had been reduced to dossing wherever he could find somewhere out of the cold night air. Listening to them talking, I imagined that the Apostles must have been like them: rough men living in rough times.

I had noticed that the typical drunken party went through three distinct stages: the humorous phase, the sentimental phase and the violent phase. As the two men bantered together, the humorous phase began.

'Boys,' Sinbad asked, 'do ye know why Ah left the Navy?'

'No, tell us, Sinbad,' I replied.

'Well, at the end-up, Ah wis in the submarine service. But they kicked me oot, because Ah wanted tae sleep wi the windaes open at night!'

On hearing this, Jimmy spat out a large mouthful of red wine all over the still unconscious Mountie. 'That's a good wan, Sinbad. There's never shortage o' laughs when you're aroon. You sailors always have a funny story tae tell.'

The gag itself was amusing enough, but I was sure I'd read something similar in the 'Merry Mac' fun page in the *Sunday Post* a few weeks before.

Sinbad was full of chat. 'There's nothin' compares tae messin' about in boats,' he told us, 'absolutely nothin'. But Ah'll tell ye this. There are many kinds o' ships – steamships, warships, cruise ships – but as we aw sit here it's proof that the best kind o' ships are friendships.'

So we'd discovered that Mountie the unconscious drunk had once been a pugilist with potential and that Sinbad had been an adventurer (and a Casanova) on the seven seas, but what about Jimmy before he had fallen to lobby-dosser status?

'Ah wis in the shipyards,' he recalled. 'Ah worked mainly as a riveter. Naebody ever uses the phrase "as pretty as a shipyard", but tae me it wis a beautiful place tae be. Everythin' wis overwhelmin'. The noise, the shoutin', the smells and the dirt were overpowerin'. But we were aw proud tae be producin' some o' the best vessels in the world. The patter wis brilliant. It wis surprisin' that we ever got any ships built wi aw the malarkey and shenanigans going on.

'Fur example, everybody had a nickname. There wis a guy called 'the Chinaman' because he had only 'wan lung'. There wis another guy who we always called 'Douglas' because his prize-winning greyhound had run away. There wis 'Polyfilla' – his real name wis Phil McCracken – and even an apprentice we called 'Brewer's Droop' because his name wis Wullie Falls. And there wis a foreman we called 'Such'.

'Why wis that?' I enquired.

'Well,' Jimmy replied, glugging from his wine bottle, 'wan o' the riveters, a wee dwarfy-lookin' guy, wis promoted tae foreman wan day. He called a meetin' o' his squad aroon him and let them know that noo he wis the big boss and the man tae be reckoned with. "And from now on I want to be addressed as such!" he said. Frae that day, we aw called him "Such"!'

Jimmy told us that the shipyards in the old days were overflowing with people, a cornucopia of colourful Glaswegian characters. Welders and riveters, along with caulkers, platers, blacksmiths, angle-iron smiths, sheet-iron workers, coppersmiths, shipwrights, loftsmen and burners comprised the 'black squad'. These were the workers who were at the hub of the shipbuilding process. In riveting alone, there was a catch-boy, a heater-boy, a putter-in, a hauder-on, a left-sided riveter and a right-sided riveter. 'The term "boy" applied tae the job, no the person,' he recounted, 'and many men were still rivet boys even when comin' near retirement.'

'It wis an experience like nae other, workin' wi people who had aw sorts o' skills and trades and aw sorts o' stories tae tell.'

'Whit about the bosses?' Albert asked.

'Ach, ye couldnae get movin' fur them. There were yard managers, engineerin' managers, boiler managers and various departmental managers. There were foremen, underforemen and chargehands. We called them "the bowler-hat brigade". We were sure their bowler hats were reinforced in case somebody dropped a rivet oan their heids. The managers aw walked about watchin' the workers and dockin' their wages if they saw any breach o' the rules.'

'Whit like?' asked Alex.

'Well,' Jimmy replied, 'fur example, it wis forbidden tae brew up oan the firm's time. If ye wanted a cup o' tea, ye posted a lookout tae keep an eye oot fur the gaffer. In some yards, they even had a "shit-hoose clerk" who wis employed tae monitor workers goin' in and oot o' the toilet. Some o' the toilets were nae mair than holes cut oot o' a board wi a trough o' water flowin' underneath. We called them "shitooteries". A lot o' the yards had a ratcatcher. But they were wurnae daft: they killed mostly male rats so's they'd never be oot o' work.

'The thing ye had tae be wary o' in the shipyards wis

sectarianism. When ye started, naebody asked ye face tae face whit religion ye were, but they clocked yir sandwiches every Friday.'

'Yir sandwiches? Why the hell would they do that?' Albert asked.

'Well,' Jimmy replied, 'if there wisnae any meat in the sandwich, they knew you were a Catholic. If ye were a Protestant and liked cheese, ye made sure it wisnae in yir sandwich oan a Friday in case folk thought ye were a Catholic. Protestants always made sure they had meat in their sandwiches oan the Friday. Ach, that kind o' thing had been goin' oan fur years. When ma faither wis 16, he went lookin' fur work, but in those days if ye were a Catholic in the shipyards, ye didnae get the chance tae learn a trade. Ye got employed as a labourer.

'Ah remember when Ah started, Ah wis shocked at first by aw the bad language and blasphemy, but that feelin' soon disappeared and before long Ah wis wan o' the boys. It wis a man's world. Ye had tae be able tae handle yirself and be prepared tae fight. Once ye showed ye were willin' tae go ahead wi anybody, things were awright. Ah rarely got in fights, though. Aw's Ah can remember is laughin' when we went in in the mornin' and we laughed aw day until we came oot.'

As more wine and beer was consumed, Jimmy's eyes welled up with tears as he began to tell us about his personal life. Here came the sentimental phase.

He'd met a pretty young girl at 'the jiggin'' in the Barrowland Ballroom and they were soon married with two children. They had a nice two-bedroom flat in Partick, but it was then that Jimmy started to drink his wages. Back then, he told us, wives would stand across the road from the yard gates on the evening of pay day, wearing their headscarves and determined looks on their faces, to ensure their men didn't blow their earnings in the pub. 'Ah remember wan o' ma pals sayin' tae me when he saw the line o' wives waitin' fur their fellas' pay pokes, "If Celtic had a back line like that, they widnae need a goalkeeper."'

Jimmy said that when his wife failed to appear one Friday night, he decided to have a 'wee bevvy' before he went home with his wages. But one thing led to another and he arrived home late. It was obvious that he had been up to no good. 'Right!' said his wife. 'Where's the pay poke?'

'Well, ye see, ma darlin',' replied Jimmy, doing his best to look sober, 'Ah had a wee bit o' trouble oan the way hame. Ma pay poke fell oan the street an' a big dug ate it. Ah've only got three pounds and two shillin's left tae gie ye.'

His wife grabbed the three pounds. 'Right, you!' she shouted. 'Keep the two bob and away and buy the dug!'

Many men, much to the concern of their families, drank most of their wages after a hard week spent in tough conditions. In the early days, the foremen paid out the wages in the pub, which more or less obliged every man who wished to continue in work to stand his gaffer a drink. But in the normal course of events, a man finished his week's work and then laid his pay packet on the kitchen table for his wife. She worked out the weekly budget and handed her husband his pocket money. The wife was the boss of the household.

But Jimmy had carried on drinking and his wife left him, taking the two young children to live with her mother in Bridgeton. 'When she left Ah hit the bottle big and wan day Ah jist packed ma job in and sold most o' the furniture tae get mair drink. Ah wanted tae be drunk aw the time. Maybe it's a family thing. Ma faither wis an alcoholic and so wis ma older brother. They're both deid noo.' The way Jimmy was drinking, even we could see that he was going to be following the family tradition soon enough.

After he'd left his job and lost his flat, Jimmy had taken to living in local 'models', model lodging houses, hostels for homeless men. When he'd found himself more often than not too drunk to be admitted to these, he'd taken to dossing on the streets. He sipped more wine and his eyes welled up as he began to sing an old street song. For a drunken old lobby dosser, he had a fine voice.

> When it's springtime in the model,
> The model in Carrick Street,

And the birds begin to yodel,
And the lodgers cannae sleep,
They get up and read the papers,
And wash their dirty feet.
When it's springtime in the model,
The model in Carrick Street.

The Diehards could feel the raw emotion in the air. It seemed to me that if the Bible had been written in the Gorbals, these men would have featured in the parables.

CHAPTER SIX

✳

SINBAD

It was autumn and the sky was already growing dark, but the garden party meandered on. The other Diehards and I had more sips of wine, and we could feel a mellow sensation coming over us. It was no wonder so many people in the Gorbals drank the cheap vino. Few people took anti-depressants; they preferred to self-medicate by getting stoned on the wine – or 'biddy' as some referred to it.

By this time, Jimmy was slurring his speech, but Sinbad looked quite compos mentis. Jimmy pointed over to Sinbad and suddenly announced, 'See that bampot there? Me and him are related through drink.'

'Aye,' Sinbad responded, 'Ah didnae know ye drank until Ah saw ye sober wan day.'

Suddenly, a large wet patch appeared on the left leg of Jimmy's trousers and a pool of pee began to develop round his feet. 'Bloody hell, Jimmy, ye're so drunk ye cannae even stand up tae pish,' Sinbad announced. Jimmy broke wind, then let out a groan and promptly fell asleep, just like his friend Mountie. 'Two down, one to go!' I thought.

'So whit about you, Sinbad? Ye say ye were a sailor. Whit did ye get up tae?' Chris asked.

'Ah'll bet ye've got a few tales tae tell,' Albert chipped in.

'Tales tae tell? Tales tae tell? They could write a book and make a movie about ma life!' Sinbad replied. 'There's an auld sayin': "Ah am the master o' my fate, Ah am the captain o' ma soul."'

Sinbad had joined the Merchant Navy when he was 16. He'd got aboard a ship in the Broomielaw 'tae escape Glesga'. 'At that time,' he explained, 'Ah wis a bit o' a wild guy and runnin' about wi gangs. Ah'd found that Ah wis quite good at usin' a cut-throat razor, so when anybody got up ma nose, Ah cut their face. Ah wis young and daft, and it wis a daft mistake tae start runnin' roon wi the wrang folk. Ach, mind you, a person who never made a mistake never made anythin'. The polis were after me, so tae avoid jail Ah jumped oan a ship and got oot o' toon fur a while. The boat wis headin' tae Bangkok, and ma way o' thinkin' wis that Bangkok wis bound tae be better than bein' banged up in Barlinnie!

'Ah had only been oan the boat a few weeks when ma navy cap flew aff. The storeman told me Ah'd have tae pay fur it. But Ah told him it wis blown aff while Ah wis oan duty. He said it didnae matter, anythin' you lose in the Navy has tae be paid fur. Well, Ah said, now Ah know why the captain always goes doon wi his ship!'

His wanderlust took him to Hong Kong, where he met 'a wonderful Chinese lassie'. 'She wis great and helped me grow up,' he told us. Sinbad had got the girl pregnant and had a son who lived in Hong Kong. In fact, he seemed to have got women pregnant all over the world. He claimed to have children in Australia, Italy, France, the USA, Ireland and South America. But to me and the boys, he was an ugly-looking character, with grey hair, rotting teeth and an extremely weather-beaten face. 'Look,' he explained, 'Ah'll admit Ah'm nae oil paintin' noo, but in ma younger days the lassies, nae matter where in the world Ah wis, would be queuin' up tae go oot wi me. Time catches up wi every man. It's a great healer, but it isnae a great beautician!'

After romancing all over the globe, Sinbad had returned for a while to Glasgow, where he met a waitress and got married. He landed himself a job as a labourer in an engineering factory, which he hated, and the couple had two boys. 'Ach, those were good times, but Ah missed the sea and kept thinkin' o' ma other children aroon the world. Ah felt trapped and wanted tae get oot but couldnae jist run aff tae sea. Ah wis supposed tae be settled but got really depressed and decided tae gas maself. Ah jist couldnae face goin' back tae the factory every day. So while ma wife and weans were oot, Ah turned the oven oan and when there wis enough gas, Ah wis gonntae stick ma heid in it.

'Ah had turned the gas oan full when Ah noticed a copy of the *Evening Times* wis lyin' oan the kitchen table. It wis open and Ah could see part o' a headline. It read "NO SUICIDE". It wis the racin' section and that wis the name o' a horse runnin' that day. Ah thought it wis message fae God. Ah turned the gas aff and decided tae carry oan wi ma life. That headline and that horse saved ma life.'

As Sinbad was finishing his story there was an almighty groan and Mountie sprang to life. 'Where the f*** am Ah?' he growled. He got to his feet and I noticed how big his hands were. They were like shovels. He had thick red hair that looked as if it had seen neither a wash nor a comb for quite a while.

'Relax,' Sinbad told him, 'you're in the Gorbals, at a wee party wi friends.'

The big fellow looked round and stared closely at us. 'Gie's a drink, Sinbad!' he cried, waving his arms wildly. Sinbad handed him a large, full bottle of El Dorado and Mountie began to drink it like lemonade. Then he started to prance around throwing right and left hooks into the air. 'Ah'll show ye that there's still a good punch left in me yet,' he exclaimed to us. We laughed, realising that Mountie was a typical punch-drunk drunk.

During our upbringing on the Gorbals streets, we had seen many men who had taken so many blows to the head that they ended up with a strange problem: they couldn't stop punching. It had become a nervous tic, an involuntary action brought on by damage to the brain.

'Sit doon, fur f***'s sake, Mountie,' Sinbad told him. 'Can ye no stop fightin' fur a few minutes at least?' Mountie sat down and glugged more wine, and as he settled down, he, like his two comrades in drink, recounted his life story to us. He had started boxing in a local club when he was 12, and he showed great promise. By the age of 16, he had a number of fine wins under his belt and had quite a few trophies. By the time he turned 18, even the newspapers were describing him as a promising up-and-coming talent. He pulled a crumpled old scrap of paper from his pocket and showed us a photograph of him as an almost unrecognisable young man with the headline 'Scotland's New Boxing Hope'.

'Ah got too full o' maself after winnin' wan fight after another,' he explained. 'Tae me, knockin' a fella oot wis as easy as squashin' a fly.' By the age of 20, he had got into the habit of celebrating every win by heading to the pub. But eventually the booze took over and he started not bothering to train. In one bout, he was knocked out so badly that he was left with brain damage. Because of his condition, the medical experts and boxing officials told him that he must never fight again. He appealed against the decision, but when he was turned down there was only one thing to do: head for a drink to help him forget his problems. From being a promising boxer with championship potential, his life sank into the bottom of a wine bottle.

'Ah could have been a champion. But those bastards widnae gie me a chance,' he maintained in his wine-sodden state. At this, Jimmy awoke from his slumber and shouted, 'Ye're talkin' rubbish! Ye couldnae batter a fish, ya big coward, ye.' Mountie's face turned red with anger. Jimmy continued, 'Call yirself a champion boxer? Come oan, then. We'll see how good ye are. Ah'll take ye oan noo.'

Jimmy rose unsteadily to his feet and carried on taunting the big man. 'Sit doon before Ah beat the crap oot ye!' Mountie shouted. It looked as if the violent phase of the party was about to begin.

'You beat the crap oot o' me? Aye, that'll be right!' Jimmy exploded. 'Come oan! Are ye man enough tae take me oan? You're a has-been and a never-gonnae-be! Ah'll show ye whit real fightin' is aw about, ya mug!'

To us young boys, the spectacle was highly amusing. Mountie was shaking his head in anger. He staggered over to Jimmy and gave him an almighty blow to the face. Jimmy went flying across the back court and hit his head hard against a brick wall. Blood began to run out of his mouth and nose.

'Ah'm gettin' the f*** oot o' here,' Sinbad muttered. 'Come oan, Mountie, take a couple o' those bottles wi ye and let's beat it before the polis turn up.' They staggered off towards the close and the street. Jimmy was moaning and he held up the left arm of his coat to stop the flow of blood from his nose and mouth. His face was as pale as a death mask. There was a little cut on his head where he'd banged it against the wall.

'Jimmy, ye awright?' Alex enquired.

'Aye, do ye want us tae call an ambulance?' a concerned Chris asked.

Albert got a rag from somewhere and began to wipe the blood off Jimmy's face. Rab helped to prop the dosser up against a wall and asked him, 'Are ye sure ye don't want us tae get help fur ye?'

Jimmy wiped more blood from his face and cried, 'F*** off, the lot o' ye! Jist leave me alone. Pass me another bottle o' that wine before ye go.'

We were concerned but we did as we were told. The sudden act of violence had taken us aback. 'Are ye sure ye don't want a doctor?' I asked again.

'Look, Ah told ye – get tae f***. Leave me alone, boys. Jist go! Ah'll be awright. Besides, Ah like ma ain company.'

By this time, it was cold and dark. We left Jimmy in the shadows and headed off, the boys to their houses and me up the stairs to our flat. As we walked away, Chris joked, 'Aye, that's the way we're headin'. In the future we'll be called the Incredible Gorbals Lobby Dossers!' We all laughed, but as I glanced over my shoulder, the sight of Jimmy sitting in the dark shadows, alone, drunk and homeless, sent a shiver down my spine. It was an image that would stay with me for ever.

CHAPTER SEVEN

*

A STRANGE DREAM

As I laid my head on the pillow, I felt a bit uneasy. The events of the day had unsettled me. But now I was away from it all – the drunks, the violence, the rats, the grubby streets and back courts. It was time to dream.

But it was not a dream that came, rather a nightmare. I was being pursued by giant metal machines, thudding their way towards me. Compared to these colossal contraptions, I was a small, insignificant creature that they wanted to exterminate. As the metal monstrosities continued to pound their way in my direction, I broke into a sweat and began to shout in my sleep. 'Help me! The machines are gonnae get me! Help me! The metal monsters are after me.'

Then I heard my mother's soothing voice. 'Wake up! There are nae machines. Wake up! It's aw a dream.' I found my mother and father beside my bed with worried looks on their faces. I was soaked in sweat. 'There, there,' my mother said. 'Ye see? It wis only a wee nightmare. There are nae big machines that want tae kill ye. Ye're safe in yir bed.'

I had had the same nightmare several times before, but what it meant I didn't know. Thinking back, I can only imagine that the machines symbolised the dangers that lay in the Gorbals streets and that my feeling of smallness represented my youth and how vulnerable I secretly felt.

I had an uneasy sleep that night and woke in the morning feeling somewhat exhausted. I glanced out of the window onto

Crown Street and saw the little girl who had been singing on the corner walking beside her frail-looking mother. They both had bruises on their faces. Fat Face had been at work again. I realised that, with everything else that had been going on, the boys and I had let our mission to get him back fall by the wayside.

The next minute, Fat Face came out of their close and shouted, 'Hurry up, ya couple o' lazy good-fur-nothin' bitches! Get the messages in and get ma breakfast made. Ah'm starvin' so be nae longer than ten minutes or Ah'll be givin' both o' you a hidin'. Get a move oan.' The mother and her daughter gave frightened nods and made off quickly to the shops, presumably to get bacon, eggs, margarine and a loaf on tick.

Watching Fat Face, I didn't feel scared of him, despite his size and his temper. I thought maybe the scary dream had toughened me up. Compared with the metal machines, Fat Face seemed no great threat. I began to wash myself in cold water in the kitchen sink, and the feeling of carbolic soap on my face made me feel a lot better. I rinsed my face, wiped it with a facecloth and now I was ready to play, ready to perform on the only stage I knew, the streets of the Gorbals.

I walked down the stairs and I could hear a commotion going on in the back court. Three women were talking animatedly in high-pitched voices. When I got to the bottom of the close, one of the women, wearing curlers underneath her headscarf, was saying, 'Ach, ye'd better call the polis. Ye cannae have that lyin' in yir midden.'

Another nodded in agreement. 'Aye, it's jist no right. It must have given ye a fright when ye first spotted it.'

Our neighbour Mrs McDougall looked as if she was in a state of shock. She was as white as a sheet and had been crying. 'Ah've called the polis and told them whit's in the midden, so hopefully they'll be here soon. Ma God, whit a shock that wis. Ah've never seen anythin' like that in ma life. It's like somethin' ye'd see in a horror film.'

I approached Mrs McDougall and asked, 'Whit's the matter, missus? Have ye found another rat in the midden?'

'Aye,' she said, 'ye could say that. Look inside and ye'll find oot. It's the biggest rat ye'll ever see.'

I didn't feel afraid as I walked towards the midden. I was used to seeing the carcasses of large dead rats lying around, but I knew women could get quite emotional when they came across one. However, when I looked into the midden a wave of shock hit me. Jimmy was lying there, face up, as dead as a doornail. He must have climbed into the midden to keep warm after we'd left the night before and died when the cold crept in.

'Aye,' Mrs McDougall said, 'it's definitely that dosser Ah caught sleepin' in ma lobby. Ah feel a bit guilty. If Ah hadnae banned him fae sleepin' in the close, he might be alive noo.'

'Don't be daft,' one of the other women said. 'It wis nothin' tae do wi you. By the looks o' him, he's been drinkin' and been in a fight. That'll be whit caused it.'

I went back over to the midden and, through the muck and blood, I could just make out the expression on Jimmy's face. He looked serene. Perhaps in death he had found the peace he had failed to achieve in life.

It wasn't long before the police arrived in the back court. 'What's the problem, missus?' one of them asked Mrs McDougall.

'Oh, we've had a dosser kippin' in our close and noo he's lyin' deid in the midden,' she replied.

The policeman walked over, glanced into the midden and shrugged his shoulders. 'I wouldn't worry. We get at least three cases like this every week. In fact, the dossers and down-and-outs seem to be dropping like flies at the moment. I think they must be poisoning the wine or something.' At this, the assembled women laughed nervously. The policeman got on his walkie-talkie. 'Yeah, dosser found in a midden at Crown Street. Please send an ambulance to remove the body.'

Then came the questions: 'Did anyone see anything? Did any of you know this man?'

One woman chirped, 'Aye, Ah gave him a shillin' last week. He told me he used tae be a riveter oan the Clyde, and before he lost his flat he'd lived in Partick.' The policeman went through the pockets of Jimmy's greatcoat. He pulled out some documents identifying him and found a photo, which he showed to us. It was Jimmy smiling with his wife and two children before he had taken to the drink.

'It jist shows ye,' one of the women said, shaking her head, 'that a man like that wi a good job and a nice family can end up as a lobby dosser and deid tae boot!'

'It would fair put the wind up ye,' added her pal. 'The demon drink has a lot tae answer fur.'

An ambulance soon arrived and took Jimmy's body away. No one mentioned the possibility of murder. To the police and everyone else, Jimmy was just another dosser who had met his end after too much drink and a mindless punch-up with another dosser.

When I met up with the other Diehards, I recounted the story to them. Chris said, 'Ach, that's a shame. He wis a nice, genuine fella as well.'

'Whit a way tae go – in a midden!' Albert observed. 'That's a fate that disnae bear thinkin' about.'

'It's nothin' unusual,' Rab told us. 'We found wan in oor midden last year.'

'If Ah ever get that bad when Ah grow up,' said Alex, 'Ah'd rather go oot and smash the windaes o' the local polis station tae get somewhere tae kip. Better lyin' in jail than in a bin! The guy had nae sense. The booze had rotted his brain.'

We walked along Cleland Street, through Gorbals Street and along Bedford Street to Eglinton Street. There, I saw Fat Face and another man pushing a barrow full of scrap. Fat Face shouted to us, 'Come oan, boys, we're takin' this tae the scrappie tae get weighed. Gie's a hand tae push it.'

'Push it yirself,' Alex shouted back. 'And while ye're at it, push it intae the Clyde and haud oan tae it when it falls in.'

Fat Face was not amused. He kept going and called out, 'Ya cheeky wee bastard! If Ah wisnae so busy, Ah'd kick yir heid in!'

'Aye,' Alex retorted, 'in yir imagination . . . ya fat pig, ye!'

But Fat Face was too preoccupied to carry on with the

exchange and continued on with the other man, huffing and puffing as they pushed the wheelbarrow along Eglinton Street. He knew that once he got to the scrap-metal dealer he would have enough for a good bevvy that night, and the remarks of a cheeky little boy did not matter to him in the scheme of things.

As we watched him go, Chris said, 'He wis lucky we didnae get him last time. But there'll be other chances, jist wait and see.'

Albert agreed. 'Aw's we've got tae do is wait fur the right moment. Then we'll come doon oan that fat heidcase like a ton o' bricks.'

'Yeah,' Rab joined in, 'Ah cannae wait. It's great tae get yir own back.'

'Good old-fashioned Gorbals vengeance!' said Alex.

The day soon turned to night, and around 10 p.m. I was at the Bank Close in Crown Street buying a copy of the next day's *Daily Record*. The other boys had gone home. Fat Face appeared, well the worse for wear. He must have got a good price for his scrap. He staggered over, shoved in and said to the man selling the papers, 'Gie's a *Record* and Ah'll see whit shite's in the paper.' He paid his money and before making off glanced at me and said, 'Who're you f***in' lookin' at? Do ye want ma fist in yir face?'

I decided to play it shrewd and replied in the most innocent voice I could muster, 'Naw, mister, Ah'm only here tae get ma *Record*. Ah don't want any trouble.' I sounded like a choirboy.

'A good job fur you!' Fat Face grunted and headed off rather unsteadily towards his close. I darted across the road and stood in the back court opposite Fat Face's tenement. I could clearly see him but he couldn't see me hiding in the shadows. I picked up a half brick and hurled it through the air. It hit him full in the face. 'Aaaarrgh!' he screamed, clutching his face. He staggered, then fell into the close. I ran off through the darkness and several back courts. I eventually made it to our close and then to our flat and my bed. I put my head on the pillow knowing that that night there would be no nightmares, just sweet dreams.

CHAPTER EIGHT

✳

IN THE CHIPPIE

When winter came on and it got too cold and dark to wander the streets, there was always a safe haven in the local chippie. The people of the Gorbals, no strangers to poverty, saw chips as the most convenient and cheapest meal. Fish and chips, black pudding and chips, steak and kidney pie and chips and (much later) even a deep-fried Mars Bar and chips were part of the staple diet. Everything was done with chips. It's no wonder Glasgow has been nicknamed the heart-attack capital of the world. But the chip shops also provided a social function. They were an alternative to the pub, meeting places for people who were between drinks, couldn't afford to drink or were trying to avoid drink altogether.

In Cha Papa's in Crown Street, there were tables and booths where people could have their chips and socialise over a cup of tea. There was no shortage of similar cafés, and we frequented several, including a place in Gorbals Street run by an old Italian woman called Mrs Zeki and another place in Thistle Street run by a younger Italian woman called Mrs Manurita. The advantage for us Diehards of going to the chip shop in Thistle Street was that we would get a free plate of chips if we agreed to assemble the flat-packed paper chip cartons for the owner. But although we got free chips there, we always preferred going to Cha Papa's, as that was where you met the real characters, the fly men, the chancers, the storytellers, all whiling away the time between bevvies. We would sit in one of the booths and watch people coming and going. To us, it seemed like the centre of the universe.

One evening, an irate woman stormed in and shouted to the Italian fish fryer, 'Hey, you! Aye, you! Ah sent ma boy in here fur three fish suppers and ye only gave him wan, ya robbin' bastard, ye!'

'Look, missus, Ah gave the boy three fish suppers,' the fryer replied.

'Well, how come he only came back wi wan?' the woman retorted.

'Have ye tried weighin' yir wee boy?' the Italian asked coolly.

Another time, a drunk guy staggered in, reeking strongly of cheap wine, and asked the owner how much a fish supper was. He was told it was two shillings.

'Two bob? That's too f***in' dear fur a fish supper.'

'Aye, it might be tae you, pal,' said the fryer, 'but you're oan a different planet. Livin' oan Earth is expensive. But, remember, it does include a free trip roon the sun every year.'

One person we often saw in Cha Papa's was an elderly woman who sat in a booth most days drinking cups of tea and eating the odd plate of chips now and again. She'd worked out it was cheaper to sit in the chip shop and do her knitting than to stay in the house and have to heat it all day. She never seemed to stop knitting and the regulars in the chip shop gave her orders for things like woollen cardigans and jumpers and hats. Presumably this paid for her numerous cups of tea and her chips. The knitwear she turned out was of extremely high quality and we speculated that if she had had some business acumen, she could probably have sold her goods to the high-class shops in the city centre. But money was not her life, knitting was. We always had a bit of banter with her. Alex would say things like, 'Hey, missus, can ye knit me a twenty-pound note?' She'd laugh and carry on knitting.

The old dear explained to us one day that she could tell if a person was happy or sad by the way their knitting came out. 'Ah've noticed over the years that when somebody that's sad, worried or angry knits somethin', the stitches are always tight, because even if they don't realise it, they pull a wee bit too hard oan the wool or hold their needles too tight.'

'So whit are you, missus, a happy knitter or a sad knitter?' Albert asked.

She laughed and replied, 'Ach, Ah'm a happy knitter! Ye've only tae look at the stuff Ah turn oot. Happy, contented people, friendly people, knit looser, slacker stitches, and as a result everythin' is softer and warmer.'

Over in the next booth, there was a little girl who was definitely not happy. She was crying loudly and shouting, 'Mammy, ma feet are killin' me!'

Her mother looked down and said, 'Nae wonder. Ye've got yir shoes oan the wrang feet.'

'But, Mammy,' the little girl tearfully replied, 'these are the only feet Ah've got.'

One colourful character who often joined us for a plate of chips was Old Joe. He was a real patter merchant, full of stories, and had been all over the world. He would impress us with graphic, detailed tales of fighting in Borneo, getting drunk with African tribesmen in the jungle, cavorting with prostitutes in South America – you name it, Joe had been there and done it.

After returning to Glasgow, he fought a long battle with alcohol and just decided one day that he'd had enough. 'Ah woke up feelin' terrible, almost suicidal, and Ah jist thought, "Whit am Ah daein' tae maself?"' he told us. 'That wis ten years ago. Ah'm happy now tae come here, have ma fish and chips and meet people who are always glad tae hear o' ma adventures.

'Besides, Ah've got a great missus who keeps me oan the straight and narrow. She's also the best bird impressionist Ah've ever came across.'

'Whit d'ye mean?' Alex asked. 'Can she sing like a nightingale?'

Chris enquired, 'Does she talk like a parrot?'

'Naw,' Joe laughed, 'she watches me like a hawk!'

The banter with Old Joe was certainly fun and his stories from around the world set our imaginations on fire.

Joe loved to have a bit of banter with the beautiful young girls who passed us with their bags of chips. He was in his early 70s but always had a sparkle in his eye when he chatted to these pretty young things. At our age, we were a bit too timid to talk to such beauties, but Joe had all the confidence in the world. 'The thing about women,' he explained, 'is that they like a guy wi a bit 'o' cheek, a guy that looks game, a guy who's cocky enough tae face up tae them. Women are the same the world over. Cheek gets ye everywhere. Watch this.'

One of the most beautiful young women I had ever seen in the Gorbals was walking away from the chip queue. Just looking at her, I felt extremely shy. She must have been about 19, with long dark hair, and she was perfectly formed. Joe was quick off the mark. 'Awright, hen? Where are ye headin', then?' he asked.

She gave a gallus smile and replied, while eating her chips, 'Ah'm meetin' a fella in the Central Station.'

'Oh, that's nice – love's young dream.' Joe commented. 'Have ye met him before?'

'Naw, it's a blind date. Wan o' ma pals fixed it up.'

'Heavens!' Joe replied. 'Ye've been oan that many blind dates, hen, the government should gie ye a free guide dug.'

She looked momentarily flummoxed. 'Ah'll have ye know Ah've been asked tae get married loads o' times.'

'Who asked ye? Yir mother?' Joe said.

The young lady, a streetwise creature, did not give up easily. 'Ah'm tellin' ye, a whole lot o' men are gonnae be miserable when Ah get married.'

Joe smiled, took a sip of his tea and said, 'Oh aye? How many men are ye goinnae marry, then?'

The young woman's face turned bright red and she laughed, uttering the line, 'Cheeky auld bastard!' before moving off munching more of her chips.

A few minutes later, a rather heavy woman passed us. Joe shouted, 'Hey, Sadie, Ah heard ye got married last month. How's it goin' wi you and that new man o' yours?'

'See him,' replied Sadie, 'Ah've got him eatin' oot ma hand.'

'Ach, well,' replied Joe, 'Ah suppose it saves ye havin' tae wash the dishes.'

Big Sadie was not amused and stormed out of the chip shop in a huff, shouting that Joe should go away and do something to himself that even we knew was physically impossible.

In another chippie towards the town centre, we got to know a regular we called Harry the Hard Case. He had been a mean fighter in his day but, in his late 50s, had settled into a more serene life. Harry's speciality was talking about violence. We'd heard him talk about it so much we thought he should have written a book on the subject. He had a large scar running down his left cheek, a reminder of his gang days.

'Boys,' he said to us once, 'Ah'll let ye intae a wee secret.'

'Oh, aye?' Alex said. 'Whit's that?'

'Well, surprise is always the best form o' attack. There are two basic forms o' street attack. First, ye can stick the heid oan somebody, gie them the good old Gorbals kiss, and tae follow up kick them right in the baws.'

'Ach, we know that awready, Joe. Gie us news, no history,' Albert said.

'Aye, ye're preachin' tae the converted oan that wan,' Chris told him.

'Tell us somethin' we don't know,' Rab said. 'Gie's a couple o' moves that we can use against aw the bampots goin' about.'

'Awright,' Harry replied, 'Ah'm givin' away the tricks o' the trade here. If ye want tae break somebody's jaw, act calm and offer him a cigarette. When he puts the fag intae his mooth, gie him an uppercut. That's usually guaranteed tae break a fella's jaw. An elbow in the face is another good wan – never fails. Also, ordinary everyday things, like a rolled-up newspaper or an Irn-Bru bottle, can be powerful weapons. An Irn-Bru bottle can knock sense intae a guy!'

One night, we were sitting with Harry chatting and eating our suppers when two young tough-looking types walked into the chip shop. Both of them looked as if they had been drinking or were high on pills. I recognised one of them as the older brother of one of my schoolmates. He had the classic Gorbals hard-man walk. He sauntered straight up to the counter, right to the top of the queue, and stared at the fish fryer. 'Oh, aye, here comes trouble,' Harry said. 'Let's see whit that cardboard hard case is gonnae do.'

The young guy shouted at the fish fryer, 'Gie's two fish suppers pronto, ya peely-wally tally bastard.'

'Hey, cut oot the language, boys,' said the fryer. 'And Ah'm no a bastard. Ah know who ma faither is, no like you. Get back tae the end o' the queue!'

The young hard man and his cohort refused to go to the back of the queue and it was clear from their attitude that they had no intention of paying for the suppers they were demanding. Harry whispered to us, 'They've got nae chance. Ah've given that tally some good tips oan how tae handle a situation like this.'

The fish fryer looked at the two hard men for a few seconds and said, 'Awright, boys, Ah don't want any trouble. Ye'll get yir fish suppers.'

The two guys smiled broadly, sure that their attempt at intimidation had paid off. Then the fish fryer picked up a small saucepan, dipped it into the hot fat, turned round and threw it into their faces. The two hard cases began running around holding their scalded faces, with skin peeling off, and screaming with pain. 'Ye've burnt ma face!' one of them cried. Someone had nipped out to the nearby police box when the two tough guys had appeared in the café, and two big policemen promptly arrived and arrested the young men for breach of the peace. They were later taken to hospital for treatment to their blistered faces.

The fryer approached our table and said, 'Thanks fur that tip, Harry. Chips oan the house fur you and the boys here!' As we tucked into our free plates of chips, we agreed that what Harry had told us might come in handy for the future.

Harry laughed. 'Aye there's wan thing fur sure.'

'Whit's that, Harry?' I asked.

'Those two guys have had their chips!'

'Aye,' Chris added, 'they were well battered!'

CHAPTER NINE

✳

THE RAZOR KING

One of the chip-shop regulars we got to know was Wullie. We speculated that he was called William because his parents were staunch Protestants and he had been named after William of Orange, or King Billy, as he was better known in Glasgow. We were all too afraid to ask him, though, because Wullie had aspirations to be the area's razor king. From an early age, he had read and reread the 1930s book *No Mean City*, in which the central character is Johnnie Stark, the 'razor king' of the Gorbals. Like Stark, Wullie lived in Crown Street. Like his fictional hero, Wullie was a handsome bloke with thick black hair, and the women loved him. He even took a job for a while as a coalman, humping huge heavy bags up tenement stairs, just as Johnnie Stark did in the book.

Wullie had been born into the right era, too. When we met him in 1967, Glasgow was awash with razor gangs, just as it had been in the '30s. Wullie had slashed his first victim at the age of 16 and now, at 21, he had built up a considerable reputation amongst the hard-man elite. In his younger days, the old hard cases had derided him as a 'bampot', a young idiot who would soon burn himself out. But as his reputation grew, the older guys stopped treating him as a joke and a degree of respect developed for this young upstart.

Wullie was always well dressed – dark three-button suit, white shirt and tie – and he must have spent hours every day polishing his shoes. They shone like mirrors. He had a string of beautiful girlfriends, mostly blonde with short skirts and long hair, exceptional-looking young women. But Wullie was in love with none of them. The only thing he loved was his razor.

He showed it to us once when we were sitting in the chip shop. It was a beautiful thing, as highly polished as his shoes, with a varnished wooden handle. Alex, a game guy who often threw caution to the wind, had the audacity to ask Wullie how many guys he'd slashed with it. He shrugged his shoulders, poured thick brown sauce over his fish supper and replied nonchalantly, 'Ach, it's got tae be aroon 50. Aye, there must be about 50 guys aw walkin' roon Glesga wi wan o' ma scars.' Wullie sounded as if he thought these guys ought to be proud, as if they had been stamped with the logo of a famous brand.

Wullie's obsession with *No Mean City* baffled me. I had read it and it just seemed a bit ridiculous. Stark, the part-time coalman, married a girl with bandy legs and moved into a single-end in Crown Street. Then things began to go downhill. His wife had an affair with a man whose wife was disabled. Stark, with his wife's permission, took a series of young girls, 'housekeepers', to be his lovers.

First of all, I thought that, although the Gorbals could be a filthy and violent place, most of its inhabitants had old-fashioned values when it came to marriage, and taking a young girl as a live-in lover while married would never have been tolerated. Second, Stark wasn't interested in money, only slashing people, whereas all the razor guys and hard men I knew were always on the lookout for an easy way to make money. Third, Stark went to dances and slashed women. This was taking things a bit too far. No razor guy would ever contemplate slashing a woman; even the suggestion seemed ludicrous. The book, by Alexander McArthur and Kingsley Long, had been an international bestseller. The dialogue, provided by McArthur, was slightly suspect in places, and some of the scenarios painted by English wordsmith Long were so preposterous that they made me laugh out loud. In fact, I thought the problem with the book was that it had an Englishman's pawprints all over it. I was in a good position to judge: I lived in Crown Street and knew most of the local hard cases by name or sight.

As one old-timer said to me, 'Folk are livin' in cloud cuckoo land if they think the way people are portrayed in that book is anythin' like the real people who live here.' He had a point, although to be fair to McArthur and Long, they were describing the Glasgow of the 1930s. This was the swinging '60s, man! So perhaps the area and the people had changed dramatically since then. But I had my doubts.

Certainly, there was no shortage of gangs, and according to the various crime reporters, they used open razors without batting an eyelid. The wild young guys also armed themselves with Gurkha knives, Stanley knives, bayonets, pokers and broken bottles. A lot of the trouble was caused by youths fortified with the cheap red wine going off to the dancing, or 'jiggin'', as some referred to it.

The rot had first set in during the 1930s, but by the late 1950s, just after I was born, gang warfare had returned as a means of settling old scores. If you picked up the *Evening Times* or the *Glasgow Citizen*, you would read about mass gang fighting in the streets. One particular story reported that the state of affairs had deteriorated so badly that the Royal Infirmary was running out of blood for transfusions to treat the growing number of victims. One summer in the mid-1960s, 50 cases of assault were dealt with by the casualty department and staff had to cope with numerous razor slashings and stabbings. It's no wonder the police, doctors and nurses prayed for rain to clear the streets, especially at the weekends.

During the 1950s and '60s major gangs began to appear or be revitalised: the Cumbie from the Gorbals, the Tongs from Calton, the Fleet from Maryhill, the Shamrock from Blackhill, the Govan Team, the Drummie from Drumchapel, the Young Team from Castlemilk. Then there were smaller gangs such as the Derry from Bridgeton, a revamped San Toi from the Gallowgate (their heyday had been the '30s), the Bal Toi, the Bar L (named after Barlinnie Prison) and the Torran Toi. Cheap wine gulped down with 'pep pills' gave the young gang members the

Dutch courage to carry on slashing and stabbing to their hearts' content. Eminent sociologists who visited the Gorbals and other parts of Glasgow concluded that the emergence of the many junior gangs was, in subcultural terms, like junior-league football teams playing each other. The gangs even referred to themselves as 'teams'. But instead of kicking a ball, the members preferred kicking into rival gang members.

As an illustration of how out of control the gangs were becoming, take the example of the leader of the Calton Tongs. He was sitting in a café near Dundas Street Bus Station in the city centre when he made a bet with his pals that he would jump on the next bus that came along and stab the first person he came across. He won the wager. The resultant court hearing was appalled to learn that the victim was an elderly cripple who had been visiting his sister. But a bet was a bet in gangland Glasgow.

My relatives, neighbours and older friends often walked the short distance over the bridge to Glasgow's High Court in the Saltmarket to see the familiar gangland faces standing in the dock. But the Scottish judiciary had had enough. They were fed up with the gangland palaver and, led by Lord Cameron, judges started handing out severe sentences, especially after Easter 1967. It was nicknamed 'Bloody Easter' because there were 22 stabbings and slashings in the city on the Friday and Saturday nights alone. No doubt some of those cases were down to Wullie, but he was lucky because he'd never been arrested. 'Too quick aff ma feet!' he boasted to us.

Young guys like Wullie were only the most recent incarnation of the Gorbals hard man. In the 1930s, the Beehive Boys were the mob to be reckoned with in the area. They had major rival mobs, however, and it was a near-run thing holding their ground against such battalions as the Protestant Billy Boys, the Catholic Norman Conks from Norman Street, the Derry Boys from Bridgeton, and the Antique Mob from Shettleston. Also, there were the Hammer Boys, the Black Diamond Boys, the Dirty Dozen from the South Side, the Romeo Boys from the East End and the Kelly Boys from Govan. The predecessors of the Cumbie gang that ran the streets when I was young, the

Beehive hung around Cumberland Street. They were not just into fighting; they made money by breaking into shops and blowing open safes. Their leader was a wild guy called Peter Williamson, a street fighter who became a legend throughout Glasgow. The Bee Hive disintegrated during the Second World War and Peter Williamson joined the army, where he was promoted to the rank of sergeant. After the war, Williamson went back to safe-blowing and ended doing a couple of long sentences in Peterhead Prison.

In the old days, a gang leader like Williamson would send a message to the leader of a rival gang challenging him to a 'square go', meaning a fair fight. They usually met, like the fictional Johnnie Stark and his opponents, at some out-of-the-way spot on Glasgow Green. The fight would take place and afterwards the combatants would shake hands and head to the nearest pub or shebeen for a drink.

As we sat there with Wullie in the chip shop, Albert jokingly asked him, 'Whit's your ambition, Wullie? Whit are ye gonnae do wi yirself?'

'Aye,' Rab joined in, 'any big plans?'

Wullie grinned, flashing a Hollywood-style smile. He had brilliant white teeth. They were sparkling – unusual for a Gorbals guy. 'Aye,' he said, 'Ah've got a few things up ma sleeve. But Ah'm no tellin' you idiots.'

'Come oan, Wullie, gie's a clue,' Rab said.

Wullie rose from the table, wiped his chin with a paper napkin, then pulled out his razor. 'See this here? This thing is gonnae make me famous, mair famous than any o' you guys'll ever be. People say Ah'm like Johnnie Stark, but Ah'm better than him. Besides Ah'm real, no fiction. Ah'm me, no him. Always be a first-rate version o' yirself, no a second-rate version o' somebody else. Ah'm gonnae go places and make a name fur maself. Jist wait and see. When ye see a guy at the top o' a mountain, he didnae get there because he fell there. It's aw about the climb upwards.'

With those ominous words and a dazzling white smile, he laughed and left.

CHAPTER TEN

✳

A FIGHT

A few weeks after our chat with Wullie, the Diehards and I were walking along Eglinton Street, past the Coliseum and Bedford cinemas. The place was teeming with people. The pubs had just come out and the air was filled with the smell of alcohol and the sound of swearing drunks. One man was standing outside the Mally Arms singing 'I Belong to Glasgow' at the top of his out-of-tune voice. As he stood there, he slurped from his carry-oot, a quarter-bottle of whisky, and we all laughed, thinking that no doubt it was true: Glasgow almost certainly was going roon and roon for this guy.

Two women who had just come out of the bingo looked at the unfortunate soul and one shook her head, tut-tutting, before saying to her acquaintance, 'Would ye look at the state o' that. He's pished.'

'Aye, ye're right,' her pal replied. 'He disnae know whether it's New Year or New York!' The two of them laughed loudly before making off for the last Corporation bus home.

The intoxicated man emptied the rest of the contents of his whisky bottle down his throat and then staggered to the nearest corner. He fumbled under his coat for a few minutes, searching for his fly. 'Ah've got it!' he exclaimed, before urinating heavily against the wall. It wasn't exactly his lucky night. As the piss bounced off the wall and ran along the street, two burly policemen appeared on the scene.

'Look at that imbecile!' one of them said to the other.

'Let's lift the drunken bastard,' replied his fellow officer.

They got hold of the bevvy merchant by both of his arms and, as they say in Glasgow, he was 'huckled aff' for what would be described in court as 'urinating in a public place' (we called it 'pishin' up against a wa''). The guy would probably face a night in the cells and a £10 fine. But if he was too cheeky to the police, there would be an added fine of £25 for breach of the peace, so it wouldn't exactly turn out to be a cheap night out for the drunk. The police liked to make such arrests. They were easy to do and it got them back to the station to enjoy a cup of tea while they filled in some simple forms and, at times, wrote up exaggerated prosecution statements. Lifting a drunk for urinating was far less hassle than dealing with the numerous young, violent and volatile gang members.

A few yards up the road, a patter merchant was standing outside a pub recounting a variety of jokes and stories to his pals. The man's storytelling technique was so good that some of his friends had tears of laughter in their eyes, and we stopped to listen.

'Here's a good wan fur ye,' he said. 'Before the big fight, David and Goliath have a weigh-in. A reporter says tae David's manager, "Whit d'ye think o' yir boy's chances?" And he says, "Well, the odd stone could make a difference!" The men all guffawed, slapping each other on the back, and then they went their separate ways.

On another corner, a gang of well-dressed teenagers were standing around, quiet and sullen. We recognised them. They weren't Gorbals people but from nearby Tradeston, and this could only mean trouble. The Gorbals gangs' power extended as far as Eglinton Street, and Tradeston began a block or so away. The Tradeston boys sometimes ventured into the Gorbals looking for trouble, and vice versa. It was obvious these guys were up to no good, but there was not a policeman in sight. The two on the beat were dealing with the innocuous drunk back at the station.

'There's gonnae be bother soon,' Chris muttered.

'Aye,' Alex said, 'like Elvis says, if ye're lookin' fur trouble, ye've come tae the right place.'

'Ye're right, Alex,' Albert said. 'Look who's comin' doon the street!'

Rab looked excited, 'Fur f***'s sake! It's Wullie wi his bird. There's bound tae be a bit o' action noo!'

It was indeed Wullie, arm in arm with a beautiful blonde. He was, as always, impeccably dressed, wearing a dark suit with a fancy striped tie and a white velvet hankie sticking out of his breast pocket. His lady was wearing a short skirt and had possibly the best pair of legs that the Gorbals had seen in many a year. Both had obviously been enjoying a few refreshments. As they walked down Eglinton Street, Wullie smiled at his girlfriend and in the light from the street lamps his brilliant white teeth shone. But the smile disappeared from his face when the saw the Tradeston mob.

As he and his girlfriend walked past the Tradeston boys, they exchanged glares, but the confrontation was never going to be left at that. When Wullie and his gal had walked a few yards further up the street, one of the Tradeston guys shouted to him, 'Hey, pal, where did ye dig up that dirty hing-oot ye're wi?' Now, this was probably one of the worst insults you could utter to a guy about his girlfriend. To call a girl a 'hing-oot' suggested she was a woman of low morals whom every man had had. 'Come oan, Wullie,' we heard the girl say. 'Never mind them.'

But Wullie had a dangerous look in his eye. He flashed his brilliant white teeth, giving the guys his gamest look. He walked towards them. 'Who called ma bird a hing-oot?' he shouted.

There was no reply for a few seconds, but then one of the Tradeston mob shouted back, 'Ah did. Whit ye gonnae do about it?'

We stood aghast watching the action unfold. Wullie launched himself straight at them. We saw his razor gleaming in his right hand. He struck one fellow along the right cheek and when another moved towards him he slashed his throat with as much proficiency as a foreman at an abattoir. The slashing continued until the Tradeston guys were either lying bleeding on the pavement or had run off, with Wullie chasing after them, wildly waving his razor. He had slashed ten of the teenagers and he had not a bruise or cut on him. He shouted after the retreating Tradeston boys, 'Naebody calls ma bird a hing-oot and gets away wi it!'

The next minute, the two policemen who had arrested the drunk appeared on the scene. Wullie hid his razor in his jacket pocket and walked off with his girlfriend. The police looked at the wounded guys lying moaning in the street and demanded, 'Who the hell did all this damage?' A respectable-looking woman standing at a nearby bus stop had seen it all. She pointed to Wullie walking down the street and said, 'It was him there, officer.' The officer gave chase, but Wullie was too quick off the mark, bolting towards Gorbals Street. The other officer called for an ambulance for the injured guys, who were holding hankies to their wounds, scarred for life but thankful to be alive. The guy whose throat had been slashed was lucky; no major arteries had been cut and his injuries were not life threatening.

Two ambulances arrived to take the slashed guys away, and meanwhile the policeman was still pursuing Wullie, who managed, during the course of the chase, to discard the razor by lobbing it over a wall into a dark back court. The policeman caught up with him several streets from the scene of the crime, posing as an ordinary punter waiting at a bus stop with several other people for the last service to Castlemilk. Reinforcements arrived and Wullie was bundled into a Black Maria, protesting his innocence and insisting that the police had arrested the wrong man. Of course, he was thoroughly searched but there was no sign of incriminating evidence, namely the razor.

After the victims had been carted off, one of the policemen, whom we knew well, told us, 'That fella's claiming that we got the wrong guy and he was just an innocent bystander waiting for his bus, but the woman at the bus stop in Eglinton Street saw it all. She'll be a witness when the case comes to the High Court. That bastard will end up getting 15 years, and it'll serve him right. You can't go about slashing people just because they insult you. But I suppose that's the way it is in the Gorbals – the razor comes before any sense.'

The next day, the local paper declared: 'Ten Slashed in Gorbals Gang Fight'. In later editions, Wullie's name appeared in connection with charges of attempted murder and serious assault. So his wish had come true. He had achieved fame as a razor king at last. But how was he going to get away with this one? It didn't look good for him, especially as the woman at the bus stop, who turned out to be a head teacher from middle-class Giffnock, was ready and willing to testify, something that no Gorbals person would do.

'That wee posh woman saw it aw,' Alex said. 'If Ah wis Wullie, Ah'd be a wee bit worried.'

'Aye,' Chris agreed, 'that posh auld cow will be singin' like a canary.'

'Ach,' said Rab, 'she's aw fur coat and nae knickers. Wullie will think o' a way tae get aff wi it. Jist wait and see!'

Albert agreed: 'The polis have wan major witness. Aw's Wullie's got tae do is get a few false witnesses and build up an alibi. He knows enough people in the Gorbals who'll say he didnae do it.'

'Where there's a will there's a way,' I said.

'Mair like where there's a Wullie there's a way!' Alex joked.

Chris shrugged his shoulders and said, 'Those Tradeston guys had better start writin' their wills before they show their faces in the Gorbals again.'

Alex began to sing to the tune of 'Please Help Me, I'm Falling':

> Please help me, Ah'm fightin' and slashin' you.
> Jist dropped in tae chib you, right out o' the blue.
> Don't want tae make love tae you, jist wan rip will do.
> Please help me, Ah'm hackin' and slashin' you!

There was blood on the pavements, menace in the air and a bizarre cheerfulness on the faces of the Incredible Gorbals Diehards.

✳

THE TRIAL

'What's the verdict, then, boys?' I asked.

Chris: 'Guilty!'

Rab: 'Guilty!'

Albert: 'Guilty!'

Alex: 'Not proven.'

In Scotland, unlike in England, juries have a third option: a case can be found not proven as well as a defendant guilty or not guilty.

'Oh, aye?' I said to Alex. 'How did ye come tae that verdict? Surely Wullie'll go doon?'

'Naw, you guys are aw wrang,' Alex told us. 'Remember, when folk roon here are dealin' wi the polis, it's a case of see nae evil, hear nae evil, speak nae evil. Naebody'll testify against Wullie.'

'But whit about the posh schoolteacher at the bus stop?' Albert asked.

'Ach, Wullie'll get roon that. Jist wait and see,' Alex replied.

'Aye, but what about the guys he slashed, then? Whit happens if they testify?' asked Rab.

Alex shrugged his shoulders. 'Ah don't think they will.'

'Ah agree wi Alex,' Albert decided. 'A gang member isnae gonnae testify against another gang member, scar or nae scar. In fact, Ah've changed ma mind. Ah think Wullie'll get found not proven.'

So there we were. The Incredible Gorbals Diehards had formed their own little surrogate street jury and had made their decision. But what would the reality be? Would the court convict or clear Wullie?

Over the weeks, news had begun to filter out. Most of the charges against Wullie had been dropped, not only because the police had failed to find the razor but also because the slashed guys had changed their testimony or refused to give further evidence to the police. As Wullie waited on remand in Barlinnie prison, the news just got better for him. Of the ten gang members he had given skin carvings to, nine had dropped the charges. Only one guy remained, and he was considered a bit backward and not really a full-blown gang member at all. We had heard that he had told people that he was seeking compensation for the large scar on his right cheek.

'Ach, he's a joke,' Alex said. 'Anythin he says in court, they'll never believe.'

'There's still the schoolteacher,' I pointed out.

'If Ah wis Wullie, Ah widnae worry about her. She's sure tae buckle under the pressure when she has tae stand in the High Court and give evidence,' Albert said.

'Aye,' Chris agreed, 'the public gallery'll be full o' Gorbals people starin' at her. Noo that would scare the shite oot o' anybody!'

After Wullie had been on remand for almost two months, with bail refused twice, he appeared for trial on one charge of serious assault and another of breach of the peace. The charge of slashing a man was serious enough to be tried in the High Court. We mingled with a crowd of other people from the area and managed to get places in the packed public gallery. The judge was a fellow who had recently made a name for himself by handing out stiff sentences of around 12 to 15 years for the kind of violent offences with which Wullie was charged.

Wullie appeared in the dock accompanied by two burly police officers, one at each side. He nodded up at the public gallery and we all nodded back. He had changed his appearance since we last saw him. His hair was in a crew cut and he had a small goatee beard. Also, he was dressed in surprisingly scruffy clothes

– a wrinkled denim shirt and jeans. We were surprised, because we had never seen Wullie in such shabby garments. He always wore smart suits to go with his brilliant Hollywood smile.

The prosecutor was a well-known QC, a large, fat man with a posh accent. First to appear in the witness box was the fellow who had been slashed. He was a guy of around 21 with thick red hair. Although he was from Tradeston, I often saw him standing around Gorbals Cross. I had spoken to him several times and he certainly struck me as being not the full bob. Every village needs an idiot, and here he was. He was certainly no gangster. He ran errands for the Tradeston gang guys and was often the butt of their jokes. He had just been in the wrong place at the wrong time when Wullie had started using his razor.

The prosecutor cleared his throat, stroked his moustache, and said, 'Can you please describe to the court what happened that night.'

'Whit night?' the witness replied.

'The night you were slashed!'

At this, a member of the jury began to giggle. I wasn't surprised. We were having to suppress laughter. It was like watching a sketch at the Pavilion Theatre. The guy in the witness stand was funnier than Stanley Baxter.

The judge hit his gavel on the bench. 'Order! Order in court! No laughter, please! Let the witness continue.'

The witness did indeed continue: 'Well, Ah wis wi ma Tradeston pals when this chib merchant appeared and slashed me oan ma dial wi his malky.'

The judge intervened: 'Chib merchant? Dial? Malky? What is this man talking about. This is not the sort of English, or Scots, I understand.'

'Well, Your Honour,' the prosecutor replied, 'a "chib merchant" is a Glaswegian colloquial phrase for a man who uses a razor, which is known as a "chib" or "malky". A "chib merchant" is one who deals in the trade of slashing or wounding people. "Dial" simply means the face.'

'Continue,' the judge ordered, 'but it might be easier for all of us if the witness made an attempt to speak proper English.'

The witness carried on: 'Ah had jist left ma drum in Tradeston when me and the troops decided tae go fur a donner intae the Soo-Side. We were aw malarkyin' about Eggie Street when this big tube appears wi a Malky Frazer and sets about us aw.' The proceedings had to be halted once again as the prosecutor, a man much experienced in Glasgow gangland cases, translated for the judge.

'Can you see the man who slashed you, or rather chibbed you, in court now?' the prosecutor asked the witness.

He looked round the court then suddenly pointed at Wullie in the dock. 'Aye, he looked a bit like that fella there sittin' between the two polis.'

'Are you sure that is the man?' the prosecutor asked.

The witness rubbed his eyes and looked over at Wullie again. 'Well, it looks a bit like him. The dial's the same. But the guy that chibbed me had mair hair and didnae have a beard. So Ah cannae say fur certain if it wis him there.'

Now it was the defence lawyer's turn to question the witness. Wullie had been shrewd in his choice. His lawyer had built up a brilliant reputation for getting gang members off on technicalities. 'Do I look like the man who chibbed you?' the lawyer asked the witness.

'Aye, ye do a bit,' the witness replied.

'And does the judge look like the man who slashed you?'

The witness looked at the judge carefully. 'Naw, Ah don't think it could have been him.'

'Why not?' asked Wullie's defence counsel.

'Well, the guy that slashed me wisnae wearin' a wig.'

The court was in uproar at that. Even the judge was laughing. But when I looked over at Wullie in the dock, he was keeping a straight face.

The next witness to take the stand was the Giffnock schoolteacher. From the public gallery, we all stared intently at her, hoping to intimidate her. She looked extremely nervous.

'Can you please describe the events you witnessed on the night in question?' the prosecutor asked.

'I had just come out of the Citizens Theatre and I was

standing at a bus stop when I saw a bunch of youths at a nearby corner. Then a well-dressed young man launched an attack on them with an open razor. It was like a scene from one of the gorier plays I've attended. There was blood everywhere and the injured fellows were all staggering around shouting for help. It turned my stomach to see such mindless violence happening in this modern age. The man who slashed the boys behaved like a savage, and they should lock him up for ever.'

'Can you see the perpetrator in court today?' the prosecutor asked. It was make-or-break time for Wullie. The reply would surely swing the jury. The teacher looked over at Wullie in the dock and pointed at him. 'He looked something like that young man there. But the fellow who slashed the others had longer hair, was clean-shaven and was wearing smart clothes. But I can say for certain if the man in the dock stands up and smiles. Then I will know for sure. The fellow was smiling while he did it, and he had the most brilliant white teeth.'

Wullie was ordered to stand up in the dock and give the woman a smile. When he did, the Diehards and I were taken aback. For when he showed his teeth, they were brown and rotten looking, or, as Albert put it, 'like a row of condemned buildings'.

From that moment, the case against Wullie collapsed like a line of dominoes. Two of his friends testified that he was a 'law-abiding man' who had never been in trouble and that on the night in question they had had a few drinks with him and his girlfriend in a pub before he'd escorted her to the bus stop.

Wullie's girlfriend took to the stand and told the court that she and Wullie were 'winchin'' (courting), that her man 'widnae harm a fly' and that he was at heart a 'shy, lovin' fella'.

Wullie himself told the court that it had simply been a case of mistaken identity. He said he didn't blame the police for 'the cock-up', as he knew they were under a lot of pressure in the Gorbals, especially at the weekends.

The jury adjourned for a short time and returned with their verdict – not proven on both charges.

Outside the court, I asked Wullie how he'd managed to get his usually brilliant teeth so brown. He shrugged, laughed and told me, 'Broon boot polish! Ah'll always be able tae say a dab o' boot polish saved me doin' 15 years in jail!' He wiped his teeth several times with a hankie and their sparkling whiteness returned. Sure enough, Wullie had plenty to smile about that day.

CHAPTER TWELVE

✳

THE SHEBEEN

After his victory in court, Wullie and his followers, including the blonde girlfriend, were in need of a drink. The blonde's uncle ran a shebeen – an illicit drinking den – in Florence Street, at the top of a crumbling tenement. I don't think the uncle lived there; he just used it as business premises to sell alcohol to the ever thirsty Gorbals punters. As kids, we would never normally have been invited to such a place, but Wullie insisted that we come along. 'These are ma wee pals,' he declared, 'and they've got tae come tae ma party!' We walked over the bridge into Crown Street, along Rutherglen Road and then into Florence Street.

Outside the close, there was a gaggle of women in headscarves and rollers, and a crudely drawn poster proclaiming 'Welcome Home Wullie!' It was as if Wullie was a war hero returning home after a long period of service overseas. As he approached the close, the women shouted out, 'Well done, son! It's good tae have ye back hame!' Wullie didn't actually live in the building, but he was recognised as one of their own. He flashed his magnificent smile in thanks and we all climbed the stairs to the top floor.

When we entered the flat, a single-end, Al Jolson, a perennial favourite at Glasgow parties, was blaring out from an old gramophone. The song was 'You Made Me Love You'. A woman called Bella was standing behind a small bar. There were rows and rows of cheap wine, beer and whisky waiting for Wullie and his pals. These small bars were common in the 1960s; it gave ordinary tenement-dwelling Glaswegians a sense of glamour having their own bar in their flat. Lounging about on sofas and chairs was a conglomeration of what can only be described as dodgy characters.

Albert whispered to me, 'If the Devil could cast his net noo, he would have a bloody good catch.' I could only agree.

'Congratulations, Wullie!' the drunken throng shouted. Wullie nodded in acknowledgement and headed straight for Bella and the bevvy.

Although Wullie was, as we have seen, a pretty wild guy and popular with the ladies, he seemed quite a shy fellow when mixing with a crowd of people. One bevvy merchant got to his feet and shouted, 'Come oan, Wullie, gie's a song. It's no every day ye get cleared at the High Court!' But Wullie explained that he was 'a wee bit tired' after the trial and needed to settle down and have a quiet drink before any major partying began. He took two glasses of red wine and sat in the corner with his girlfriend.

Much to our surprise, Bella handed me and the boys large glasses of wine, saying, 'Ach, ye might be too young tae drink in a pub, but ye can have a drink here. Besides, if you boys were in France, ye'd be allowed. Over there, the weans drink wine aw the time.'

'Ah think Ah'll move tae France!' Chris joked. I took a sip of the wine and a warm, glowing feeling overcame me.

The boys and I sat down with the regulars to listen to their patter. We got talking to one old-timer, 'Tam the Bam', who was no stranger to a bevvy or two. He looked pretty ancient and Alex asked him, 'How auld are ye, Tam?'

He took a sip of his wine like a real connoisseur before replying, 'Ah'll be eighty-two ma next birthday.'

I could tell the wine was already making Alex just that wee bit cheekier. 'Eighty-two?' he replied. 'Ah'd hate tae live tae that age.'

But auld Tam, who had lived in the Gorbals all his life, was used to dealing with young upstarts like Alex. He retorted, 'You widnae hate it if ye were eighty-wan!' After that ice-breaker, there was much laughter and merriment in the shebeen. I got the feeling that the older guys took a great deal of pleasure in ridiculing us and winding us up. We were a novelty.

Another fellow, Mad Mick, asked us what we were going to do when we grew up. I replied that I'd probably be a chef, like my father.

'A navvy oan a buildin' site, cos the money's good,' Chris said.

'Ah'll be a wheeler-dealer, buyin' and sellin' gear,' Alex replied.

Rab had a similar plan, adding that he wasn't averse to the idea of dealing in 'dodgy gear', as that was where the money was.

Albert took a large sip of wine and gave his answer, which surprised us: 'Ah'm gonnae be the leader o' the Labour Party.'

Mad Mick was taken aback at this bold response. 'Oh, aye? Why do ye fancy that?'

The cheap wine seemed to be making Albert even more philosophical than usual. 'So that Ah can help homeless people like ma cousin,' he told Mick. 'Ah'd gie him money tae get a flat.'

On hearing this, Mad Mick grinned mischievously. 'Ah'll tell ye whit. Ah need a hand paintin' ma flat. If ye help me paint, Ah'll gie ye a few bob tae gie tae yir cousin.'

Albert replied, 'Ah've got a better idea: why don't ye get him tae help ye paint and gie him the money?'

Mad Mick laughed loudly and said, 'Welcome tae the Conservative Party!'

Al Jolson's 'April Showers' began to play and the gramophone was turned up full blast. When the chorus started, everyone joined in. The party was getting into full swing. More drink was consumed and I noticed that Wullie was still deep in conversation with his girlfriend. He had a serious look on his face and his brilliant teeth were no longer flashing. 'You've got tae be kiddin' me. Ye cannae be right,' I heard him say. Probably a bit of a lover's tiff, I decided.

Sitting next to Mad Mick was Tony the Tim. Tony was well known as a fanatical Celtic supporter. As he sat with us drinking a 'hawf and hawf' (a half pint of beer and a large whisky), his chat was limited to the subject of his beloved Celtic.

'How do ye know the Hunchback o' Notre-Dame is a Rangers supporter?' he asked.

'Don't know, Tony,' I replied.

'Cos he looks like wan!' Tony guffawed.

Wullie got up and walked away from his girlfriend, who was crying. I thought perhaps the trauma of the trial and the effects of the wine had caught up with her. Wullie stood in another corner, staring into space. I walked over to him and asked, 'Whit's happenin', Wullie? Ye look as if ye've seen a ghost.'

He shrugged his shoulders, took a sip of the wine and said, 'That silly cow is pregnant, in the puddin' club, whatever ye want tae call it. It looks like we'll have tae get married pronto. Ah'll be a daddy in five months. Ma days as the razor king are over. The game's a bogey.'

Wullie looked genuinely shocked. I'd never seen him like that. He was usually such a gallus guy. He walked back over to his girlfriend and hugged her. Then he announced to the party, 'Ah've got somethin' tae tell ye aw. Ah'm gettin' married. Ma missus is pregnant and Ah've decided tae make an honest woman o' her.' Everyone was taken aback at the announcement as most people had concluded long ago that Wullie, razor and all, was not exactly the marrying kind.

Mad Mick was quick to recover from the surprise, though. 'Raise yir glasses tae the happy couple,' he cried. 'Hip, hip!'

'Hooray!' we all shouted.

'Hip, hip!'

'Hooray!'

'Hip, hip!'

'Hooray!'

Wullie and his bride-to-be left the shebeen in comparatively high spirits. He gave a flash of his famous gnashers and was gone.

By this time, Alex was half cut. 'The razor king is deid, long live the new razor king,' he declared.

'Aye,' the members of the party said, raising their glasses. 'Long live the new razor king!' We didn't have a clue who this new razor king was, but there were certainly plenty of contenders.

Mad Mick was the first to comment on the change in Wullie's circumstances. 'The thing is, ye cannae plan life. Everythin' is aw worked oot fur ye. Take Wullie, fur example. He wanted tae be a real hard man, but a bird and a baby have intervened. It's jist as well, because he's a nice fella at heart and it'll suit him givin' up aw that gang fightin' nonsense. Don't ye think, Tony?'

'Aye,' his pal replied, 'but when a woman meets a man she loves him fur who he is but then she tries tae change him intae something else. Take ma wife,' he continued, steering the conversation back round to his favourite subject. 'She knew Ah wis mad about Celtic when we met, but after a while she tried tae bar me fae goin tae the matches. "It's either me or Celtic," she said.

'"Ah'll miss ye, hen," Ah told her straight aff. Got a divorce after that. Naebody but naebody is gonnae stop me followin' the Celtic and if they try, tae hell wi them!'

The gramophone was turned up to full volume again, and playing on it was Andy Stewart singing 'We're No Awa Tae Bide Awa'. The whole party, including us Diehards, sang along:

> Fur we're no awa tae bide awa,
> Fur we're no awa tae leave ye,
> Fur we're no awa tae bide awa,
> We'll aye come back and see ye.

Everyone felt emotional about Wullie's new path in life. Some people were even crying, but Bella wasn't getting carried away. 'Ach,' she said, 'the mair they greet, the less they'll pish.'

CHAPTER THIRTEEN

✳

THE REGULARS

From that day on, we were always welcome at the shebeen – Wullie or no Wullie – and we got to know the regulars well. Apart from Mad Mick, Tony the Tim and Tam the Bam, there was Holy Harry, who had got kicked out of the ministry for drinking and was always good for a story, and a guy called Phil, who was forever coming away with funny jokes and anecdotes.

A fellow in his early 60s who called himself Al Jolson turned up sometimes and we reckoned he was a real nutcase. Our suspicions were confirmed when he told us that he was often in and out of Gartnavel mental hospital. To put it mildly, Al Jolson was a character like none we had never met before. After seeing the biopics *The Jolson Story* and *Jolson Sings Again*, he had had a nervous breakdown and he was convinced that he actually was the reincarnation of the man. He took to spray-painting his assumed name on walls all over Glasgow.

We had been mystified as to who could have been spraying the words 'AL JOLSON' all over the place, but when he had been arrested for defacing walls, the court case had appeared in the paper and the headline read, rather cheekily, 'Al Jolson Arrested'. The magistrate fined him £25, saying, 'There are doubts about your mental health and the psychiatrist says it is all to do with your having a breakdown after your mother died. But this does not give you the excuse to go around Glasgow defacing walls with the Jolson name. I will fine you this time as a show of leniency, but it will be prison for you if it ever happens again.'

Al often turned up at the shebeen with a tin of Cherry Blossom black boot polish. He would then black up his face and, putting a Jolson record on the gramophone, sing along and do all the actions. It brought tears of laughter to our eyes when he got down on a bended knee while singing 'Sonny Boy'. The guy might not have been the full shilling, but he was great entertainment. His favourite song was 'My Mammy'. He always gave it laldy, with plenty of drama and tears flowing down his cheeks. Another Jolson number he liked to perform was 'When You Were Sweet Sixteen':

> I love you as I never loved before,
> Since first I met you on the village green.
> Come to me or my dream of love is o'er.
> I love you as I loved you,
> When you were sweet,
> When you were sweet sixteen.

After a performance, applause would ripple round the room and people's faces would be wet with tears, either of laughter or emotion.

While Al was doing his routine one evening, Chris looked me and said, 'Who wis the first black millionaire, Al Jolson or Muhammad Ali?'

'Al Jolson,' I replied confidently.

'Got ye!' Chris said. 'Al Jolson wis white!'

Al Jolson wasn't the only one who kept us entertained. Phil turned up one time wearing a 'Barlinnie blazer', with a badge bearing the motto 'Ad Sum Ard Labour'. He told us he'd bought the blazer from a gents' outfitters in Govan a few years ago and wore it often, as it always guaranteed a laugh and got people talking to him. They say that in Glasgow talk is cheap because supply exceeds demand, and Phil certainly had a lot of patter on offer.

He reckoned he could tell a story or joke about any subject in the world and challenged us to come up with a word at random, which he would then match with a joke. Albert shouted out,

'Spaghetti! Ah bet ye cannae come up wi a joke fur that!'

Phil smiled, took a sip of his wine, and contemplated the word for a few moments. 'Spaghetti . . . Noo that's a tricky wan. But hold oan, Ah think Ah've got a joke about that somewhere in the back o' ma mind.' He cleared his throat and continued. 'There wis a doctor havin' an affair wi a nurse. Wan day, she turns up and tells him she's pregnant. The doctor says he's happily married wi two kids and he cannae risk the scandal or the expense o' gettin' divorced. He promises her he'll pay fur her tae get oot o' town and hide in Italy until the baby's born. "When ye have the baby," he tells her, "send me a postcard straight away and jist write oan it 'plate of spaghetti', and ma wife'll never know."

'So she flies aff tae Italy and everythin' is goin' accordin' tae plan. Then, wan mornin' his wife hands him a postcard that's jist arrived fae Italy. He reads the message and collapses wi a heart attack. After he's been rushed away tae hospital, the wife looks at the postcard and it says, "Three plates of spaghetti – two with meatballs, one without."' There was much laughter, with shouts of 'That wis a good wan, Phil!' and then Al Jolson started singing 'Swanee' at the top of his lungs.

In the corner, there was an old fellow in a drunken stupor with a copy of the day's paper sticking out of his jacket pocket. I went over and picked the newspaper from his pocket. The report on the front page was all about the poor standard of public health in Glasgow. It stated that alcoholism was a more severe problem here than in any other city in Britain and gave statistics showing that Glasgow had the worst housing in Europe, with overcrowding and more substandard and municipal dwellings than any comparable city. Glasgow also had the dubious honour of being leader in the unemployment league. The sombre article also said that Glasgow's mortality rates were scandalous. Leading sociologists were quoted as saying that Glasgow had been one of the most violent areas in Britain ever since it had been designated a city and that the prison population was far above the average. The city's vast array of problems was put down partly to historical factors, including the continuing problem of sectarianism. The piece made Glasgow out to be some sort of living hell. I suppose for some it was, but it was the only home I knew and I wouldn't have changed it for the world.

I had just finished reading the gloomy story when the old drunk suddenly woke up and staggered towards the kitchen sink. He then began to urinate into it. This was not uncommon in the shebeen. It was generally accepted that those who were too drunk to make it to the outside toilet were allowed to 'pish in the sink'.

I went over to the boys, who were sitting in a corner listening to Holy Harry's stories. Harry wasn't a wine drinker. Whisky was his passion, and the more he drank the more he sounded like a clergyman giving a sermon. He was a real fire-and-brimstone madman. Much to the amusement of his fellow regulars, he was given to shouting out things like, 'My friends, be careful how you live! Set a good example! You may be the only Bible some people will ever read! And remember, if the only prayer you ever say is "thank you", that will suffice!'

I thought it was ironic that, while an old drunk was urinating in a sink only a few feet away, Harry was telling us yet another story with a religious message. 'When I was a young chaplain,' he recounted, 'I went to visit one of my older parishioners in hospital. When I got near her bed, I noticed that with the index finger of one hand she was touching, one by one, the fingers of the other, with her eyes closed. When she opened her eyes, she told me she was saying her prayers the way her grandmother had taught her years before.

'"I hold my hand like this," she explained, "my thumb towards me. That reminds me to pray for those nearest to me. Then, there is my index finger, so I pray for those who point the way for others – teachers, leaders, parents. The next finger is the biggest so I pray for those in high places. After that comes the weakest finger – look, it won't stand up by itself – so I pray for the sick and the lonely and the frightened. And the little finger – well, last of all, I pray for myself."'

'Ach, Harry,' Alex said, 'this is aw gettin' a bit heavy fur us. Have ye no got a story that'll make us laugh?'

'Aye,' Chris added, 'gie's a Bible story that'll bring a smile tae oor faces.'

'Nothin' too serious, Harry!' Albert agreed.

'At school, they were teachin' us about Noah's ark and aw the animals oan it. Have ye got a story about that?' Rab asked.

'Noah's ark?' Harry asked. 'Certainly! Do you know why dogs have wet noses?'

'No, tell us!'

'Well, when all the animals were on the ark, it sprung a leak and they were having difficulty stopping the water coming through a little hole. But then a dog came forward and stuck his nose in the hole, and it fitted perfectly and stopped the leak. So that's why even today dogs have wet noses.'

Harry laughed and broke into 'Amazing Grace'. Everyone sang along, including us.

> Amazing Grace, how sweet the sound
> That saved a wretch like me.
> I once was lost but now am found,
> Was blind, but now I see.

> T'was Grace that taught my heart to fear
> And Grace my fears relieved.
> How precious did that Grace appear
> The hour I first believed.

When the last verse was sung, Holy Harry rose from his chair. He looked as if he was about to start foaming at the mouth. He shouted, 'I would rather be a doorkeeper in the house of God than to dwell in the tents of wickedness!' He said he was quoting Psalms 84:10. If ever the Reverend Ian Paisley needed a stand-in, this was the guy he should call.

As we were about to leave, Al Jolson staggered over. He was clutching a can of gold spray paint. 'Boys,' he said, 'Ah wonder if ye can do me a favour?'

'Whit's that, Al?'

'Well, Ah want tae spray ma name aw over that big wa' in Florence Street. As big as possible tae show folk that Al Jolson is back in town! Will ye keep a lookout fur me?'

We followed Al down the stairs to the street. He walked over to a large gable end and we kept an eye out as he spray-painted the words 'AL JOLSON' on it in giant letters. We couldn't stop giggling at the ridiculousness of it and probably weren't doing the best possible job as lookouts. Just as he was about to finish his graffiti, a police van whizzed round the corner. He'd been spotted. Two big policemen jumped out of the vehicle and one of them shouted, 'Jolson, you've been warned before about this carry-on! You're lifted for vandalism!'

Al was unceremoniously bundled into the back of the van and carted off to the Central Police Station. As he was being whisked away, we could hear him singing 'My Mammy' in the back of the van. Poor soul! He could have done with his real mammy around to help him out of the jam he'd got himself into.

CHAPTER FOURTEEN

·····································

✳

A DAY OOT

Tony the Tim invited us to be his 'personal guests' on the Celtic supporters' bus leaving from the Seaforth pub in the Gorbals for a match in Dundee. We were all mad about football, but we had never been to an away match. We looked on it as a 'day oot', the perfect excuse to escape the grim reality of everyday life in the Gorbals. In fact, for many people in the area, whether they were Catholic or Protestant, Celtic or Rangers supporters, such trips were often cathartic, offering a chance to just let rip for the day.

We boarded the bus on the Saturday morning and it was just as we had expected. All the men were clutching bottles of wine and cans of beer, and everyone was in a jovial mood. In fact, we were the only sober people on the coach. The supporters began to sing a variety of songs, starting off with:

> Oh, when the Celts go marchin' in,
> Oh, when the Celts go marchin' in,
> Ah want tae be in that number,
> Oh, when the Celts go marchin' in.

The coach party was a mixed bag of Gorbals characters like Tony and his cronies and younger guys who were members of the Cumbie razor gang. There were also a great many Irishmen who worked all week as navvies on the building sites. For some, the best part of their tough existence was going to the football, home and away, every week. It was the same for some Rangers supporters. On the bus, Chris said to me, 'Wan side o' the city's singin' about the Pope and Irish freedom fighters, and the other side's singin' about 1690 and King Billy. It's nae wonder folk fae outside Glesga think we're aw mad!'

In Glasgow, there were really only two sorts of supporters: the 'Tims' (Celtic fans) and the 'Huns' (Rangers). Of course, there were also Partick Thistle supporters, but, as far as we were concerned, they never had the same passionate enthusiasm as the Old Firm fanatics. At least you never heard a Partick Thistle fan singing a sectarian song. Many Celtic and Rangers fans considered them objects of ridicule. In fact, the well-worn joke was that the team should have been called Partick Thistle Nil.

As we motored along, more drink was consumed. Sitting in the seat in front of us was an inebriated Irishman in his late 50s. He began to sing in a Donegal brogue, 'F*** them all, f*** them all, the long and the short and the tall!'

'Aye,' Alex shouted to him, 'and f*** you as well, ya Irish bastard!'

At times like this, Alex could be well out of order, but he didn't really mean it. The insult was just his way of taking the mickey. The intoxicated fellow rose from his seat turned round and glared at me and Alex. 'Who said that?' he growled.

Alex was quick off the mark and pointed at me: 'It wis him, mister!' He had just played the oldest trick in the book, but it was my own fault. I had been too slow, and, as the old saying goes, there are two sorts of people: the fast and the unlucky.

The Irishman bashed me in the face and I went sprawling onto the deck of the coach. Blood was pouring from my nose. 'Hey, Paddy, leave the boy alone! He's wan o' us!' one of the mob shouted. Paddy growled and sat down, muttering more threats. Somebody handed me a hankie and I used it to try to stem the flow of blood from my nose.

Alex knew his prank had maybe gone a bit too far. 'Ach, sorry,' he said. 'Ah didnae think that big gub wis gonnae belt ye! Are ye awright?'

I put on a brave face and looked out of the window. I saw a sign reading 'Dundee 60 miles' and thought of the song 'The

Road and the Miles to Dundee' as blood trickled into the hankie.

'Don't worry, it's only a wee belt oan the nose,' said Chris.

Rab agreed: 'Ye'll be awright by the time we get tae Dundee.'

We were about 40 miles from the city when the blood stopped flowing, but the blow had somewhat taken the wind out of my sails. Then the engine began making strange noises and the vehicle slowed down before coming to a complete halt as the driver pulled up in a lay-by. He called out, 'Sorry, boys, the engine has packed up. This bus'll no be makin' it tae Dundee today. The best thing is if everybody gets aff and tries tae hitch a lift oan another bus headin' tae the match.'

In a way, I was relieved because this was a perfect opportunity to get away from the guy who'd hit me, who I believed still had it in for me. The other Diehards and I stood by the side of the road and tried to flag down passing supporters' buses, but most of them were full. Then a half-empty bus pulled up at the lay-by and a fellow, obviously the worse for wear, shouted to us, 'Come oan, boys, there's plenty room!'

The guys from our bus had a look, shook their heads and turned down the man's offer. 'Ah'm no f***in' gettin' oan that bus,' one of the younger guys said to us.

'How no?' I enquired.

'It's full o' the Calton Tongs, and there's no way Ah'm gonnae be sittin' beside them,' he said.

The Tongs were a legendary razor gang based in Glasgow's Gallowgate and long-time adversaries of the Cumbie. It would have been virtual suicide for any of the Cumbie guys to have boarded, but we reckoned we were OK, as we would be treated as 'daft wee boys'. Besides, I preferred to take my chances in the company of the Tongs rather than face the Irishman again.

We boarded the bus feeling a bit apprehensive, but we were greeted like old comrades. 'Hey, it's the young Gorbals mob!' one of the Tongs shouted. 'Sit doon, boys, and enjoy yir trip tae Dundee!'

We did as we were told and soaked in the atmosphere. Most of the gang members had scars, but they were all well dressed. Their patter was loud and aggressive, and there were frequent shouts of the gang's slogan, 'Tongs, ya bass!' The atmosphere somehow managed to be both friendly and intimidating at the same time.

Once again, I looked out the window for a sign to tell me how far we were from Dundee. It said 20 miles, but, given the way the journey had gone so far, I had a feeling that we would be lucky to make it. It wasn't long before I was proved right. A drunk Tong walked up to the front of the bus and shouted at the driver, 'Stop the bus, Ah need a pish.' The driver ignored him. The Tong got more aggressive: 'Fur f***'s sake, ya tube, stop the bus or Ah'm gonnae pish ma troosers.'

The driver told him, 'Ye'll jist have tae hold it in. We're no far fae Dundee and Ah'm no stoppin' fur you or anybody. So away and sit doon and pish in an empty bottle.'

I thought it was a mistake to address a gang member in such a fashion and, once again, I was right. The Tong picked up an empty beer bottle and whacked the driver over the head with it. The bus veered from side to side as blood began to flow from the driver's head. He managed to pull over before slumping unconscious in his seat.

'Whit the f*** have ye done?' one of the other gang members yelled.

'He widnae let me aff fur a pish. Serves him right,' the culprit replied. He then got off the bus and began to urinate loudly against the side of the vehicle.

They laid the driver out on a passenger seat and someone declared, 'He's awright! At least ye didnae kill him! Let him rest fur a wee while and he'll come to. But we've got tae get this bus tae Dundee. Who can drive us there?' he asked the passengers.

One old guy stuck his hand up. 'Ah'll do it. Let me take over the wheel.' The old fellow was extremely drunk. The rest of the way to Dundee, the bus swerved from side to side and it was lucky we didn't crash. We eventually arrived at a car park and the Tongs and the Incredible Gorbals Diehards alighted. The concussed driver was left on board.

The leader of the Tongs said to the gang member who had assaulted the driver, 'Whit did ye do that fur, ya bampot? Because o' you we might miss the game and because o' you we might no have a bus hame.'

'Ach,' the guy replied, 'Ah didnae like his attitude!'

More words were exchanged and a fight developed between the two men. I knew they must both be carrying razors, but they didn't use them on each other. It was a rule never to slash a member of your own gang. The two Tongs began punching into each other, but the leader showed that he had not gained his reputation for nothing. He head-butted his cohort, who fell to the ground. The fellow lay there for several minutes before the leader picked him up and led him away in the direction of the football stadium.

We all grinned at each other. 'Welcome tae Dundee!' Chris said.

'Aye,' I added, 'the home of jam, jute, journalism – and noo the Calton Tongs!'

CHAPTER FIFTEEN

....

✳

HEADIN' HAME

After the laughter had died down, we realised we were in a tricky predicament. We were stuck in Dundee with no guarantee that we would get back to the Gorbals. Also, the match had long started. Besides, we didn't have the money to get in. Tony the Tim had promised to pay for our admission or get his pals to lift us over the turnstiles, but we had lost him along the way.

We had a short walk about Dundee and decided the best bet was to get back to the car park to see if we could hitch a lift on another bus back to Glasgow. When we got there, there was no sign of the Tongs' bus. The driver had obviously come to his senses and vamoosed before they returned. Another victim of the terror of the Tongs!

After a while, a few coach drivers began to reappear, but when we asked them if they had any places on their buses, it was the same answer every time. They were all full. The match was now over and hundreds of supporters were making their way to their coaches. A number of the Tongs turned up. One of them shouted, 'Where the f*** is oor bus?' I explained to him that the driver and bus were nowhere to be found, no doubt as a result of the assault. 'How the f*** are we gonnae get back hame?' he enquired.

It was a question we were all asking ourselves. Chris, however, couldn't stop laughing. 'There's nothin' tae worry about,' he said confidently. 'We'll get back hame by hook or by crook. Jist wait and see!'

Alex agreed: 'Aye, nae bother. We always get oot o' a fix, and this is nae different.'

'The Incredible Gorbals Diehards will never be beaten!' declared Albert.

'Too right!' Rab said, inspired. 'Gettin' back hame is a wee problem pretendin' tae be a big wan!'

I was surprised by how optimistic the boys were, but I reflected that the bash on the nose I'd received might have affected my outlook and put me in an unusually gloomy state of mind.

The leader of the Tongs turned up with the rest of his cronies. He looked like a general ready to lead his troops into battle and oozed semi-inebriated self-confidence. 'If that bastard o' a driver has f***ed aff wi the bus, there's only wan thing fur it. We'll have tae steal another wan tae get back tae Glesga,' he said. Around 20 of his comrades agreed.

They walked over to a still empty bus and looked inside. 'That'll do nicely!' the leader cried. He then picked up a brick and smashed the window of the door. He pulled a lever, the door opened and all the Tongs climbed aboard. 'Come oan, boys, get in,' he told us. 'Jimmy'll get us started and drive us back tae Glesga!' As he was saying this, the man he was referring to, who was a professional car thief, was busy getting the engine running. We hesitated, a bit unsure as to whether it was wise to ride with the notorious Tongs in a stolen bus all the way back to Glasgow.

As I was considering this, the driver of the bus appeared. 'Hey! You lot! Whit the hell are ye doin' oan ma bus? Get the hell aff before Ah call the polis!' He tried to climb on board but a member of the Tongs sprang into action and kicked him full force in the balls. The man fell to the ground moaning.

The bus began to rev up. A big fat policeman, who looked very much like PC Bob from the 'Oor Wullie' cartoon strip, appeared. He saw the driver lying moaning with pain on the ground. 'What happened to you?' he demanded.

The driver moaned and pointed at the bus. 'They guys there have attacked me because Ah caught them stealin' ma bus!'

PC Bob pulled out his thick wooden truncheon and made an

attempt to board the coach, shouting, 'Right, boys, off the bus. You're aw under arrest!'

I thought that was rather a bold statement from this Dundonian polis, but then he didn't know he was dealing with arguably the most violent razor gang in Glasgow. The leader of the Tongs appeared and said calmly, 'Officer, Ah think there's a wee bit of a misunderstanding here.'

PC Bob held his truncheon tightly. 'What do you mean, misunderstanding?'

The leader of the Tongs smiled and moved towards the officer. 'Well, ye see . . .' he was saying. Then he head-butted the policeman hard in the face. PC Bob's nose exploded like a smashed egg. He fell in a heap on the ground beside the wounded bus driver. But it didn't end there. Around ten of the Tongs came off the bus and began to kick into the two of them until they were both unconscious.

'Right, boys,' the leader shouted to his fellow gang members, 'let's f*** off back hame.' The bus pulled out of the car park with gang members shouting out of the windows, 'Tongs, ya bass!'

We were at a loss as to what to do. We were still stranded in a strange town, unwilling witnesses to a bus driver and a policeman being beaten senseless. When more police turned up there would be plenty of questions, and we didn't fancy providing the answers.

While all the action had been taking place, Rab and Alex had gone for a wander to see if they could get us seats on another bus back home. They returned in a jubilant mood. Rab said, 'They've got seats fur us oan a bus over there!'

'Aye,' Alex said, 'Ah know the driver. He used tae drive the bus that takes me tae ma school.' Alex had had trouble keeping up and the education authorities had decided that he needed to attend a special school.

Chris looked at the two unconscious men lying on the ground. 'Thank goodness fur that!' he said. 'Let's blow before mair trouble blows in.'

We boarded the bus and the driver pointed to the back, where there were seats free. As we sat down, I realised that the bus was completely silent, which surprised me because the other supporters' buses we'd travelled on had been deafening.

As the bus pulled out of town, we could see speeding police cars, sirens blaring, heading towards the car park. 'Phew!' Albert said. 'That wis a close shave!'

'Yeah,' Chris agreed, 'we got oot o' that wan by the skin o' oor teeth.'

'There's never a dull moment when we get together!' Alex laughed.

'Aye,' Albert said, 'maybe a bit too interesting at times.'

There was still silence from the other passengers on the bus. My first reaction was to wonder whether they were none too pleased at picking up a bunch of ruffians like us. But what happened next took me by surprise. The fans began waving their hands wildly in the air, still making no noise.

'Whit the hell's happenin', Alex?' I asked.

Alex laughed, 'There's nothin' tae worry about. Ah know some o' these guys fae school. They're aw deaf and dumb.'

'But why are they waving their hands and arms about?' asked Albert.

'Oh, simple, ya thick bastard! They're singin' "The Celtic Song"!'

Although they didn't have the power of speech, they put great energy and fervour into 'singing' 'The Celtic Song' using sign language. We began to mimic them, copying their hand movements, much to their amusement. One of the supporters noticed us, smiled and used some sign language we could all understand – the V sign.

'Imagine Parkhead wis like this every week,' Chris said. 'The polis would be right pissed aff.'

'Why's that?' Rab asked.

'Well,' Chris replied, 'they widnae be able tae arrest anybody fur breach o' the peace!'

We were soon back in Glasgow and Alex's mates invited us to a disco in West Regent Street. Inside, the music was playing full blast through high-powered amplifiers and bright lights were flashing. There were young men and women dancing away, but most of them couldn't hear a note being played because many of them were deaf. I looked on in disbelief. If they couldn't hear the music, how come they were all dancing in time?

'The lights flash in time tae the rhythm o' the music that's bein' played,' Alex explained. 'Also, the vibrations travel through the air and the floor.'

'Ah see whit ye mean,' Albert said. 'Even though they cannae hear the music, in a way they can see and feel it well enough tae be able tae dance tae it.'

'But if ye cannae hear or talk, how the hell do ye chat up a bird ye fancy?' Rab asked.

'Easy-peasy. Jist look over there,' Alex replied.

In a corner of the disco there was a group of young guys chatting up their birds using sign language. They were all smiling. 'Blimey!' Chris observed. 'Silence really is golden!'

CHAPTER SIXTEEN

····································

✳

THE GORBALS CROSS TOILETS

It was late autumn 1967. The weather was getting colder and as the boys and I walked down Crown Street the Glasgow rain was pouring down like a drunk urinating against a wall. It was decided that the Incredible Gorbals Diehards needed somewhere to hang out. After all, every gang needs some sort of headquarters. Alex proposed that we gather together hammers, nails and wood and build a gang hut in the back courts between Crown Street and Thistle Street, 'a place we can aw hang about in when the snow and rain are comin' doon'.

'Don't be daft,' Chris said. 'We'd spend aw that time buildin' it and then it would disappear overnight.'

'Aye,' Albert agreed, 'people would steal the wood for their fires. Coal's expensive and if folk see a pile o' wood standin' there, it'll be gone before ye know it.'

They had a point. Money in the Gorbals was as scarce as stairheid windaes and some people would steal anything, particularly if it was to keep warm. People were always fighting against the cold in the Gorbals. Dealing with the numerous cold draughts that haunted the crumbling Victorian tenements became a bit of an art form. The makeshift gang huts we had built in the past hadn't lasted long. Building them had proved to be a waste of our time and energy.

'Ach, let's go fur a walk and think about it,' Rab said. 'Somethin' is bound tae turn up.'

We found ourselves at the hub of the local community:

Gorbals Cross. During the 1960s, the Cross was a really busy place. It seemed as if all of humanity converged there. Gorbals Street itself housed numerous cash-and-carry warehouses and a plethora of shops run by Asian people, Jewish folk and Italians. It was arguably the most cosmopolitan part of the area. The street was also home to the area's most popular public baths and swimming pool.

On Gorbals Street, we saw a man struggling to lug his heavy suitcase to a nearby bus stop. We gave him a hand. He was a bit out of breath and seemed grateful for the help. 'Thanks a lot, boys,' he panted. 'Well, that's the worst part o' the journey over!'

'Where are ye headin' tae, mister?' asked Rab.

'Sydney, Australia,' he replied, laughing.

It was an unusual day, weather-wise. The rain turned to sleet, then the sleet turned to rain, then the sun came out and promptly disappeared behind a black cloud; a strong wind blew up from nowhere and there was a nasty chill in the air. Four seasons in one day!

'Ah wish God would make his mind up about the weather. He keeps changin' it aw the time!' Albert said.

'Aye, it's confusin',' Chris agreed. 'Wan minute ye need sunglasses, the next an umbrella.'

Rab laughed, 'It's nae wonder people roon here are considered crazy. It's the weather that's turned us aw hawf-mad!'

'Whit d'ye mean?' Alex asked. 'We're no hawf-mad, we're pure mental! And it's got nothin' tae do wi the weather!'

The strange weather only strengthened our resolve to find a headquarters, somewhere we could hide out, preferably in the warmth, during the winter months.

As we walked through the streets, we saw the unusual sight of a young girl struggling inside her jumper. Because of the sudden cold, she had decided to put the garment on but had got her head stuck in the sleeve. 'Help me! Help me!' she was shouting. Alex and Rab ran over and pulled her out of the woollen prison in which she had inadvertently found herself. 'Oh, thanks, boys! Ah tell ye whit, some people can get very lonely in a jumper!'

That was the thing about living in the Gorbals: at times, it could be tough, or just mundane, but sometimes the funny things people said could transform a run-of-the-mill situation into something that made you smile. The residents might have had little or no money, but the main currency was words.

For example, a few nights before, we had witnessed a fight between several hard men. They were waving knives and in the melee one of the guys had his ear cut off. He fell to the ground clutching his head as the ear lay in a puddle. An ambulance was on the scene in no time and the medics bundled the injured guy and his severed ear (in a hankie) into the vehicle. As the doors were closing, someone shouted out, 'Happy New Ear, pal!' It might have been a disconcerting situation, but the Gorbals people had a unique sense of black humour that could, for a moment, transform a grim and violent situation into a farcical comedy.

Interesting conversations were always in the air. After a heavy downpour, I heard one man complain to his wife, 'These bloody puddles are terrible. The streets roon here are always covered in puddles.'

His wife, a stout woman, looked at him and said, 'Hey, stop complaining' Have ye no heard about the droughts in Africa? The people there would do anythin' fur water. If they saw a puddle, they would think they'd hit the jackpot.'

There was also a lot of unconscious humour going about. I was once waiting at a bus stop in Crown Street with three old ladies when I heard one of them say, 'Windy, isn't it?'

The second shook her head, 'Naw, Thursday.'

The third old biddie said, 'Me tae. Let's go and have a cup o' tea.'

Another time, I passed a group of women in their 30s standing on a street corner having a bit of banter. One of them proclaimed loudly to her pals, 'Ma maw's gettin' dead embarrassin'. She's obsessed wi her age. She'll have tae stop makin' herself oot tae be younger than she is, because soon Ah'm gonnae be aulder than her!' It was that kind of humour that kept the people going as they struggled with everyday life.

On that cold and windy day, the boys and I meandered

through the streets, and ended up back at Gorbals Cross. As we passed the public toilets, we could hear a sing-song going on. It was coming from the toilet attendant's room at the bottom of the stairs:

> It's a long way to Tipperary,
> It's a long way to go.
> It's a long way to Tipperary,
> To the sweetest girl I know.
> Goodbye, Piccadilly!
> Farewell, Leicester Square!
> It's a long, long way to Tipperary,
> And my heart lies there.

Alex said, 'That's a strange song. Whit do they want tae tip a fairy fur? It sounds like there's a wine party goin' oan in there.' We trooped down the stairs to investigate. At times like this, Alex was fearless, as if a sudden madness had overtaken him. He banged on the attendant's door with his fists and shouted, 'Open up! It's the sanitary inspector here. Ah know ye've got drink in there. Open the door noo, or there'll be trouble!'

There was silence for a moment and then suddenly the door was opened. A rather sheepish-looking toilet attendant peered out. 'Ach, it's no the sanitary inspector. It's a bunch o' daft boys!' he said over his shoulder to his pals.

Alex smiled and said, 'Sorry tae put the wind up ye, but we heard aw the singin' and we jist wanted tae join yir wee get-together.'

The toilet attendant, who introduced himself as Tommy, said, 'Nae bother. Come away in and join the party, ye're very welcome.'

We walked into the small room. It was comfortable and warm. Two men were sitting on chairs and a sizeable carry-oot of wine and cans of beer, whisky and a large bottle of lemonade was arranged on a table. It was easy company to fall into and we knew one of the men, Jim, from the shebeen. He was known as a bit of a storyteller. He said to the toilet attendant, 'Hey, Tommy, Ah know these young guys. They're awright, they widnae harm a fly. But Ah'll tell you whit, it's better fur you tae be oan their good side rather than their bad side!' The toilet attendant looked slightly worried at this remark and stayed silent.

The other bevvy merchant introduced himself as 'Big Billy'. He was from Partick and he had a massive scar running down each cheek. I thought that having one scar was bad enough but two was really unfortunate. We were all offered glasses of wine but plumped for lemonade instead.

Big Billy poured himself a large Bell's whisky and announced, 'Ah want tae gie you guys a wee tune. Livin' in Glesga has made me feel as though Ah wis born 10,000 years ago!' I knew what he meant. I already felt I had lived at least three lifetimes, with all the preposterous and outrageous situations I'd witnessed. Billy began to sing an old blues song:

> I was born 10,000 years ago,
> There's nothin' in this world I don't know,
> I saw Peter, Paul and Moses playing ring around the roses,
> And I'll whip the man who says it isn't so!
>
> I saw Satan when he looked the garden o'er,
> Then saw Adam and Eve driven from the door,
> And behind the bushes peeping,
> Saw the apple they were eating,
> And I'll swear that I'm the guy what ate the core.
>
> I saw Jonah when he embarked within the whale,
> And thought that he'd never live to tell the tale.
> But old Jonah'd eaten garlic
> And he gave the whale a colic,
> So he coughed him up and let him out o' jail.

Tommy had landed the job as toilet attendant only a few weeks before, and he'd invited his best pals down to his 'wee office' to celebrate. As we sat there in the warmth – there was a glowing three-bar electric fire – and listened to their patter, the thought came to me that this would be the perfect headquarters for us. While we were inside the cosy little room, people were coming and going in the toilets, unaware that we were having a wee party. This gave me a feeling of mischievous contentment.

Albert asked Tommy why he had become a toilet attendant. Tommy, a small man with a thin, almost skeletal frame, replied, 'Well, Ah used tae work wi these two jokers aw over the place. But when the work dried up, Ah had tae take anythin' that wis goin'. When Ah went doon tae the broo, there wis nothin' doin' until a few weeks ago when this job turned up. Ah never thought Ah'd end up as a lavvy cleaner, but tae tell ye the truth it's no a bad job, quite cushy. And because Ah'm a man o' the world Ah know how tae deal wi the drunks and vandals. Mind you, sometimes there's so much bother fae them Ah think that when somebody comes in jist fur a shite, it's a breath o' fresh air!

'Aye, who ever said life wis easy anyway? It's a struggle most o' the time. But listen, boys, Ah'll tell ye somethin': whatever the struggle, carry oan climbin'; it might only be wan step tae the top!

'This job is fine fur me at the moment. Ah've done ma wee office oot jist like a palace and ma pals can call in whenever they want.'

'Aye,' Jim chipped in, 'when it's freezin' the baws aff ye ootside, ye know ye can always call in oan Tommy in his office, and there'll be a drink, warmth and a friendly word.'

'This wee job is a nice change,' said Tommy. 'When Ah wis a boy ma faither taught me a wee rhyme about change that Ah've never forgot: "If ye always go where ye've always gone, if ye always do whit ye've always done, you'll always be whit ye've always been!"

Big Billy raised his large glass of whisky and said, 'Ah'll drink tae that! Here's tae Tommy, the boss o' the Gorbals lavvies! A change is as good as a rest!'

We raised our glasses, saying, 'Tae Tommy, the boss o' the Gorbals lavvies!' It was an unusual toast, but then again what wasn't unusual about the situation?

Chris smiled at me. Albert smiled at me. Alex smiled at me. Rab smiled at me. I smiled back. The Incredible Gorbals Diehards had found their headquarters.

✳

TEN SHILLINGS EACH

So that was it. The Gorbals Cross lavatories were to be our nerve centre, our own wee social club for the winter. Basing ourselves there had numerous advantages: we were bang in the centre of the south-side community; there was no shortage of parties where we met characters and heard stories that would curl your hair; and it was free, with exceptional WC facilities.

Our new centre of operations also had its own motto, which had been composed on one of the toilet doors:

> Here I sit broken hearted,
> Paid a penny and only farted.

The boys and I liked it immensely. Tommy's office was comfortable and warm, with the added bonus that he always had a cheery word for us and a story to tell.

'Ach, this'll do us fur the winter,' said Chris. 'Nice and cosy and a great place tae hide. Anybody that's after us would never think o' lookin' in Tommy's office.'

Albert agreed: 'Aye, it'll be a bit like hibernatin' in the warmth. We'll be jist like tortoises!'

Alex laughed and told him, 'Aye, but we've got thicker skins than tortoises!'

'Ah knew oor lives were goin' doon the toilet,' Albert commented, 'but Ah never thought we'd end up hangin' about wan!'

'It's no so bad,' Rab joked. 'Ah'm flushed wi excitement!'

During the course of the following weeks, we sat in Tommy's office and marvelled at all sorts of shenanigans and were surprised by all kinds of human behaviour. Drunks would come in and try to use the cubicles as their own private drinking booths. With as many as four drunkards squeezing into a confined space with their carry-oots, Tommy would moan, 'Oh, naw! The jakes are in again and Ah'll only get a load o' abuse if Ah try tae throw them oot. Whit can ye do fur me, boys? Any ideas?'

As Tommy had been so kind as to let us use the toilets as our gang hut for the winter, we felt duty bound to help. 'Ah know!' said Chris. 'We can water-bomb them!' We decided to carry out his plan at the next opportunity.

One morning, we were sitting in the office when we heard a crowd of drunken fellows coming down the stairs. They were all talking loudly and aggressively, and when I looked through the gap in the office door into the toilet I could see four jakes, all armed with drink, squashing themselves into a cubicle. They were bearded, shabby men, who, even in the less than fragrant atmosphere of the public toilets, stank to high heaven.

'Hurry up and get in!' one of them shouted to the others. 'It's f***in' freezin' oot there!' His companions did as they were told and squeezed into the small space.

'Awright! First the heavy and then the wine!' I heard one of them cry.

There was the sound of beer cans being opened and laughter. A few yards away at the urinals, men were coming and going, spending the proverbial penny.

Tommy looked worried. 'That's the third time they've been doon here this week and Ah'm fed up throwin' they alkies oot. Sort it fur me, boys!'

We gathered up several plastic bags, went to the sinks and filled them all with water. In a coordinated movement, we lobbed the water bombs into the jakes' cubicle. We swiftly made our way back the few yards to Tommy's room.

'Aaaargh! Fur f***'s sake!' one of the jakes shouted. 'Whit the hell is happenin'? Somebody's tryin' tae droon us!'

They all staggered out of the cubicle, soaking wet, and Tommy confronted them. 'Hey, Ah've told you guys no tae come here again, and if ye do, Ah'm gonnae set ma wild young dugs oan ye!' he said, pointing at us. The jakes moaned and groaned and quickly made their way upstairs and out into the cold. Tommy was laughing. 'Ah'll bet ye that's the first time in years those guys have had a bath or a shower!' he said.

'Shower? They guys are a shower o' bastards,' Albert commented.

Bizarre incidents like that were commonplace in the lavvies. We met all kinds of characters. One regular visitor to the office was 'Sammy the Shilling Thief'. He would often turn up out of breath and banging on Tommy's door as if he was being chased. Sammy, who was in his late 20s, described himself as 'a belly thief . . . Ah steal tae eat.'

He had been thieving since the age of six and regarded it as his profession. He told us he would steal 'anythin' at any time' if it would make him money. His exploits ranged from going shoplifting and nicking lead and other scrap from tenement roofs to his latest scam: robbing shilling meters. At the time, it was estimated that up to 100 shilling-in-the-slot meters were being robbed in Glasgow every weekend.

Sammy told us, 'It's the best and easiest way tae make money. But Ah would never rob a meter in the Gorbals. Ye never shite oan yir ain doorstep.' He and an accomplice would travel to posher districts like Hillhead and find a respectable 'wally close'. He explained that the advantage of going to such areas was that most people were out working during the day and their gas and electric meters were usually quite full. 'Me and ma pal Frankie find a nice quiet close, then we go intae action quietly and slowly. Slowly, slowly, catch the monkey,' Sammy told us. 'Ah go up the close and Frankie stands at the bottom. Ah knock oan a flat door Ah think is empty, then Ah boot it in and head fur the meter. If Frankie sees anybody comin' towards the close, he starts whistlin' tae let me know. It's almost foolproof. We're rakin' it in.'

The other Diehards and I thought that he was exaggerating until one day he and Frankie turned up at the toilets loaded with shilling coins. They had had a good day: ten posh meters in a row and not a witness or policeman in sight. Sammy placed piles of shillings on the office table and gloated, 'The meter reader'll no be gettin' his hands oan these!' Tommy had no objection to him counting out his booty in his office because he was on a bung to provide refuge in such moments. As he counted the mass of coins, Sammy joked, 'Ye might think Ah'm no the full bob, but Ah've got plenty o' them!'

Sammy's cohort Frankie was a different kettle of fish. He was in his 60s and didn't seem like a criminal at all. Soberly dressed, he explained that before his meter-robbing days he had always been in respectable employment. Until he was laid off in 1962, he had been a tram-car conductor. He would often sit in the lavvy office and talk about the days when trams were the main means of transport in Glasgow. He described in detail his life on the swaying, coloured trams, which he referred to as 'shooglies'. They had been a fundamental part of Glasgow transport for 90-odd years, and Frankie had stories about 'wee drunk men', singing passengers, wise-cracking conductors and clippies, and passengers meeting and falling in love on the trams.

As an example of the banter, he told us that one time when he declined to let a passenger with a dog on because the tram was full, the passenger shouted, 'Away and stuff yir tram up yir arse!' to which Frankie replied, 'If ye'd have stuffed yir dug up yir arse, ye both might have got oan!'

When a passenger complained to Frankie, 'We're aw gonnae be late fur oor work,' he would retort, 'Naw, we'll no be. Ah'm awready at ma work!'

'It wis the best job Ah ever had,' he told us. 'Every day, there wis always great patter. It wis like performin' in the music hall. Fur example, a passenger might say tae me, "Does this tram stop at Clydeside?" and Ah'd reply, "Well, if it disnae . . . there's gonnae be a big f***in' splash!"'

When Frankie talked enthusiastically about his old job, it was like listening to a history lesson. He described in great detail how the old trams didn't turn around when they got to their destination. At the terminus, he flipped over the backrests of the bench seats 'like a set o' dominoes'. Destination boards were at both ends of the tram; what had been the back of the vehicle became the front. As the conductor, it was also his responsibility to 'swing the bow collector aroon'. This was the current collector that swivelled on the roof of the tram, reaching skyward and pressing against the electrical cable above.

'But how did ye end up in the robbin'-meters game?' I asked.

'Aye, Frankie,' Alex enquired, 'wis a life o' crime better than bein' oan the trams?'

Frankie shrugged his shoulders, 'Well, after the trams, Ah went oan the buses, but Ah got caught fiddlin' the fares. Ah wis pocketin' some o' the money and an inspector caught me at it. Because Ah wis sacked fur theft, it wis nigh oan impossible tae get another job. Then Ah bumped intae Sammy, who came up wi the meter idea and offered me the job as his lookout. The money's better than bein' a conductor but the stress can get ye doon.'

Sammy laughed as he counted piles of shillings. 'Aye, you're like the trams – you've gone aff the rails! Whit ye worried about? We're quids in. Anyway, they rich people in their wally closes'll no be worried about missin' a few shillin's. Besides, it's the gas and electric boards that'll be missin' oot and they're loaded awready.'

Sammy dealt Frankie a pile of shillings and gave Tommy his cut. Then he handed me and the other Diehards ten shillings each. 'Right, boys,' he said, 'ye never saw nothin'. Have a couple o' bob oan me tae keep yir mooths shut. It's a bit like the war: careless talk costs lives!' He and Frankie bade us farewell, with Sammy shouting, 'A shillin' in the hand is better than two in the meter.'

We all laughed, but as I looked at the ten ill-gotten shiny shillings in my hand, I could sense that trouble was coming.

CHAPTER EIGHTEEN

＊

PAYBACK TIME

'Ten bob!' Alex exclaimed. 'That's twenty tanners! A score o' sixpences!'

As we walked through Gorbals Cross, along Rutherglen Road and into Crown Street, we all began to sing:

> Ah've got sixpence,
> Jolly, jolly sixpence,
> Ah've got sixpence tae last me aw ma life.
> Ah've got twopence tae spend
> And twopence tae lend
> And twopence tae send hame tae ma wife!

Passers-by were looking at us as if we were 'aff oor heids' but we didn't mind because we took pride in the fact that we were 'aw hawf-mad' anyway.

'Whit are ye gonnae do wi yir windfall?' I asked the other Diehards.

Chris answered first: 'Ah'm gonnae get maself a big apple pie and gorge maself oan it. Then Ah might go tae the pictures. An apple pie is two bob and the kids' matinee at the George is a shillin', so this'll cover it nae bother.'

Albert thought for a few moments and said, 'This money's goin' straight tae Murray's newsagents and Ah'm gonnae buy as many comics as Ah can. Ten bob can buy a lot o' good Superman and Spiderman comics.'

Rab said, 'Ah know this wee bird that might gie me a hand job fur two bob. She's a right line-up merchant. They say she'll do anythin' fur a shillin'!'

I was unsure what to do with my ten sparkling shillings. Perhaps stuff myself with cakes and chocolate and have a jubilee. A jubilee was a frozen ice lolly; they were good value – it took ages to finish one, but the process was highly pleasurable.

'So, Alex, have ye made yir mind up?' I asked.

'Aye. Ah fancy tryin' a Ruby Murray. Ah've never had wan before, but the older guys Ah talk tae say curries are the new in thing. Nice and hot and spicy, no like the cauld, damp, freezin' Gorbals. Yeah, Ah'm gonnae go tae a place up the toon and get maself wan.'

I thought it was a good idea. I'd never had a curry before either, but I'd heard they were highly addictive and a lot tastier than the stodgy fried food we were used to. Alex and I headed over the Clyde to Argyle Street, past Boots and into Union Street. Just opposite the side entrance to the Central Station there was a downstairs cafeteria that had signs outside claiming that it sold 'the best, cheapest and hottest curry in Glasgow'. The whole thing felt not like simply going for meal but an exotic adventure.

As we got to the entrance, I noticed half a dozen gangster types going into the restaurant ahead of us. It was obvious that they were a bunch of fly men and con men. Leading the way was a short, plump fellow with a mop of thick black hair. Like his friends, he was immaculately dressed, wearing a jet-black woollen suit, a white shirt and thin black tie, with a white velvet hankie sticking out of his breast pocket. 'When I grow up I want to look like that,' I thought.

At the time, the gangsters of Glasgow all dressed exceptionally well. When they were gallivanting around causing trouble and making money, you never saw hoodlums shabbily dressed, because they really did believe that clothes maketh the man. Scruffy clothes were looked down on as the uniform of the working class and unemployed. The gangsters didn't think of themselves as working class or middle class; as far as they were concerned, they were in a class of their own. They got their dress sense from watching movies starring James Cagney and Humphrey Bogart. They copied the patter, the body language, the gaze, the threatening tones and the humour of their Hollywood heroes. Some of the Glasgow heavies had even visited New York and come back speaking in pseudo-American accents. To Celtic supporters, Jock Stein was the hero; to Rangers fans, it was John Greig; to Glasgow's gangsters, it was Al Capone.

As they walked down the stairs, the boss was laughing with his pals, saying, 'Right, let's get stuck intae the hottest curry in Glesga. It's like sittin' in front o' ma auld maw's coal fire!' As we entered, he shouted to his comrades, 'Smell that curry in the air! Man, we are in heaven.'

The chef behind the counter greeted them like old friends. 'Whit's it tae be, boys? The same as usual?'

'Aye,' the boss replied, 'six o' the hottest Ruby Murrays ye can knock up, and nae scrimpin oan the chilli powder!'

The chef was glad to oblige and got to work. Alex and I stood in the queue, remaining silent, while the gangsters waited and the chef prepared the steaming-hot exotic dishes.

Suddenly, Alex blurted out, 'Hurry up, fur f***'s sake! We've no got aw day!' The gangsters turned round and looked at this cheeky little boy, surprised at his impudence.

'Hey, you! Aye, you!' the boss said to Alex. 'None o' yir cheek or yir daft mooth'll be meetin' ma fist!'

It was then I recognised his face, he had been in the paper, photo and all, only a few weeks before under a bold headline that declared 'Gangland Boss Cleared of Double Murder'. I kept my mouth shut and concentrated my gaze on the floor.

Alex was far braver and madder than even I could have predicted. He replied, 'Aye, who are you f***in' kiddin', Humpty Dumpty? Curries are fur skinny guys like me, no fat bastards like you, so hurry up!'

The boss's face grew bright red and I swear he would have killed Alex right there and then if there had been no witnesses. One of the others grabbed the boss's arm. 'Leave it. He's only a stupid wee boy and he disnae know whit he's talkin' about or who he's talkin' tae. If he did, he'd shite himself.' The boss backed off and luckily the six plates of curry arrived just in time to defuse what could have been an ugly situation.

The gangsters went to one table and after we got our curries we went and sat down at another, but I could see the boss glancing over at Alex every now and again. Alex just carried on as if nothing had happened. I'd often noticed that he had a short attention span, which was perhaps part of the reason why he'd been sent to the special school.

'Mmmm!' he exclaimed, 'Ah'm right intae this curry lark. Nice and hot and spicy. Mind you, ye always get the shits afterwards. They call it Gandhi's revenge. They should feed this tae aw the big fat women in the Gorbals. They might lose some weight then!'

Alex had me laughing out loud, especially when he remarked that the curry was so scorching he would have liked to have put it into his hot-water bottle to keep him warm in the damp single-end where he lived.

We devoured our curries and I noticed that the gangsters had also finished their meal. The boss and his cronies seemed in a better mood now and, much to my relief, were looking less murderous. As I was thinking this, a hot, burning feeling began in my stomach as if someone had set fire to my insides.

'Alex, ma belly feels as if it's oan fire,' I said, sweat forming on my brow.

'Ah've got the same feelin'. In fact, Ah think Ah'm gonnae shite maself.' Alex got up rather quickly and headed for the gents' toilet.

I was ready to do the same, but I heard the gangster boss say, 'That curry is the best laxative ye can get. Ah'm away tae the lavvy tae flush ma system oot.'

Two of his cronies agreed and followed him into the toilets. I wanted to do the same, but I decided to wait until Alex came back out before taking any further action. However, as I waited the fire in my belly just seemed to be getting hotter and hotter, and Alex was taking a long time. I headed for the toilet and was greeted by the sight of Alex being pinned up against the wall by the boss.

'Who the f*** did ye think ye were talkin' tae in there? Don't ye know who Ah am?' he was shouting. The blood had drained from Alex's face, giving it a deathly pale colour.

'Oh, no!' I thought. 'I just hope Alex manages to keep his mouth shut. He doesn't know he's dealing with a gangland hit man!'

Alex spluttered, 'Put me doon, ya big liberty-taker. Let me go!'

The boss, in a moment of unusual common sense, released Alex from his grip. 'Noo,' he shouted, 'are ye gonnae say sorry?'

Alex regained his breath and I thought that perhaps he had seen the light when he said, 'Aye, Ah'll say sorry. Ah'm sorry . . . Ah'm sorry Ah didnae insult ye mair, ya big fat bastard, ye!'

The boss looked aghast, his pals looked aghast, I was aghast. I thought that Alex must have a death wish, and now it was about to come true. He was going to be murdered.

The mobster grabbed Alex by the hair and began to swing him to and fro. Then he threw him into the air like a rag doll, and he fell onto the floor. The boss picked Alex up, shouting, 'Ah'll teach ye, ya cheeky wee bastard. Ah'll teach ye no tae talk tae me like that.' He then gave Alex a Glasgow kiss, sending him back to the floor again.

I did think this really was taking a liberty, as one of the unwritten rules in the Gorbals was that no real man, especially one of the gangster types, would ever contemplate beating up a kid. As Alex lay on the floor, the boss booted into him several times and I could strongly smell shit. The guy had literally kicked the shit out of Alex.

'That's it!' one of the gangsters shouted. 'The boy's had enough!'

'Aye,' said another, 'the cheeky wee bastard has had his just deserts. Let's go.'

Their boss bent over Alex's crumpled body and put his ear to his mouth. 'Ach, there's nothin' tae worry about. The wee bastard's still breathin'. No like that other imbecile we done up the Gallowgate.' Then he looked in the mirror and coolly began to comb his hair. He looked over at me and said, 'You were the sensible wan o' the two. Where are ye both fae?'

My hands were shaking and the fire in my belly was raging. 'The Gorbals,' I replied.

'The Gorbals?' the boss laughed. 'Ah should have known. Aw the cheeky bastards come fae there. When yir pal comes to, tell him tae button his lip in future, comprende?'

'Comprende!' I replied.

The boss laughed again. 'Ye see, you're a cheeky bastard as well, but the difference between you and yir pal is you're a nice cheeky bastard. You know how tae play the game.' With that, he and his cronies left.

Alex was still lying unconscious on the floor. 'Alex! Wake up! Wake up!' I shouted in desperation.

Suddenly, he came to, as if he had been in a dream or, in this case, a nightmare. 'Whit the f*** happened?' he asked. He couldn't remember a thing.

As he cleaned the blood from his face and the mess from inside his trousers, I went into a cubicle and dealt with Gandhi's revenge. When I emerged a few minutes later, Alex looked as if nothing had happened to him. He had a few slight bruises on his arms and face, and that was it.

We walked up the stairs and out into the fresh air. As we strolled along the bridge over the Clyde towards Eglinton Street, Alex suddenly said to me. 'Ah, it's aw comin' back tae me.'

'Whit, can ye really remember whit happened, Alex?' I asked.

'Aye, it wis a smashin' curry, very hot. In fact, it wis so hot it knocked me oot completely. Let's go fur another wan soon,' Alex said.

'Sure, nae bother, Alex,' I replied.

It was as if Alex had a knack for blotting out the trouble he'd caused – not a bad skill given the amount of bother his mouth got him into.

CHAPTER NINETEEN

✳

TEN-BOB TALES

Our ten-shilling adventure was certainly something I wouldn't forget in a hurry, but what about the other boys? Did Chris get his apple pie and visit to the pictures? Did Albert get his comics? Did Rab, to put it politely, have his passionate liaison? The next day, all was to be revealed.

We met up and, as the day was crisp and sunny, we sauntered over to the Glasgow Green. Chris was sporting two black eyes, Albert had a large bruise on his forehead and Rab's hand was bandaged. The Incredible Gorbals Diehards looked as though they had been in the wars, and I felt somewhat guilty, as I was the only one with not a scratch on me.

We stopped near the People's Palace and Chris began to tell us his story. 'Armed wi ma shiny bobs, ma plan fur the day wis simple: spend aroon two bob oan a big apple pie and once Ah'd scoffed that Ah wis aff tae the George tae spend another shillin' oan seein' a hawf-decent picture. Anyway, Ah bought this big apple pie and sat doon in the back court tae get stuck intae it. In fact, ma mooth wis drippin' jist at the thought. Ah'd put the apple pie doon beside me when two bampots appeared and wan o' them shouted, "Gie's that pie or Ah'll kick yir heid in." The next thing Ah knew, Ah wis wrestlin' wi the two o' them. They couldnae get the better o' me, but wan o' them managed tae punch me in the eye. Ah wis hawf-blinded, but Ah still gave them a doin'. They ran away and when Ah looked doon, a big Alsatian dug wis eatin' ma pie. Ah booted it right up the arse and it howled, but it wis too late tae save the pie and aw's Ah wis left wi wis a pile o' crumbs.

'Ach, Ah jist thought it wis wan o' those things, wan o' those days, so Ah headed aff tae the pictures. Ah had only jist sat doon when a bunch o' boys came in and sat behind me. They were aw laughin' and jokin' and then Ah felt somethin' wet oan the back o' ma neck. Wan o' the bastards had spat at me, a real big, filthy, greasy spittle. Ah turned roon and punched wan o' they boys full force in the face, but his pals jumped oan me and were punchin' and kickin'. That's how Ah ended up wi this other keeker [black eye]. The manager turned up wi a couple o' usherettes and we were aw flung oot. In the fight, Ah lost the rest o' ma shillin's.'

Then it was Albert's turn. 'Ye think you had a bad day? Ah went tae Murray's tae buy some comics, but they were low oan supply, so Ah decided tae try another shop, the wan in Eglinton Street near the Coliseum picture hoose. Anyway, Ah'd got the latest Superman and Spiderman comics and Ah wis walkin' along Bedford Street near Nicholson Street, real bandit country. Four scruffy-lookin' bastards appeared fae nowhere and wan o' them shouted, "Drop the comics noo!" He wis a big tube aged aroon 16, and he looked like he hadnae seen a bar o' soap since the Pope wis an altar boy. Ah tried tae run aff, but the fella got a grip oan me, threw me intae a puddle, then kicked me in the heid wi his manky wellington boots. That wis it. They were gone, ma comics were gone and aw's Ah wis left wi wis this bloody bruise oan ma napper.'

As visitors were coming and going from the People's Palace, which tells the story of Glasgow's history, I thought that what I was hearing here was far more amusing and interesting than anything any museum could offer.

Rab was next to put us in the picture with his incredible tale. 'Ah goes roon tae see Fat Bessie and offers her the goin' rate fur a hand job, two bob. But she tells me her rates have gone up tae three bob – supply and demand and aw that. Anyway, Ah managed tae knock her doon tae hawf a crown – two and a tanner – and we headed fur a back lane. Ah nae sooner had it oot when her two big brothers appeared oan the scene and wan o' them wis wavin' a thick leather belt. He wis shoutin' at Bessie, "Whit did Ah tell ye? Ya dirty hing-oot! Maw says ye've got tae stop this carry oan." Then he hit her right across the heid wi the belt and she bolted aff screamin' like a maniac.

'Then Ah wis next. The two o' them gave me a right beatin' wi the belt. Ah tried tae put ma hands up tae defend maself, but the belt jist kept rainin' doon oan me. Tae make matters worse, after they gave me the doin' they made aff wi ma money. Aw's Ah wanted wis a hand job, but Ah ended up wi a hand that needed a bandages job!'

After our tales of woe were told, we decided to walk back over the bridge to the Gorbals and make for our headquarters. When we got to the toilets, Tommy was sitting alone drinking a large bottle of El Dorado wine. He was slightly drunk but in very good spirits and full of absurd patter.

'Ah'm a bit worried about ma position,' he said to us.

'Why's that, Tommy?' Alex enquired.

'Well, a stocktaker came this mornin' and he found that there were two shits missing!'

We sat and chatted and after a while there was a loud knock on the door. It was Sammy and Frankie, really out of breath. Both of them were wearing large black coats, the pockets jingling and bulging with shilling coins.

Sammy said, 'We had a good mornin', screwed ten meters, but we might have a wee problem.'

'Oh, aye?' Tommy asked. 'Why's that?'

'Well, the last meter we screwed wis goin' well,' Sammy said, 'until Ah heard Frankie whistlin' at the bottom o' the close tae warn me that somebody wis comin'. Anyway, Ah ran doon the stairs and when Ah got tae the street there wis a fat fella in a suit comin' towards the close. Me and Frankie walked roon the corner but the next minute the big fella appears, shoutin', "Come back here, you two bastards! Ye've screwed ma meter!" We were quick aff the mark and he couldnae catch us, but Ah'm worried.'

'Why's that?' asked Alex.

Sammy's hands began to shake. 'Because Ah know the guy. He wis in Barlinnie at the same time as me. He's a real gangster, wan o' the heavy mob fae the Gallowgate. He's well known fur beatin' the f*** oot o' people fur money. He runs a protection racket. He knows ma face, knows ma name, and he's gonnae be after me and Frankie big time. How wis Ah supposed tae know whose meter Ah wis screwin'?'

There was only one thing for it: more wine was needed to steady the nerves of Sammy and Frankie. Both of them were shaking so uncontrollably that Chris commented, 'They two look like a pair o' pneumatic drill operators.'

Tommy also looked worried, for he was the man that was providing a safe haven for the meter robbers, and when – not if – the mobster found out, he would receive the same unmerciful punishment that was being prepared for Sammy and Frankie.

A large carry-oot appeared on the scene and the nerves began to fade as the effects of the wine took hold. Indeed, at one point Frankie shouted jokingly to Sammy, 'That's another fine mess you've got me into, Stanley!'

We were all interested to hear how Sammy had got into this mess. We wanted to know how and when he started in crime. It was a bit like having a TV chat show, where Sammy was the celebrity and we were the hosts.

'So, Sammy,' I asked, 'how did yir life in crime start?'

'Well, Ah wis about 12 at the time and ma family didnae have any money – no a bean, no even a pot tae pish in. We were nothin' special, poor but dishonest. In fact, we were so poor the Red Cross used tae send us parcels. The last straw fur me wis when ma drunken faither came in wan Christmas Eve and told me and ma two brothers and three sisters that there would be nae presents fur us oan Christmas Day.'

'Why wis that?' Albert asked.

'That auld bastard told us that Santa Claus had committed suicide after an argument wi Rudolph and the elves. We aw burst oot cryin' and that Christmas wis the worst ever. Especially when aw ma pals got presents and told me Santa wisnae deid, he had come doon their chimneys. Frae then oan, Ah vowed that if Ah wanted somethin' Ah'd take it – Santa or nae bleedin' Santa!'

'So how did ye start aff?' Chris enquired.

'Ah asked God fur a bike and Ah waited and waited, and then Ah sort o' remembered that it disnae work that way. So, instead, Ah went oot and stole a bike and asked God fur forgiveness. The bike proved a great way o' gettin' roon Glesga. Ah could pinch things and make aff quite quickly. It wis the best getaway vehicle ye can imagine.'

'And how did ye end up in Barlinnie?' Rab asked.

'Ach, it jist happened over time. Shopliftin' led me tae approved school and Ah loved it there. Good food, clean clothes and Ah wis away fae ma drunken lyin' faither. Also, Ah made a lot o' great pals. The problem wis they were aw thieves like me. When Ah got oot o' there, Ah teamed up wi some o' them and started breakin' intae shops and stealin' lead fae roofs. It wis after that that Ah ended up in borstal.'

'Whit wis borstal like?' asked Albert.

'Good!' Sammy said. 'It wis like goin' tae criminal finishin' school. Ah learned a load o' tricks there and met guys fae aw over Scotland who had much the same background as me – shite and poor. Afterwards, Ah did wan bank job but got caught straight away and ended up in Barlinnie fur a stretch. When Ah'd served ma time, Ah worked oot that screwin' meters wis a boomin' industry, so that's where Ah'm at noo. Besides, breakin' intae a meter gets ye a much shorter sentence than a bank job. The money's good, too, so in a way it's the ideal job. They say that crime disnae pay, but that sayin' wis thought up long before shillin' meters were invented!'

Sammy was funny, but deep down we knew it was no laughing matter. Somewhere in the city, there was a psychotic criminal planning retribution against him and his sidekick.

CHAPTER TWENTY

✳

VENGEANCE

They say that time is a great healer of wounds, but it can also provide menacing people with the chance to form a plan to inflict the injuries in the first place.

A few days after Sammy had told us of his encounter with the top gangster, we called into the lavvy only to find Tommy absolutely steaming drunk. It was obvious he was worried about something. Sammy was sitting with him, not quite as inebriated, but ashen-faced. Tommy, on a wine-fuelled high, shouted to us, 'Welcome, boys. Ah've turned vegetarian – Ah only eat wine noo!' But there was no laughter from Sammy, who sat glumly in his chair with the look of a man who was about to face a firing squad.

I noticed that Tommy was wearing a new pair of expensive-looking glasses, and, in the hope of lightening up the atmosphere, I asked him, 'Where did ye get the specs, Tommy? They almost make you look intelligent!'

He took another slug of his wine and said, 'The meter money. Ah bought them fae ma cut o' the stolen shillin's. Ever since Ah wis a wee boy, Ah've always wanted a nice pair o' glasses. Ah used tae wear horrible NHS wans and the other kids used tae taunt me at school, callin' me "specky four-eyes", so Ah saved up aw ma bobs and got these. Crackin' glasses, aren't they?'

'Aye,' said Chris, laughing, 'can ye see yir way tae lendin' us a pound?'

But there was still no laughter from Sammy and no sign of Frankie. 'Whit's up?' I asked Sammy. He shook his head and his face contorted into a tortured expression. 'Frankie's in hospital,' he said. 'They got tae him.'

'Who got tae him?' I asked.

'The f***in' Glesga Mafia. They've been aw over the place lookin' fur us. Ah told Frankie tae keep his heid doon fur a while, keep a low profile. But the stupid bastard widnae listen. He's a regular at a bookie's in the Gallowgate. He went in there wi a few shillin's tae stick a bet oan and who wis there? Aye, you guessed it – the hood whose meter we screwed. They bundled Frankie into a motor, kidnapped him. They took him tae a single-end in Bridgeton, tied him tae a chair and beat the f*** oot o' him wi baseball bats. At first, he widnae talk, widnae tell them where Ah lived, but they ended up pullin' oot two o' his teeth wi pliers. O' course, he ended up spillin' the beans.'

'How is he noo?' Rab asked.

'In a bad way,' Sammy said. 'He's lyin' up in the Royal Infirmary wi two broken arms and two broken legs and o' course a couple o' missin' teeth. He's oan a drip. They dumped him near the hospital and phoned fur an ambulance. Ah've jist been tae his bedside. He says they're scourin' Glesga lookin' fur me. The problem is they know where Ah live noo, so it's no safe tae go back hame. Also, they might know we sometimes divvy up the money here, so it's no even really safe fur me here.'

As he said this, he pulled a bunnet over his head and arranged a thick tartan scarf so that it partially covered his face. 'Right, boys,' he told us, 'Ah'm fur the aff. If anybody comes lookin' fur me, ye've no seen me, right?'

'Aye, right, Sammy,' we all replied.

He'd been gone less than an hour when there was a loud knock on the door. Chris opened it and three gangsters walked in. I was taken aback because leading the way was the hoodlum who had almost beaten Alex to death. He was accompanied by a guy who had 'CUT HERE' tattooed on his throat and another fellow who had tattoos on his right and left knuckles proclaiming 'LOVE' and 'HATE' respectively.

The fat gangster looked taken aback at seeing me and Alex,

but he covered it up well, shouting, 'Ah, the Gorbals curry boys! You been behavin' yirselves?'

Tommy and the rest of the boys looked frightened, and a bit alarmed that this guy knew us, but I kept my cool and replied, 'Aye, sure. Whit are ye doin' in the Gorbals? Is this no a wee bit aff yir patch?' I thought it was a good line, as I had heard it uttered many times by older hard men greeting each other.

'Good question, young man,' the hood replied. 'Well, the problem is that two guys broke intae ma hoose and stole a right few bob fae ma meter. As if that's wisnae bad enough, they broke intae ma auld maw's hoose and stole aw the meter money. The shock put her in a bad way and she wis rushed tae hospital wi a suspected heart attack.'

'Aye,' added the 'CUT HERE' man, 'the auld woman is 82 and the shock's nearly killed her.' As he spoke, I could see tears of emotion welling up in the boss's eyes. For a few minutes, he was struck dumb. I could sense that he loved nobody in the world but his old mother, and someone had had the audacity to break into her house – a suicidal move.

'LOVE' and 'HATE' was next to join the fray. 'We've caught wan o' the guys awready,' he said. 'A big bampot called Frankie. He'll be in the hospital fur a while, though. That's him sorted. Noo we're lookin' fur another joker, a f***in' liberty-taker called Sammy. Has he been aroon recently?'

The boys and I stayed silent and shrugged our shoulders. But the wine had given Tommy more Dutch courage than was good for him. 'Whit the fuck are ye talkin' about? We don't know nothin' about nothin'!' he yelled.

The boss looked angrily at Tommy and broke his silence: 'By the way, whit's yir name?'

'Tommy.'

The leader walked over and punched Tommy right in the face, knocking the new glasses off. Tommy fell to the floor and the three gangsters began kicking into him, leaving him moaning and groaning.

'Tommy, eh? You're the bastard that's been lettin' them divvy up here!' the boss shouted angrily. As he said this, he tramped on the specs, crushing them under his foot. Tommy's expensive new glasses had suddenly become a jigsaw puzzle. 'Well, we want compensation fur aw the trouble you bastards have caused,' said the gangster. 'Five hundred quid by next week or you and yir pal Sammy are deid.' Tommy moaned in agreement and the three gangsters climbed the stairs to Gorbals Cross.

The attack had certainly sobered Tommy up. 'Five hundred quid?' he said, spluttering through blood. 'How are we gonnae raise that sort o' money?'

'Ach, don't worry,' Albert said, as we helped clean the blood from his face. 'You and Sammy'll jist have tae beg, borrow and steal. Sure, that's whit ye've been doin' aw yir lives!'

During the next few days, Tommy searched all over the place for Sammy, but he was nowhere to be found. Eventually, he twigged that his pal had probably gone into hiding at his sister's house in Paisley – far enough away to conceal himself from the denizens of Glasgow's underworld.

On an urgent visit to Paisley, Tommy was told by the sister that she hadn't seen Sammy, but that was just what he'd expected to hear. He left a note for his pal 'just in case he passes by'. The note was short and to the point: they had to raise £500 by the following week, otherwise the two of them would end up like Frankie or even worse. It emphasised that they were both safe for a few days to give them leeway to get the money but they were in the danger zone if they failed to meet the deadline. The note did the trick and Sammy turned up at the Gorbals Cross toilets.

It was like watching a strange sort of business meeting. 'Right,' Sammy said to Tommy, 'how much can ye raise?'

Tommy thought for a moment. 'Well, wi the shillin's Ah've got left, some savin's, plus ma pay at the end o' the week, probably a hundred quid.'

'F***in' hell! That means Ah'll have tae find four hundred! At the moment, Ah've probably got a hundred, so that leaves another three . . . Ah'd better get tae work.'

Albert's prediction came true. Sammy had to beg steal and borrow to get the balance. A hundred quid was begged from the seriously injured Frankie, another hundred he borrowed from his sister – 'The poor wee soul's life savin's,' he explained – and the final hundred he acquired by 'screwin' a few upmarket hooses' in Paisley.

The money was placed in a brown envelope and, because Tommy and Sammy were too afraid to meet the gangsters face to face again, Alex and I were entrusted with the task of handing the money over at Gorbals Cross.

At the appointed time, a huge silver Ford Zodiac pulled up at the Cross with the three gangsters inside. Alex and I walked over and the boss wound down the driver's window. 'Ah, the curry boys! Is it aw there?' he asked.

'Aye,' I replied, 'Five hundred quid compensation in crisp Bank of Scotland notes!'

The gangster smiled, opened the envelope and counted the money. 'Wan . . . two . . . three . . . four . . . five. Spot oan! Tae make bread, ye need dough! Thanks, boys, and tell they two idiots they're in the clear noo. Ma maw's recovered and Ah'll be payin' fur a holiday fur her oot o' this cash. Money's like muck – nae good unless it's spread about.' He thought for a moment and then said to us. 'Good work, lads. Ah'm fair impressed by ye! Ah'll tell ye whit, do ye fancy a curry? It's oan me.'

I looked at Alex uncertainly. Then suddenly he replied, 'Thanks fur the kind offer, mister, but ma doctor told me no tae try curry again.'

'Oh, aye? And why's that?'

'It causes me tae have blackouts,' Alex answered, with a sardonic expression on his face. We all guffawed as the Zodiac sped off over the Glasgow horizon.

CHAPTER TWENTY-ONE

✳

MIDDEN MONEY

In the Gorbals, most people faced an everyday struggle with money, and poverty can make people do strange things. Take, for example, 'Malky the Midgie-Raker'. He was a fellow in his late 50s, with a slim build and a mop of grey hair. When I wandered around the back courts with the Diehards, we frequently spotted Malky going from midden to midden, dustbin to dustbin, searching for any discarded items that might raise money.

Unusually, he was not a drinker, but, as Alex and Chris observed, he was certainly 'no the full shillin". Rab quipped that Malky was 'two cans short o' a carry-oot'. But there was no doubt about it, he was an extremely hard worker, and being a self-employed 'midgie-raker', he had to be. A normal working day for him started at around 9 a.m., and he sifted through the rubbish in the middens until it got dark.

Sometimes he had a pal with him, a scruffy-looking alcoholic who was his right-hand man, and they would share the spoils at the end of the day. The alcoholic would take his stuff and sell it on, then head for the pub to obliterate reality. Malky was a different kettle of fish. He made off with whatever he considered of value then sat on it for a while before finding a buyer who would pay a reasonable price. The alcoholic was homeless, but it was rumoured that Malky had a 'smart wee flat' in nearby Govanhill.

Midgie-rakers fascinated us lads. There was an apocryphal story going round that one of them had started off with a pram to cart around the goods he found in the middens. He made so much money he was able to buy a cart and then a car to transport what he began to call 'discarded antiques'. He steadily progressed over the years from taking his stuff to the local rag stores and scrap merchants to having a stall of his own at the Barras, and eventually he opened up an antique shop. Although it seemed plausible enough, we surmised that it was just another Gorbals fairy tale. The area, with some of the worst unemployment, violence, poverty and drunkenness in Britain, thrived on such stories. They gave people hope that one day they just might, if they were lucky, escape from it all and make good.

To transport his goods, Malky used a big Victorian-looking black pram, which had itself been one of his finds in a 'lucky midden'. The middens fell into two distinct categories: the ordinary midden, where no real treasure was to be found, and the lucky midden, where all sorts of discarded treasures were lurking.

One day, we spotted Malky in the back courts between Crown Street and Thistle Street. The middens there were a mixed bag; some were considered lucky and others not so. This was because the residents of Crown Street lived in what they considered to be superior housing to that available in Thistle Street. It was working-class snobbery, of course, but Malky did believe that the Crown Street middens were better hunting grounds than the Thistle Street ones. As he said, 'The people o' Crown Street have jist that bit mair money and they can afford tae throw away things that the Thistle Street mob would hold oan tae.' It was a debatable theory, but who were we to argue with a man who had spent the last decade sifting through middens?

When we caught up with him that day, his alcoholic sidekick was nowhere to be seen. Malky stopped for a break, rolled himself a cigarette and explained his pal's absence: 'That nae-good bastard has failed tae show. We had a good run yesterday. He found an old gold brooch in wan o' the middens. Ah wis aw fur keepin' it till Ah could find a good buyer, but he wis straight aff tae the pawnbrokers. They handed him ten quid fur the brooch. Five pounds fur him and five pounds fur me – no a bad wee windfall. But the problem is, once an alcoholic like him gets money, he heads straight tae the pub tae drink himself stupid. That's why he's no turned up the day. He's probably lyin' somewhere in a stupor or spendin' the rest o' his money in the pub. Ah think Ah'll have tae gie him the sack.'

We all burst out laughing at that last remark. 'Imagine gettin' the sack fae bein' a midgie-raker,' Alex muttered under his breath. 'Ye cannae get much lower than that!'

'Aye!' Chris agreed, before addressing Malky: 'So, Ah think ye'll no be givin' him a reference fur his next job!'

Malky looked concerned, took a puff of his Woodbine and said, 'It's no a laughin' matter. Ah'm wan man doon and Ah wis plannin' tae hit a few lucky middens in Hillhead this afternoon. Ah'll be needin' help.' Hillhead was a posh area of Glasgow and we realised there were sure to be quite a few lucky middens there. Malky took another puff of his cigarette and looked us up and down. 'Ah'll tell ye whit, boys, why don't ye come along and help me oot? Jist fur the day. Ah'll split anythin' we find fifty–fifty, hawf fur me and hawf fur you guys. We're sure tae make money. Ah never leave Hillhead wi'oot a profit!'

It was an offer we found hard to refuse. Besides, the unofficial motto of the Incredible Gorbals Diehards was 'Never turn down an experience'.

'Awright, Malky, we'll do it,' I said.

'Aye, nothin' ventured, nothin' gained,' Chris agreed.

Albert chipped in, 'Ma auld man is always sayin', "Where's there's muck, there's brass!"'

'But we're no professional midgie-rakers like you, Malky, so ye'll have tae gie's a few pointers, a few tricks o' the trade,' Alex said.

'OK, it's settled then,' Malky said. 'You guys can join me fur the day and Ah'm tellin' ye, it's gonnae be worth yir while. Right, first, tricks o' the trade. When we get tae the middens, keep yir eye oot fur things like weddin' or engagement rings in the bins.'

'Rings?' Chris said, 'People willnae be thowin' them away!'

'Naw, ye're wrang,' Malky said. 'They Hillhead tenements are full o' posh young birds that have jist got married or are about tae get married. When they put the rubbish oot, the ring often falls fae their fingers and right intae the bin. They're either too posh, too upset or too daft tae search through the manky rubbish tae get the ring back, and that leaves the coast clear fur us tae rake it in.'

'So is it only rings we're lookin' fur?' Albert asked.

'Naw, naw, naw, naw. Ya stupid wee eejit,' Malky said. 'The older wans throw oot aw sorts o' valuables: clocks, paintin's, vases, plates and saucers, aw kinds o' bric-a-brac that can be sold oan at the Barras or tae a dealer. So keep yir eyes open at aw times.'

'But how are we gonnae get tae Hillhead?' I enquired. Malky told us he had a cousin called Gordon who worked as a chauffeur for a company that provided limousines for weddings and funerals. We made our way to a telephone box in Bedford Street and Malky was soon on the blower to his cousin.

'Aye, Gordon. That's right. Pick us up and take us tae Hillhead, will ye. Ah've got five boys wi me and they're gonnae do a wee bit o' graft in the lucky middens.'

Half an hour later, a large black Daimler arrived and we all piled in. 'Right, lads,' Gordon said, 'we'll have tae be fast. Ah've got a funeral lined up in hawf an hour.' We were driven in luxury to Hillhead. It occurred to me that we must have been the poshest midden-rakers ever.

'Whit's it like bein' a chauffeur, Gordon?' Albert asked.

'It's no a bad job, but Ah'm jist a lowly driver. Aw the high heid yins look doon their noses at me. Ah jist ignore that and get oan wi ma job, thinkin' about the monkey tree principle.'

'Whit the hell is that?' Rab asked him.

'Well,' Gordon replied, as we glided through the streets of Glasgow, 'the monkeys at the top o' the tree look doon at the monkeys at the bottom of the tree and aw's they can see is smilin' faces lookin' up at them; the monkeys at the bottom o' the tree look up and aw's they can see is a bunch o' arseholes above them.'

That made us laugh, and then it was out of the car and into the back courts to begin our search of the so-called lucky middens.

Malky had been right. It didn't take us long to find some things
of value. In one midden, Albert came across a little painting that
depicted the Colosseum in Rome. Meanwhile, Alex stumbled
across a clock that looked as if it might be Victorian. In yet
another midden, Rab found an old decorative plate, which had
the maker's name and the date 1925 stamped on the back of it.

But no matter how hard we searched, Chris and I were turning
out to be the least successful. Our haul so far was two empty
ginger bottles (worth tuppence each) and a smashed framed
photo of a First World War veteran.

In one back court, a woman appeared carrying a pile of old
dusty-looking comics. She said to us, 'My man's been comic mad
since he was a boy. He's got all these old ones hanging about the
house and they're just causing a mess. I'm throwing them out
while he's at work. You can have them if you want.'

We stopped work for a few minutes and rifled through the
pile. The comics certainly looked ancient. They dated back to
before we were born, some to before the war. There were old
editions of *Detective Comics* with Batman and of *Action Comics*
with Superman. Albert said, 'Ah've never seen such auld comics
before. The guy who collected these has got good taste.'

Then Malky shouted over at us, 'Come oan, boys, drop they
daft comics and get back tae work. There's nae money in readin'
comics. Get a move oan! Time is against us.'

Alex got the pile of comics and threw them into the midden.
'If we've no got the time tae read comics, naebody else is gonnae
read them.' He took a box of matches out of his pocket, lit a
match and dropped it on the pile. Albert must have been about
ready to murder him, but he knew better than to argue with
Alex when he was in that kind of a mood.

Over the next few hours, we all continued searching through
the middens with a ferocious zeal. It was getting dark and we
were about to give up when Chris shouted out, 'Oh, ya beauty,
ye!' He sounded like a prospector who'd just come across a gold
nugget, and he had indeed come up with gold. For in the bottom
of the bin he was searching through was a magnificent-looking
gold ring. It was no ordinary gold ring, either, Malky told us,

having scrutinised it through a magnifying eyeglass that he kept in his pocket, but a 21-carat Edwardian antique.

'Aye, this ring is the business!' he declared. 'Let's get the f*** oot o' Hillhead before the owner turns up!' We all scarpered out of the back court and Malky made another phone call from a nearby box, asking Gordon to come and pick us up.

As we sat in the back of the limo, Malky did his calculations. 'Right. The ring'll probably fetch a hundred, the paintin' a fiver and the clock and plate another fiver – that's a hundred and ten quid in total.' Much to our surprise, Malky put his hand into his waistcoat and pulled out the money right then and there – £55 for us to share. He couldn't be that daft, after all. He laughed, saying, 'Ah told ye Hillhead is full o' lucky middens, and you guys have brought me luck!' He then handed a fiver to Gordon to cover his petrol.

As the limo dropped us off in Crown Street we all agreed that being a midgie-raker was not a bad life at all. But even though the money had been good, we would never have considered taking it up full time. 'Leave the midgie-rakin' tae professionals like Malky,' Chris said, waving a ten-pound Clydesdale Bank note in the air.

Years later, I realised that setting fire to those old comics had been absolute folly. In February 2010, a May 1939 copy of *Detective Comics* featuring the first appearance of the Caped Crusader was sold in the USA for a record $1,075,000. Earlier that month, a copy of the June 1938 edition of *Action Comics* that introduced Superman to the world had sold at an auction in Dallas for $1 million.

✳

CHAPTER TWENTY-TWO

SEMPER VIGILO

During our ride in the limo, Gordon had said to us, 'Look, boys, if ye come across anythin' big that can make us some money, gie me a shout. Ah can shift the gear in this car easily and get us a good price. The firm disnae pay me that much tae be a chauffeur, so Ah've got tae make ma money up in other ways, if ye know whit Ah mean.' As he pulled up at a set traffic lights, he turned his head round, laughed and then winked, a real dodgy wink, I thought, typical of a fly man on the make. Gordon also gave us his business card with a phone number on it should we ever need his services.

When we'd got out of the car and were walking through the Gorbals with Malky, a woman ran up to him, sobbing, and shouted, 'He's gone! Yir pal's gone!'

Malky look confused. 'Who's gone?' he asked.

The woman revealed she was referring to Malky's alcoholic right-hand man. This tearful lady was his unfortunate sister.

Malky looked visibly shocked. 'Whit the hell happened tae him?' he asked.

The tears flowed down the woman's cheeks like a waterfall as she blurted out, 'It wis the drink. The last time Ah saw him wis late last night. He had a carry-oot, and we were havin' a wee joke together. Funny enough, Ah said tae him, "Ah hope ye're no gonnae drink yirself tae death!" Ah wis worried about him, o'course, but Ah wis only jokin' really. He shrugged his shoulders, laughed and told me, "Chance would be a fine thing!"

That wis the last time Ah saw him. They found him lyin' deid this mornin' in wan o' the closes. There wis an empty bottle o' whisky beside him.'

On hearing this, Malky began to shake and he said to her, 'Listen, Ah'll handle the funeral arrangements. Don't worry about the money.'

The woman brushed the tears from her face and said, 'Oh, thanks, Malky. Ah don't want tae see him get a pauper's funeral.'

In the Gorbals, it was most people's worst nightmare to end up having a pauper's funeral. That was why so many paid a few shillings a week to the local Co-op or the Provident man who knocked on the door every Friday for insurance money. Their lives might have been poverty-stricken, but it was considered essential that they have a dignified exit.

Thinking of death reminded me of a joke on that subject. A Gorbals man died and awoke in the afterlife. He saw familiar crumbling tenements and equally familiar old faces. 'Ah never thought that Heaven would be jist like the Gorbals!' he exclaimed, and a voice replied, 'Who said this was Heaven?'

We walked with Malky along Crown Street. His face was pale with shock and he told us he was going to head home to his flat in Govanhill. Before he got on his way, he said to us, 'That news wis a real kick in the baws. Ach, Ah'll tell ye whit, Ah'm gonnae gie up the midgie-rakin' fur a while. Ah need a rest and, besides, Ah've got tae sort oot this funeral business. Listen, boys, ye can have ma pram. Do whit ye want wi it.' He disclosed the pram's secret hiding place and we were grateful. We were sure we could find some use for it. How exactly we were going to make money from an old Victorian pram was another matter, but we decided to wait until someone or something provided an idea.

A few days later, we were walking through Cleland Street and we went into nearby Cleland Lane. There was a timber shop there, complete with benches and saws. We got talking to the boss, a friendly hard-working fellow, who told us he was annoyed that he had to pay for another firm to take away the discarded off-cuts of wood and the sawdust. It was then that an idea hit

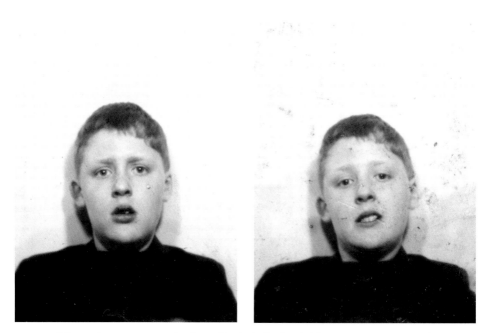

Me aged ten – a game-looking Gorbals Diehard. (Courtesy of the author)

A typical back court, between Crown Street and Thistle Street.

My dad and me in our tenement flat in Crown Street in the mid-'60s. (Courtesy of the author)

Dad and me doing a bit of sparring in our living room – it was always wise to be prepared for the streets. (Courtesy of the author)

Children at play, quite happily, in a dingy back court.

The old burial ground known as the Rose Garden.

A busy Gorbals in the old days: the corner of Cumberland Street and Commercial Road in 1955.

A man on a bike rides along a deserted Camden Street.

Row upon row of Victorian tenements at Lawmoor Street.

Crumbling but still standing – flats at Naburn Street.

The new Gorbals emerges
with the construction
of the Queen Elizabeth
high-rise flats.

An old shop in
Rutherglen Road, pictured
in the early 1970s.

me: we could divide the off-cuts into bags and sell them around the tenements to people with open fires. The sawdust could be sold to local butchers for their floors and to people who had pets, for bedding and cat litter.

We agreed a deal to take the stuff away for nothing and, using our giant Victorian pram to cart our goods around, we bagged up the wood and began to knock on doors. We even thought up a catchphrase to say to people as they opened their doors: 'Do ye want tae buy a bag o' sticks fur wan and six?' The one and six figure had been decided on mainly because it rhymed with 'sticks'. Much to our surprise, our little scheme did a roaring trade. People were only too glad to pay a shilling and sixpence for a large bag of sticks. It was certainly a lot cheaper than coal, and our sticks worked out less expensive than the little bunches they sold in the corner shops for threepence or sixpence. The butchers were glad of fresh sawdust and the people with 'indoor cats' were eager to pay for our cheap cat litter. Our business gradually expanded and we developed a new sideline when we bumped into a fellow who was selling off a load of cheap Beatles magazines. If a young lady opened the door saying her mammy was oot, we would often convince her to buy a Beatles magazine, and we made nearly as much on them as on the sticks for a time.

So the sticks and sawdust game was providing all of us Diehards with regular pocket money, but it was hard work humping bags up and down tenement staircases. One day, we had just sold another couple of bags and were walking from the Clydeside end of Hospital Street towards Ballater Street, when we came across an opportunity to make easier money. A few vans were pulling up next to a warehouse building. We had heard that a new wholesaler warehouse, owned by a foreign businessman, was opening up in the area. We watched as the owner instructed his workers to unload the goods from the vans and take them indoors. We had a peek inside, and the place was packed with radios, watches, tape recorders, lamps, vases, mirrors, jewellery and clothes. A short time later, the owner locked the heavy front door and drove off in his flash Mercedes.

We had a look around and found that there was a lane at the back, where Alex noticed a small window that belonged to the warehouse. In a moment of madness, he picked up a brick and smashed the glass. With his slight frame, it was easy for him to climb inside. He shouted, 'Man, it's unbelievable in here!' and then started to hand stuff out through the window. He passed out all sorts of things – clocks, radios, an assortment of jewellery – but there was far too much stuff to fit everything in our pram.

'We need somethin' bigger,' Rab mused.

'Aye,' Albert said, 'a motor would do the trick.'

'Ah know!' Chris cried. 'Why don't we give Gordon a bell?'

We ran round to Gorbals Cross and phoned Gordon, leaving Alex inside the warehouse with Rab as a lookout. Less than 20 minutes later, Gordon turned up in his long black Daimler, fresh from a wedding, and we all loaded gear into the vehicle.

As we did so, though, we noticed a couple of 'windae-hingers' (gossiping housewives who sat with their elbows on pillows on their windowsills chatting and watching the world go by) in a nearby tenement had spotted us, and a man who was passing by at the end of the lane stopped and looked for a few moments, too. It was time, as they say, to 'clear the pitch' before the police arrived. Gordon sped off in his Daimler, which was jam-packed with our spoils. It was getting dark and we hid in the shadows.

About half an hour later, two police vans arrived on the scene. At first, they were walking around inspecting the front of the warehouse. Then they found the broken window. We watched from the shadows as the policemen forced open the front door with jemmies. Much to our surprise, four policemen began to load goods into the vans. It was a surreal moment.

'Would ye look at that!' Chris whispered. 'The polis are worse than the thieves they're arrestin'.'

'Ah, well, at least they've no arrested us!' said Alex.

'Robbin' bastards!' Albert observed. 'They should be ashamed tae wear their uniforms.'

'Maybe we should go oot and arrest them!' Albert joked.

We tried to stifle our laughter. As the police vans were being driven away, full of the stolen stock, the motto 'Semper Vigilo' was clearly visible on the vehicles.

'Whit does that mean, *semper vigilo?*' Alex asked.

'Ma teacher told me it means "always watching",' said Albert.

'Aye,' said Chris, 'the funny thing is, it's us watchin' the polis actin' like tea leaves!' We couldn't stop giggling. If this was how the scales of justice operated, no wonder there was so much lawlessness in the Gorbals.

The next day, a headline in the local paper read 'Gorbals Warehouse Targeted in Burglary'. A police spokesman said he believed 'an organised gang of professional criminals' was behind it.

Despite what we'd seen, we were just a wee bit relieved. At least they weren't looking for five daft boys with a pram and a fellow in a Daimler.

CHAPTER TWENTY-THREE

✳

THE LIMO DRIVER

While we'd been up to no good, Malky had set about organising and paying for his pal's funeral. There was a big turn-out, and it was revealed that the midgie-raking alcoholic had once been a promising footballer with the world at his feet. In his early days, he had trained with top Celtic stars. But he, like many talented Gorbals people, had succumbed to the allure of alcohol. He'd scored an own goal by putting booze in front of a career as a footballer.

More than 200 people came for his big send-off and there were extravagant floral tributes. One giant one spelled out 'THE GREATEST FOOTBALLER THE WORLD NEVER SAW'. In his last days, the midgie-raker had had no dignity. Many who attended the funeral had avoided him towards the end. But, in death, he was eulogised as if he'd been a saint.

'It jist shows ye,' Rab said as the funeral cortège went down Thistle Street, 'the only time some people aroon here will gie ye any respect is when ye're deid!'

After the big send-off most of the mourners packed into the Wheatsheaf Bar in Crown Street. Malky had put up the money for a first drink for all the mourners. Soon there was a lot of sentimental singing coming from the pub, with 'Danny Boy' the favourite. The drunks were fairly out of tune, but moving nonetheless, as they sang, 'Oh, Danny boy, the pipes, the pipes are calling from glen to glen.' We were taken aback at how sentimental the atmosphere had become. Even Alex had a tear in his eye. 'The last time Ah wis like this,' he said, 'wis when ma maw asked me tae cut up an onion.'

Time passed and we were still waiting for our cut of the warehouse plunder. It was like Billy Bunter's postal order: there was much talk about it arriving but it never did. We even took to phoning Gordon at work, but a manager picked up the phone every time and said, 'Gordon has gone on holiday.' We surmised that, laden with cash from the stolen goods, he had headed off somewhere to blow it. We didn't blame him. Given the chance, we would have done the same. A couple of weeks passed, and we decided to try again. We got the same reply: Gordon had gone on holiday.

'He must have got a right few bob fur that gear if he can afford tae go oan holiday fur aw this time,' Albert said.

'Aye, he's had mair days aff than Santa Claus,' Chris observed.

A few days later we decided to try one more time. We were getting desperate. As Chris joked, money was as short as 'a midget tryin' tae do the high jump'. Once again the manager maintained that Gordon was away. Albert lost patience and shouted down the receiver, 'Look, we know he's no oan holiday! Where is he? He owes us money.'

There were a few seconds' silence and then the manager replied, 'My best suggestion to you is that you pick up a copy of the local paper. Then you might be a lot clearer about the situation.'

We were mystified, but we went to the corner shop and bought a paper. There on page three, all was revealed. The headline screamed 'Drunken Limo Driver Had Romp with Hookers'. There was a large picture of Gordon and smaller photos of two prostitutes, one called Mandy and the other Rita. It turned out that Gordon, having made a mint on the stolen goods, had gone cruising the red-light district around Blythswood Square in his limo and had picked up the two women. He'd even had a few bottles of champagne in the car, which he'd parked in a dark lane. What the police described as 'a drunken orgy' had developed. A retired female schoolteacher had been passing by while taking her little Jack Russell, Jock, out for a walk. She told the court, 'My dog stopped for a wee at a lamppost and I noticed a limousine parked nearby. I could hear noises coming from it and I thought someone was being strangled. I went over to investigate but when I looked through the window I saw a naked man cavorting with two women. I was so shocked I went to the nearest telephone box and dialled 999.'

The newspaper report gave more lurid details. A sergeant had testified, 'We were called out to an incident involving a black Daimler limousine near Blythswood Square. When we arrived on the scene, we looked through the window and spotted a man committing indecent acts with two women. We banged on the window. I asked the man what he thought he was doing and he responded, "I was only playing, officer." I recognised the two women as local prostitutes whom we have dealt with several times before in this very court.'

When asked by the sheriff to give his side of the story, Gordon had apparently replied, 'I can't remember a thing, Your Honour. The only thing I know is that I came into some money unexpectedly and bought some champagne to celebrate. Where the two women come into the picture, I really don't know.'

The court heard that Gordon was a 'highly respected' chauffeur who had been in his company's employ for the past five years and was a popular employee. He was said to be a hard worker, often working at three or four weddings or funerals every day. His employers had given a character reference declaring that their man was trustworthy and had never been in trouble with the police. His manager wrote, 'It seems because of the pressure of his work he has had a moment of madness and turned to drink and women. Unfortunately, if he does get a criminal conviction, he will be immediately dismissed from his job.'

Gordon was on a losing streak. The Sheriff he was in front of was well known to be a stern character who handed out heavy sentences. Using prostitutes and driving under the influence were two crimes he particularly despised. First of all, he dismissed the two women with a £25 fine each and told them off for being 'naughty girls'. When he came to Gordon, though, the Sheriff said. 'You are a man of supposedly good character. Indeed, your employers say you are a hard-working individual who works long hours with no complaints. Unfortunately, you have made a grave mistake. The people of Glasgow must be protected from social deviants such as you.' He sentenced Gordon to six months in prison and banned him from driving for three years. The newspaper reported that as Gordon was being led away, he shouted, 'Ah'm ruined! Ruined!'

We all shook our heads. 'That's oor money up in smoke!' Alex said.

'Aye,' Chris agreed. 'Sent tae jail fur a moment of madness, eh? We have them aw the time.'

'There's somethin' wrang wi the Scottish legal system,' Albert said. 'The sheriffs seem tae come doon hard oan anybody that likes a drink or the birds.'

Rab told us, 'That's because they old judges are no gettin' any nookie. That's why they send people doon. They're jist jealous o' anybody that tries tae be a good-time Charlie, any guy that wants tae be a man about toon.'

Looking back, I can only agree. Drinking and illicit sex were certainly frowned upon by our so-called betters. There seemed to be some sort of hidden agenda to punish the working classes for enjoying themselves.

Rab summed it up: 'Why do ye think the courts are full o' drunks and prostitutes? It's aw about money. The judges are oan good wages, the lawyers are oan good wages, the polis are oan good wages. Even the court clerk and his staff are oan good enough money. Crime is big business in Glesgaw and aw the fines go towards keepin' those people in work. Have ye ever seen a lawyer or a judge oan a bike? They drive big fancy cars, live in big fancy hooses and eat and drink in the best restaurants. It's the wee man in the street who gets done fur breach o' the peace or bein' drunk noo and again that pays fur it.'

'Aye,' Chris nodded, 'they say that crime disnae pay, but it pays the wages o' aw those greedy stuck-up snobs!'

Later, we bumped into Malky, who, much to our surprise, was staggering out of the Wheatsheaf. We had never known Malky to take a drink, but I thought that the grief of losing his pal must have taken its toll on him. He was just about compos mentis enough for us to explain Gordon's court case to him.

He looked at the paper and shook his head. 'Stupid bastard. He had a good job and a big motor. Noo he's thrown it aw away. Champagne and two prostitutes! At least he gets the sack and goes tae jail in style. That's the problem wi bein' a chauffeur wi a limo, though. It starts tae gie ye a taste o' the high life. Ye get ideas above yir station.'

'When Gordon comes oot o' jail, do ye think he'll get another job?' Alex asked Malky.

A wide grin came over Malky's face. 'Course he will. He can join me in the midgie-rakin' game. Sure, a vacancy has been created. It's a golden opportunity. Ah'll have plenty o' work fur him as long as he disnae mind gettin' his hands dirty.' With that he lurched off up Crown Street, singing, 'Danny boy, the pipes, the pipes are calling . . . '

CHAPTER TWENTY-FOUR

✳

SELLING STICKS

There was no alternative: if we wanted money, it was back on the sticks for us. So it was up and down the stairs, up and down like yo-yos, five crazy Gorbals boys trying to make some extra cash. The good thing about selling the bags of sticks around the tenements was that we got to meet plenty of characters we would never normally have bumped into.

In Florence Street, one of our customers was old Mary, a woman in her 80s who lived alone in abject poverty. Although she had little or no money, she kept her little single-end immaculate. We felt so sorry for her that we dropped our going rate of one and six and ended up giving her a bag of sticks for nothing every now and again. It was the least we could do, and she did repay us by inviting us into her tiny home for a cup of tea, biscuits and, of course, a few kind words. She brewed a beautiful cup of tea and it never failed to comfort us on a cold day. Mary told us, 'Ye cannae beat a wee cup o' tea. They call it the cup o' cheer! Ah never take it fur granted and Ah cannae imagine ma life wi'oot a cup o' tea. If ye're cold, tea will warm ye up. If ye're too hot, it'll cool ye doon. If ye're doon in the dumps, it will cheer ye up. If ye're excited, it'll calm ye doon.' Then she burst into song: 'Ah like a nice cup o' tea in the mornin', and a nice cup o' tea fur ma tea . . .' She even had a dish towel with the words of Rudyard Kipling printed on it:

> We had a kettle; we let it leak;
> Our not repairing made it worse,

We haven't had any tea for a week . . .
The bottom is out of the Universe.

Mary's man had been shot dead in the war and she lived on a small widow's pension. As we dunked our digestive biscuits into our tea, she would often reflect on her life. 'People are always saying time is a great healer. Ah don't know about that. When Ah met ma man, Ah wis a beautiful young woman, but look at me noo – an auld hag livin' oan a few shillin's a week. But nae matter how auld ye get, ye never lose yir beauty. It jist moves fae yir face tae yir heart.'

She showed us an old photograph of herself and she had indeed been beautiful. We liked her a great deal because, even at her advanced age, she had a delightful, funny take on life. On the wall above the mantelpiece there was a small, framed piece of embroidery that read:

I went out to find a friend; a friend I could not see.
I went out to be a friend; and friends just flocked to me.

Mary had plenty of pals. Her neighbours were always at her door or dropping in for 'a blether'. Apart from her lovely nature, she was also a bit of a philosopher and always said things that made you think. 'Neighbours are a funny mixture o' people wi whom you happen tae share the same area,' she said to us. 'After a bit o' time, ye end up becomin' pals because ye know that in the Gorbals ye're aw in the same boat, and life is better fur everybody if ye aw pull together. If that means puttin' up wi people's funny ways, ye have tae remember that they're also puttin' up wi yours as well. The best people, Ah find, are the people who've got nothin' – nothin' but good manners.'

Sometimes Mary would often pull out an old fiddle and begin playing old songs like 'Bonnie Mary of Argyle'. It was amazing to watch her perform; it was as if she had thrown her cares to the wind. She was a beautiful player, and some mornings she gave us our own private concert, playing many tunes such as 'My Love is Like a Red, Red Rose', 'Ye Banks and Braes', 'Auld Lang

Syne', 'Scotland the Brave' and 'Wild Mountain Thyme', and we would all sing the words.

We also met her daughter Stella, who would often drop in to see her. She lived in nearby Bridgeton with her man and two children. One afternoon, when Mary had popped out to see one of her neighbours, Stella began chain-smoking, a troubled look on her face. 'Ah'm worried, boys.'

'Whit ye worried about, Stella?' asked Rab.

'Well, it's ma maw. She's beginnin' tae forget things and she's always had a sharp memory. Ah know it happens tae most old folk, but Ah never thought it would happen tae ma maw. Last week, she told me tae go doon tae the shop fur a pint o' milk. Ah brought it back and we made some tea. Then about ten minutes later, she told me tae go oot and buy a pint o' milk. Ah told her Ah'd awready done it and she said she couldnae remember me doin' it. It's wee things like that that have got me worried.'

'Ach, it's only old age,' Chris told her.

'Aye, and anyway, we aw forget things every now and again,' Albert said.

'Ma maw forgot tae pay the rent last week! Maybe it wis the bingo that robbed her o' her memory . . . and her money,' Alex joked.

We laughed, but with Stella looking so anxious, we couldn't help but worry a bit ourselves.

When Mary came back in, she seemed as sharp as ever. 'Nothin' tae worry about,' I whispered to Stella. 'Look at her – as bright as a button.'

We got up to leave and, as we did so, Mary called to us, 'Remember, boys, it's no the load that breaks ye doon, it's the way ye carry it!'

'Definitely nothin' tae worry about,' I thought.

Another regular customer was Greta, who lived in a crumbling tenement in Hospital Street. She too was one of our discount customers. If we were lucky, we might get sixpence from her for a bag of sticks, and when she had nothing, we got nothing. Greta had a large grown-up family, and she fascinated us because she seemed to specialise in the subject of sex education. At school and at home, the subject was never discussed, but Greta was always willing to impart her knowledge.

Sex was a subject rarely talked about in the Gorbals when I was growing up, perhaps because of the strong Catholic and Presbyterian influences in the area. Sex, or discussion about sex, was usually confined to sniggering teenage boys and girls. Unmarried couples made love standing up in closes or middens, surrounded by rubbish and rats, because they had nowhere else to go. So in a way Greta was a kind of Gorbals sex therapist: ask her any question on the subject, and she had a ready answer. Alex put it less kindly, commenting, 'That auld cow is sex mad. She disnae do it any mair, but she talks about it aw the time.'

She often looked back on her heyday when she was 'young and full o' fun'. She went into great detail about the mating rituals of the time. Many relationships started on the dance floor in places like the Barrowland, the Palais in Denistoun or the Plaza at Eglinton Toll, as the people of Glasgow had always been known for their eagerness to 'have a night at the jiggin''.

Mary described the girls standing at one side of the dance floor dressed in all their finery – hoop skirts, fancy blouses, stockings and bright scarlet lipstick. The boys, meanwhile, hung around wearing their smart suits with their Tony Curtis haircuts: 'a big DA at the back and a quiff oan the front'. It was safety in numbers. The lads and lassies would spend the night exchanging glances and giggles. Some would get lucky and manage to get 'a lumber' before the end of the night. 'A lumber' didn't necessarily lead to sex – it just meant you'd made the acquaintance of a member of the opposite sex whom you liked – but it could lead to anything from a quick fumble in a midden to an engagement.

Single girls who found themselves 'up the duff' were shipped out of town to live with relatives and when the baby was born it was usually adopted. Even in the late 1960s there was still a degree of shame attached to being an unmarried mother. Most guys wanted to marry a virgin and did not want 'used goods'. Backstreet abortions were common and if anyone found out that a single girl was 'in the pudding club' then she would cruelly be branded a hing-oot. The stigma of being a single mother could even mean that they found it hard to get work and landlords didn't want them as tenants.

'That wis why Ah got married,' Greta explained to us. 'Ah got pregnant and there wis no way Ah wis goin' tae wan o' they dirty abortionists, so the only alternative wis tae get married. The baby wis conceived in a midden. Ah wis young and so wis he, and we didnae know much about things like contraception in those days. Most o' the boys couldnae afford condoms and a lot o' them used balloons instead. Remember, it wis no long after the war and people still had Victorian values. In ma day, we never had any sex education. Ye found oot by trial and error. A lot o' us – especially the boys – pieced together the facts o' life fae dirty jokes, seaside postcards and drawin's oan public lavatory wa's.'

Years later, I recalled our conversations with Greta when I read that in the 1950s marriage was the unassailable norm and an all-pervasive expectation. For example, never before that decade had such a high proportion of women under 30 got married, and the figures have never been equalled. In the late 1950s, the proportion of women who got married before the age of 50 was 96 per cent, compared to 81 per cent in 1900 and 68 per cent in the 1990s. Greta certainly knew enough to write a book on the subject of love, marriage and sex, but unfortunately she had left school at an early age, barely able to read or write.

'So, Greta,' Chris asked rather cheekily one afternoon, 'do ye still, ye know . . . still do it wi yir man?'

She laughed. 'Wi that nae-user? Ye're kiddin'! Fur years, Ah would lie in bed no able tae sleep while he wis oot in the pub. Then he'd stagger in full o' wine and beer, stinkin' o' Woodbine smoke. When Ah heard his footsteps comin' towards the bedroom, Ah'd pretend tae be asleep. But then he'd start maulin' me. Ah'd still kid oan Ah wis sleepin', but he kept oan and oan, and if Ah didnae give in, he'd batter me. There wis nae love in it, nae affection, nae kind words. Jist maulin' and grunts and groans. Ah'd end up lookin' at the cracks in the ceilin', thinkin',

"Oh, they need repairin'." There wis nae fun in it fur me. It wis degradin'. When it wis aw over, Ah'd jist think that at least Ah had performed ma wifely duty.'

We always left Greta's flat feeling that we had our eyes opened. Her stories were certainly worth a bag of sticks.

CHAPTER TWENTY-FIVE

✳

DOG DAYS

The sticks game was proving to be a nice little earner. We had no overheads. Our materials were free and the pram didn't need petrol. In a good week, the other Diehards and I earned well over a pound each, and in one incredible week we all earned more than two pounds.

It was an education, too. Every day was a learning curve as we knocked on tenement doors and got a glimpse into other people's worlds. Take, for example, Bobby, a big fellow in his late 20s who was never in work and hung around the house all day. He lived with his mother in Rutherglen Road. When we delivered the sticks, she was rarely in, as she worked as a cleaner for some toffs in Giffnock. But she always left the one and sixpence for our sticks with Bobby.

In the neighbourhood, Bobby was generally regarded as a bit odd, and as a bit of a layabout who scrounged from his mother. His father had died from injuries he'd sustained in a gang fight in the Glasgow Green years before, and older people who recalled the incident said that the unfortunate fellow had been 'stabbed mair times than a pin cushion'.

Having no father had left Bobby without a male influence in his life and he was thought by many to be very much a 'mammy's boy', with no real direction. In fact, because he never talked about girls, some of the older boys suspected that he was 'a poof'. But talk was talk – just gossip. Take as you find, was my philosophy, and I got on fine with him.

We knocked on Bobby's door one morning and, much to our surprise, there was loud barking. He answered the door with a huge grin on his face. 'Come in, boys, and meet ma new dug, Hercules,' he said. Standing behind him there was the largest Alsatian I had ever seen in my life. It certainly had an intimidating look about it. At that time, a lot of people in the area had invested in Alsatians. There were so many break-ins and attacks against people that buying a ferocious dog was seen as a smart move. We knew one fellow who had two large Alsatians and would walk about the Gorbals as if he was invincible.

I was very wary of such dogs, as on my way to school one morning when I was younger, a mad dog had run over to me and bitten me on the thigh. It was extremely painful and I'd needed injections from the doctor to combat any diseases it might have spread. Alex was also wary. He claimed to have been 'bit oan the willie' by a dog one night in Thistle Street. Alex being Alex, he hadn't bothered going to the doctor but, like me, he'd vowed to keep his distance from dangerous-looking dogs.

As we entered the flat to drop off the bag of sticks, Hercules began barking and growling at us. This animal had a feral, crazy look in its eyes – the eyes of a murderous hunter, I thought. 'Don't worry, boys,' Bobby assured us, 'his bark is worse than his bite. Surely you know the auld proverb, "A barkin' dug never bites"?'

'Aye,' Alex said, 'Ah know the sayin', but does that big dug know it?'

Bobby walked over and put a muzzle on Hercules, which made us feel a lot safer. 'The only thing he can do noo is paw ye tae death,' Bobby laughed,

Where had he got this gigantic creature? 'Ah went doon tae the cat and dug home and Hercules wis there in a cage. The fella in charge said he'd belonged tae a rich businessman but the guy wis away oan work trips aw the time and couldnae look after him properly. He did mention that Hercules needed mair trainin', as he has a habit o' bitin' people. Ah said Ah'd train him and Ah got the dug fur nothin'!'

As he said this I thought that, to put it politely, Bobby was off his rocker, and Hercules wasn't far behind.

Alex was obviously thinking along the same lines. He asked, 'Bobby, when ye say ye're gonnae train this dug, how exactly are ye gonnae do that?'

Bobby laughed and declared, 'Ah'm gonnae train it tae be the toughest dug in the Gorbals – in fact, the toughest dug in Glesga! It's gonnae be a real killer, a real powerhouse. He's gonnae live up tae his name. Ye see, the thing about Alsatians is they're scared o' nothin' and they're good company. Hercules'll be a good guard dug fur the hoose when Ah'm oot and a great bodyguard. Naebody's gonnae think o' messin' wi me wi a big dug like this.'

As he said this, Hercules moved towards us growling with a menacing look on his face. Muzzle or no muzzle, we made our excuses and left.

'He's the sort o' guy that should be banned fae havin' a dug,' Alex observed as we headed back down the stairs.

'The Alsatian should be trainin' that nutcase, no the other way roon,' Chris said.

'Aye, ye're right,' Rab agreed. 'Ma auld man says there's nothin' worse than a heidcase in charge o' a dug.'

'Ach, don't worry,' said Albert. 'It'll probably end up eatin' him. He'll be dug meat.'

Later that day, we were all walking along Crown Street with just one bag of sticks left, so we decided to drop in on Mary and offload it on her. We went up to her house and she was as cheery as ever. 'Oh, thanks fur the sticks, boys. Come away in and Ah'll make ye a nice wee cup o' tea,' she said. We were glad of the offer, as we felt pretty tired after a day going up and down stairs.

As Mary poured the tea, I noticed she had a one-bar electric fire on. I'd never seen it before. Mary always had a roaring open fire going during the winter.

'Where did ye get that smashin' wee electric fire?' Rab asked.

'Oh, ma daughter got it fur me,' Mary replied. 'She says it'll save me some days fae makin' the coal fire. It's got a nice heat, but Ah widnae change fae a real fire – there's nothin' beats it.'

'Go oan, then, Mary, gie's a tune oan yir fiddle before we go. It always cheers us up,' Chris said.

'Aye, gie's wan o' they auld Highland reels ye're good at,' Albert said.

Mary picked up her fiddle and put it under her chin. Then nothing. There was silence.

'What's the matter, Mary?' Alex enquired.

Her face turned a sickly white. 'Ah've forgotten . . . forgotten how tae play it. Ah cannae remember how tae play ma ain fiddle.'

Mary had once told us she had been playing the fiddle since the age of six. How could she suddenly forget? She began to cry uncontrollably, which made us feel very uncomfortable. To try to lighten up the atmosphere, Albert said, rather unconvincingly, 'Don't worry about it, Mary. We aw forget things sometimes. Ye're jist havin' a bad day.'

Mary didn't reply and the tears kept flowing. We stayed for a short time, but we felt powerless. As we walked down the stairs none of us spoke as we all thought about what had just happened. We were in a slight state of shock. It had felt like watching a human being disintegrate before our very eyes.

Suddenly, Alex broke the silence: 'Ah don't want tae get old if ye end up like that!'

'Aye,' said Rab, 'live fast, die young.'

The next day, we called back at Mary's, as we were all concerned. We knocked on the door and it was opened by her daughter Stella. She looked worried and was chain-smoking as usual. 'Come in, boys. Ma maw's jist havin' a wee lie doon.'

'How's she keepin'?' I enquired.

Stella took a deep drag of her cigarette and thought for moment before saying, 'Ach, ma maw's no well and she's gettin' worse'.

'Whit d'ye mean?' asked Chris.

'When Ah came in this mornin' she seemed as right as rain, but then she tried tae light the electric fire wi a match. Besides that, she's frail as anythin' these days.' We looked over to the new fire, which was not turned on. A single burnt match lay beside it. Stella said, 'The doctor says there's nothin' he can do but play it by ear until things get worse, then contact him again.'

A few weeks later, we were back at Mary's again. Stella had made us a cup of tea, telling us, 'Ma maw's away oot fur a few minutes. She's in seein' wan o' the neighbours.' We chatted for a while and then suddenly we heard, from outside on the landing, the voice of a drunk man shouting, 'Come oan! Fur f***'s sake, let me in. Ah'm burstin'!' We opened the front door to find the man standing outside the lavatory door looking agitated.

'Whit's the matter, pal?' Rab asked.

'Ah'm dyin' fur a pish,' the man replied, 'but there's some bastard in there who'll no come oot.' He banged on the toilet door again. 'Hurry up, there! Come oot,' he shouted.

We persuaded the drunk to go elsewhere and began kicking at the door. But it was a sturdy Victorian door that had stood the test of time and it wouldn't budge. Finally, we all battered into it and it flew open. Mary was inside, sitting fully clothed on the lavatory. She was clearly dead.

The relevant authorities were called, including the police. One of them said into his walkie-talkie, 'Body in a stairheid lavvy, Crown Street. Looks like natural causes, suspected heart attack.'

Mary's body was taken away and we all went back into the flat, where Stella was sitting in an armchair crying. 'Ma maw, ma auld maw's gone,' she sobbed over and over again.

I looked over at the dormant electric fire and remembered the burnt-out match lying beside it on our last visit. It had been an omen, I thought, a sign that kind old Mary's life was soon to be snuffed out.

CHAPTER TWENTY-SIX

✳

HERCULES

Walking along Argyle Street one day, just past Lewis's department store, the boys and I spotted Bobby and his dog coming towards us. 'Oh, naw!' Alex said, 'Here comes that idiot wi his mad dug.' It wasn't a particularly cold day, but Bobby was wearing a scarf that partially covered his face. As they approached us, Hercules began to snarl. It made us slightly nervous.

I put on a brave face and went into confident patter mode. 'How's it goin', Bobby? Whit ye daein' up the toon?'

He replied, 'Ach, Ah'm takin' Hercules a wee walk tae see if we can do a bit o' fightin'.'

'Fightin'? Whit d'ye mean?' I asked.

'Ah've been trainin' him up tae have a go at other dugs and he's up fur it big time. But tae make him mair aggressive, Ah performed a wee trick that'll keep him in a bad mood aw day,' Bobby boasted.

'Whit wee trick?' Albert asked.

He pointed between the dog's legs. 'Ah've put a tight rubber band roon his willie.'

We laughed, but then, as an old lady with a little white West Highland terrier came towards us, Bobby said, 'Watch this!' He let go of the Alsatian and it immediately darted towards the terrier, sinking its teeth into its throat. The little dog squealed, blood began to flow from its throat and it collapsed. The woman was shouting, 'Get that big Alsatian aff ma wee dug! Somebody help! Help!'

Bobby ran over and put the Alsatian back on the leash. His face was well covered by the scarf, and I realised that he was using it to protect his identity in case the police got involved.

Blood was trickling from the terrier's throat, but its owner managed to get it to its feet, and she walked off with it, presumably in the direction of the vet's.

Chris was angry. 'That Bobby's a f***in' liberty-taker. He cannae be aw there. Imagine attackin' a wee woman wi her dug!'

'He's definitely no right in the heid,' Alex said.

'There's mair oot than there's in!' Albert quipped.

'Hingin's too good fur that imbecile,' grumbled Rab. 'Guys like that should be banned fae ever havin' a dug. In fact, instead o' puttin' the dug doon, they should put him doon.'

Over the next few weeks, Bobby and his dog became the talk of the town, or at least of the Gorbals. The trick with the elastic band round the willie certainly worked. We heard numerous stories about Bobby's inglorious adventures. He and his dog were attacking at least six other canines a day, and a few people had been bitten, as well. He was often on the lookout for us boys and seemed to have an overwhelming compulsion to boast to us about the Alsatian's prowess. We decided to give him a body swerve, as we didn't want to be associated with Bobby and his vicious dog. We were sure that the whole scenario was going to end in disaster. We even stopped going to Bobby's mother's house with the sticks. It just wasn't worth the hassle.

Inevitably, though, we bumped into Bobby now and again. Usually, we just told him we were 'too busy wi the sticks tae hang about natterin''. It worked fine until one day we came across him and found it hard to get away. He and Hercules were blocking our path in Hospital Street. Bobby boasted, 'Ye should have seen it yesterday! Hercules almost ate three dugs alive. Wan old codger tried tae interfere, but Hercules bit him right in the baws and the fella wis howlin'! He wis howlin' like a dyin' wolf!' Although his words were so bizarre that ordinarily we would have laughed, we stayed stony-faced, because at the end of the day it was no joke.

Meanwhile, we had other problems to deal with. Albert and

Alex had befriended an old gent in Florence Street. He was a retired bookkeeper and stood out in the Gorbals because he had a 'pan-loaf accent'. What surprised me, though, was that he gave us two and sixpence for the sticks – a shilling over the odds. I was a bit suspicious about this, but decided that he was probably generous because he was lonely and wanted company.

Then one day Albert and Alex came up to me looking rather embarrassed.

'Whit's up?' I asked.

'Ye widnae believe it,' Alex said. 'Ye'll think we're makin' it up.'

'Makin' whit up?'

'Well, ye know that auld fella in Florence Street?'

'Aye?'

'Well, he said . . . he said . . .'

Alex, for once, was lost for words. Albert continued: 'He offered us ten bob each tae do things tae him.'

'Whit things?'

'Well, he said if we gave him a wank there wis a pound in it,' Albert blurted out.

I was dumbfounded. 'You mean he's a stoat-the-baw?' I asked, using the slang term for a paedophile.

'Aye, the auld bastard's a pervert. We'll no be goin' back there again,' Alex said.

Over the next few days, we asked around and learned that the old fellow was always inviting children into his house 'to play' and that he had even bought some toys specially. We couldn't go to the police because of our anti-grass mentality, but something had to be done, and quickly.

'Ah've got an idea,' Albert said. 'Leave it tae me.' He then went to the corner shop and bought a bottle of Irn-Bru. We had a slug each and then Albert said, 'Right, let's go fur a wee walk.'

We headed for a back court in Florence Street, where the old man was watching the children play. He smiled over at us and said, 'Nice day, boys! Nice day to play games.'

Albert said, 'Aye, mister. Ah've invented a new game.'

'Oh, yes? And what's that?' said the old fellow.

'Well, it involves an Irn-Bru bottle and a heid.'

'An Irn-Bru bottle and a head?' the old fellow said, looking bemused.

'Aye,' Albert said. 'Your f***in' heid!'

Albert then smashed the old man over the head with the bottle. He fell to the ground, blood oozing from a cut. He was moaning loudly as we ran off. Chris laughed and said, 'He'll no be wantin' a wank fur a while!'

We stopped at the Bank Corner in Crown Street and in a short while the air was full of police and ambulance sirens. 'That'll be fur that auld pervert,' Rab observed. We couldn't stop laughing. We decided that this was street justice at its best, with no need for lawyers or courts.

We were still talking about it when a guy in his early 20s approached us. He was a handsome fellow and decked out in the latest young-gangster gear – Arthur Black tailor-made shirt, Levi's Sta-Prest trousers, Doc Marten boots and a set of tartan braces. I recognised him as a leading member of the Cumbie.

'Where is that bastard?' he shouted at us.

'Where's who?' I replied.

'That c**t Bobby wi the big dug.'

'Hivnae seen him,' I replied. 'Whit d'ye want him fur?'

'That f***in' bag o' shite's Alsatian bit ma wee sister and when ma auld maw tried tae stop it, the dug bit her as well. Ah'm no a happy man, Ah can tell you,' he shouted.

Bobby was in bigger trouble than he could ever have envisaged. This guy was a 100 per cent hard case and always excelled himself in fights.

'Look, boys,' he told us, 'if ye see that joker wi the dug, gie me a shout. Ah'm away intae the pub. Do me a favour and it'll no be forgotten, cos Ah'm like an elephant and Ah never forget. Do me good and Ah'll do you good.'

We were quite excited because we believed that Bobby needed to get his comeuppance, and now was obviously the time. Fate had dealt its hand. After about an hour hanging around the corner, we were just about to give up and move to pastures new when Bobby and his dog appeared. He stopped to boast to us yet again. 'Man, ye should have seen it! Hercules got intae a scrap wi two dugs at the wan time. He almost killed the wan and the other wan wis mollicated!'

While Bobby was showing off, Alex ran over to the pub to tell the young gangster that his prey had arrived. The next minute, the angry gangster and two of his pals were crossing the road. 'Hey, you!' he shouted. Bobby looked round. 'Aye, you! Yir dug bit ma maw and ma sister. They needed stitches. Noo you're the wan that'll be needin' stitches.'

He pulled out an open razor and slashed Bobby from his forehead right down to the bottom of his right cheek. Hercules growled and leapt at the young gangster, but he slashed it as well, from the top of its head to its mouth. It gave a loud yelp then ran off, leaving its owner holding his face together as if it was a jigsaw puzzle.

A few days later, we bumped into Bobby again. He had a large bandage covering his face and told us he'd needed 66 stitches and the dog, now a lot more subdued, had needed 20.

He told us, 'This dug has brought me nothin' but a hard time. Ah'll have tae get rid o' it.' He then strode off purposefully. We decided to follow him at a distance to see what he was up to. We saw him go into the new multi-storey flats in Queen Elizabeth Square. We were puzzled about why he was going there, for as far as we knew he had no relatives or friends living in the flats. Then it all fell into place. Alex shouted, 'Look! Up there!' Bobby was at the very top of the flats, dangling the Alsatian from the roof.

He let go and the dog came plummeting towards the earth. It hit the ground with such force there was blood and guts everywhere. Albert swore he had been hit by an eyeball. Unfortunately, Hercules was one dog that would never bite or bark again.

CHAPTER TWENTY-SEVEN

✳

SAVING SOULS

When I was growing up, the Gorbals was full of churches. Apart from the usual Catholic priests and Protestant ministers, there was a wide variety of Bible thumpers of all kinds, some of whom called themselves missionaries. We got talking about it one day, and Albert commented, 'There are probably mair missionaries here than in Africa.'

Rab said, 'Aye, they've come here tae save us fae damnation, cos we've aw been bad boys.'

These missionaries generally set up small churches in converted buildings where they could preach their brand of the faith. Posters began to appear outside such churches and some of them were quite amusing. One church had a notice declaring:

> When you were christened, your mother brought you here.
> When you were married, your partner brought you here.
> When you die, your friends will bring you here.
> Why not try coming on your own some time?

Other signs appeared weekly, saying things like 'If you are heading in the wrong direction, remember God allows U-turns' and 'If your knees tremble, kneel on them'.

One of these small churches was housed in the old Glasgow Missionary Hall. When we wandered in there on a typical cold, rainy Glasgow day, we were, rather surprisingly, met with open arms, or, in biblical terms, treated like the prodigal son. The two middle-aged Christian women inside gave us tea, biscuits and sandwiches and then we were introduced to the guy who was their preacher. He was a slightly built, softly spoken man in his 50s. These people were definitely middle class, but they weren't overly posh or at all stuck up, and there was something about the way they behaved and talked that made us like them.

Indeed, when I listened to them talk and watched their kind, gentle actions I thought, 'I want to be like that one day.' This was a revelation for me, because before my aspirations for the future had been to be a gangster or a fly man, that sort of thing. But these people seemed so happy, so contented with their lives, and they weren't short of a bob or two, either.

We were encouraged to sit in on the services and the preacher's patter was certainly different to what we had been used to hearing in chapel. It had the effect of cheering everyone up, and we forgot the freezing cold, the rain and the drunks staggering along the streets outside. The pastor seemed wiser to us than anyone we had ever met before.

In the first sermon we attended, he told us, 'In your path through life, you will face many boulders and there may be a big one that stands in your way, so big in fact that you'll feel as though there is no way to rise above it. Yet by pressing on this huge boulder that blocks your way, you may find that it is no more than a pebble on your path. Remember, your eyes are placed in the front of your head for a good reason. It is more important to look ahead than to look back.'

Alex whispered to me, 'That guy's patter's so good, Ah could listen tae him aw day.' I knew how he felt, and we agreed that we would come back whenever we could. There was always a cup of tea and a few kind words at the church, so we enjoyed the whole experience, and the preacher had the knack of making us feel good.

He would stand in the pulpit and say the absurdest things: 'I am sure you know the story of Everybody, Somebody, Anybody and Nobody. Everybody was sure Somebody would do it. Anybody could have done it but Nobody did. It ended up

Everybody blamed Somebody when Nobody did what Anybody could have done.

'Any questions on that little tale?' he asked.

'Aye,' Albert shouted out, 'whit does it mean? Ma heid's nippin' jist thinkin' about it.' The congregation laughed and the preacher explained, 'Well, young man, it means that he that is good at making excuses is seldom good at anything else. Try not to be just an ordinary person but a great person. The really great person is the one who makes others feel great. We all have the potential to be a diamond, because a diamond is a chunk of coal that was made good under pressure.'

He continued, 'If you want to test your memory, try to recall what you were worrying about one year ago today. I'll bet most of you can't remember. Worry is the dark room in which negatives are developed. It is a fact that people don't injure their eyesight by looking on the bright side of things.'

The fellow could talk about anything; he even made mundane topics like the Glasgow weather sound interesting. 'People complain about the weather,' he explained, 'but there is no such thing as bad weather, only inappropriate clothing. I love all sorts of weather: the rain and the sun make things grow. It's a particular pleasure to hear the birds sing in the trees when the spring comes, and there's a story behind that. After creating the world and before creating man, God took a break. He gathered the angels around and asked what they thought of his work so far. All agreed that the Earth was a masterpiece. Then one angel was cheeky enough to say it lacked something – a soundtrack that would praise the creator. And that is why God created birdsong. So the next time you hear the birds singing in the trees, think of it as a soundtrack to your lives and a tribute to God.'

After the services, we went into a back room for our tea. There was a poster on the wall that read: 'Fear knocked on the door. Faith answered. And lo, no one was there.' We always made a beeline for the preacher at these get-togethers, and he proved to be excellent company. He was just about one of the only adults we'd met who could tell great stories without the aid of alcohol. He told us that he had once been a successful businessman but had suffered countless hard knocks. His business had folded, he was injured in a car crash and he was on the point of packing it all in.

'I was at a low ebb,' he said, 'and to cheer myself up I took my little boy to the circus. I saw this clown falling down, then getting up again, laughing as much as ever, and I thought, "I can be like that." From then on, I never looked back and with the help of my faith, I am happier now than ever. It's all about having enthusiasm. That's why I like you young guys: you have a real zest for life.'

'Is that whit ye call it, mister?' asked Alex. 'Then if ye're right, aw ma pals and ma relatives are in either approved school or Barlinnie cos they had too much zest!'

The preacher laughed and said, 'No, seriously, enthusiasm for life is a great thing and if you can hold onto it, then it'll stand you in good stead. It's all right to have enthusiasm for 30 minutes, better still for 30 days, but it's the person who has it for 30 years who'll make a success of life.'

He smiled, and walked over to a nearby table, opened a drawer and came back to us clutching a rubber ball. 'You see this?' he said, and he threw it to the ground first softly and then harder. 'The harder that ball is thrown, the higher it bounces back. What do you guys call yourselves again?'

'Eh . . . the Incredible Gorbals Diehards,' I replied, rather sheepishly.

'Well,' he said, 'I've noticed this about the Incredible Gorbals Diehards: the harder you guys are hit, the higher you bounce back. Long may it continue!' And at that, he bounced the ball so hard it hit the ceiling.

His words were still ringing in our ears as we walked home that night.

'Ah've never heard patter like that,' Chris said.

'It's better than goin' tae school,' said Alex, 'even approved school!'

'He's whit they call a philosopher,' Albert said.

'Whit's that?' Alex asked.

'It's a guy that speaks wise words, a fella that speaks sense,' Albert replied.

'There's no many o' them roon here. It's aw drunks, fly men and bampots, folk who talk nonsense. They're no a patch oan that guy,' Rab said.

The rain was still pouring down and the sky was dark and threatening, but we all agreed that the Gorbals philosopher had brightened up our lives.

✳

THE PREACHER

We were really enjoying our visits to the wee church, and besides, it seemed to be raining all the time, so we put the stick-selling game on hold for a little while until the climate improved. During the dark winter, we looked forward to our tea, biscuits and sandwiches and our nightly talk from the preacher. To us, he just seemed to get better. He was very charismatic. Indeed, Albert commented, 'Ah'm sure that guy's tryin' tae hypnotise us. Last time Ah had a cup o' tea wi him he stared me right in the eyes and Ah felt ah bit funny, like Ah wis goin' intae some sort o' trance.'

The preacher was full of stories, in and out of the pulpit. He told us over a cup of tea that in another church he had placed a large bowl of fresh juicy apples on a table, with a note beside it that read, 'Take only one. Remember, God is watching.' At the other end of the table was a bowl of chocolate biscuits. 'I came back one day and there was a little scrawled note beside the biscuits, saying, "Take all you want. God is watching the apples."'

The preacher was very quick-witted and even had some great jokes. One elderly gentleman had just made us tea when the preacher looked at him and said, 'Excellent cup of tea. You know there's a book in the Bible that's dedicated to men like you?'

'Oh, aye? And whit book would that be?' the old guy enquired.

'He-brews!' the preacher replied.

But the Gorbals Diehards were not to be outdone in the humour stakes. In a more serious moment, the preacher was telling us about the trouble in the Middle East and asked us if we knew anything about Damascus.

'Aye, mister,' Alex replied, 'it kills 99 per cent of aw known germs!'

The preacher laughed loudly and said, 'Remember, don't stop laughing just because you get older. It's because you stop laughing that you grow old. A smile in hard times is like the silver lining in a cloud.'

One night, we followed him from the back room into the main hall for a sermon, and it was clear his following was growing. Word had got round the Gorbals that this was the man to hear, and the congregation was made up of young and old. The preacher took to the pulpit. He was silent for a few moments, had a sip of water from a glass and looked over at us boys. 'We have a group of young men with us tonight,' he said, 'who admit that they are wild boys and who go by the name of the Incredible Gorbals Diehards. These young men may be rough and ready, but I can tell they have good souls. No one can give a definition of the soul, but we all know what it feels like. The soul is something higher than ourselves.'

We already felt a bit embarrassed that the preacher had singled us out, but then he then looked over at Alex and asked, 'Tell me this, son, what did you have for breakfast?'

Alex replied, 'Porridge.'

He then looked at Chris. 'And what did you have?' he asked.

'Cornflakes,' Chris said.

'And you?' he asked me.

'A cup of tea.'

The preacher thought for a moment and then shouted from the pulpit, 'Lord, don't let these young men be like porridge, slow to get ready and hard to stir. Instead, make them like cornflakes, always prepared and ready to serve. And may their humour continue to be like a cup of tea – a thing that relaxes all who meet them.'

There was much applause and we felt like minor celebrities, as the congregation had their eyes firmly pinned us. The service finished off with everyone singing:

What a friend we have in Jesus,
All our sins and griefs to bear!
What a privilege to carry
Everything to God in prayer!

Afterwards, we mingled with the rest of the congregation and got chatting to the old man who'd made the tea earlier. It turned out the old fellow was a former jailbird who had been converted to religion after reading the Bible in his cell in Barlinnie. Like most old lags, he had a great sense of humour.

'In ma younger days,' he told us, 'Ah went completely aff the rails. Drink, women, gamblin' – you name it, Ah did it. Anyway, Ah ended up lyin' in a cell in Barlinnie and somebody handed me the Bible. Ah needed advice and Ah decided tae put ma finger oan the text at random tae see whit it advised. The first time Ah did it, it said, "And Judas went and hanged himself." Ah shut the Bible and tried again. This time, Ah hit upon the words, "Go and do likewise." Hopin' fur somethin' better, Ah tried a third time and got, "What thou doest, do quickly." It made me laugh and frae then oan Ah never looked back. Ah knew God wis havin' a wee joke wi me.

'Also, Ah liked that it wis easy tae contact him. It wisnae like usin' a telephone. There wis no number tae look up, no diallin', no waitin'. When Ah wis stuck in that cell, Ah realised that he wis always there, ready tae listen, whatever time of day or night, whenever Ah needed him. Ah heard a sayin' when Ah wis inside that helped me think about ma life: "Two men looked through prison bars. Wan saw mud; the other saw the stars." Luckily fur me, Ah saw the stars.'

Over in the corner there was a group of younger children making drawings for the walls. The old guy encouraged us to have a go. Only Alex agreed, as he was game for anything. He was confident of his skills, even though I don't believe he had ever sketched before. He picked up some crayons and set to work on a large piece of white paper. The preacher noticed him at work and walked over, saying, 'What are you drawing, Alex?'

'Ah'm drawin' God,' he replied.

'But nobody knows what God looks like!'

Without pausing for breath, Alex replied cockily, 'Well, they will in a minute!'

One Friday night, after we left the church, we took to the streets and it was a typical weekend night. The pubs were coming out and there was a menacing atmosphere in the air. We wandered around for a while, and circled back to Eglinton Street, where we spotted our friend the preacher standing at a bus stop near the Bedford Cinema. Two drunks appeared to be pestering him for money. As we came closer, we heard one of them demand, 'Right, gie's yir money, otherwise we'll kick yir heid in.'

'Hey,' I shouted, 'leave that guy alone. He's wan o' oor pals.'

'Aye,' Alex called out, 'f*** off, ya pair o' tubes, and don't try tae take liberties.'

'Away ye go and mug somebody else, ya bampots!' Rab shrieked.

Chris joined in too: 'That guy's a man o' the cloth, so get tae f***!'

But, for all our shouting, the drunks wouldn't listen. The smaller of the two ran over and, with fists and boots flying, tried to lay into us. We were too quick for him, though, and managed to dodge out of the way. 'Beat it!' he shouted at us. 'Otherwise Ah'll kill the lot o' you wee bastards.'

As he said this, I noticed a crowd of young guys coming in our direction. They were led by the young gangster whom Alex had tipped off about Bobby and his mad Alsatian. Alex, realising he was owed a favour, rushed over to him and said that two drunks were trying to mug our friend the preacher.

The chib man walked over and shouted to the muggers, 'Hey, hey, hey! Whit the f*** do ye think ye're playin' at? That guy does good work in the Gorbals. Don't even think o' robbin' him.'

The drunks looked taken aback, but the smaller one put on an air of bravado. 'This is none o' yir business. F*** off oot oor way.'

It was a classic mistake. The young guy launched himself at the cheeky mugger, giving him the classic Gorbals Kiss. We could clearly hear the sound of the guy's nose breaking. The mugger fell to the ground, clutching his bloodied nose. He was moaning loudly. The next minute, the gang leaped on the other drunk and grappled him to the ground. They then took great delight in kicking the living daylights out of the two muggers. While this was going on, the preacher managed to jump on a bus and get well out of the way.

A few nights later, we turned up at the church to be greeted by our friend. 'That was a close shave on Friday,' he said. 'I must thank you guys for helping me out. But I am a great believer in the biblical saying "Turn the other cheek."'

'Aye, ye're right enough,' Alex said. 'But there's another sayin' frae the Bible: "An eye fur an eye and a tooth fur a tooth."'

CHAPTER TWENTY-NINE

✳

COMPETITION

Having had a little break from selling our bags of sticks, we decided that perhaps our days in that business were numbered, but we thought we would carry on for a few more weeks until we came up with another idea to raise funds. However, when we started up again, we found that we had stiff competition. Another gang of boys of a similar age had seen our success and had set up business in opposition to us. We first realised this when we trundled our trusty old pram around to the sawmills only to be told that another group of youths had been there an hour before and loaded up the majority of the off-cuts. But the thing that alarmed us most was that our rivals had not only been quicker off the mark, but they also had *two prams* to take the sticks away.

'They guys are fly,' Chris said. I had never studied business practice, but I was beginning to learn the basic rules. Chris was right: our rivals were shrewd. The only solution, Albert said, was to be 'flyer than them'. 'We'll play them at their ain game,' Alex vowed.

We managed to get hold of another old pram to bring our transport stock up to two, and from then on we made sure we went earlier than our rivals to the sawmills to ensure we got the best and the most of the wood.

After we'd loaded up one morning, we bumped into our competitors. There were six of them, led by a teenager with a mop of red hair. We felt no real animosity towards them; it was all a game, really, and we were in it for the laughs as much as the money.

'Hey, you! Aye, you! Carrot Heid!' Alex shouted to the leader. 'Whit d'ye mean, musclin' in oan oor territory? We're the stick guys roon the Gorbals, no you!'

The red-haired youth laughed loudly but his pals looked wary. I didn't blame them. Alex was well known to be a formidable character and had built up a reputation for having an unpredictable personality. The guy with the red hair walked towards us, still pushing his pram. He wasn't aggressive at all but very diplomatic. He had what we would call 'a real gallus manner'.

'Ah'm sorry, boys, if we've trod oan yir toes. But we're aw in the same boat and we don't want any trouble. Besides, there's enough sticks fur everybody. And, as ye know, imitation is the best form o' flattery!' The guy was a good talker, I gave him that, but I couldn't shake off the feeling that he was getting one over on us.

I was right. A few days later, when we knocked on the door of one of our customers to offer her her usual bag of sticks, she told us, 'Sorry, boys, Ah've got a bag awready fae the new boys. They're cheaper. They're only chargin' a shillin' a bag. The boy wi the red hair said that he'd undercut any price that you guys were quotin'. Money's scarce, ye know, and if Ah can save even a tanner, then Ah have tae do it. Loyalty is wan thing, money is another.'

We got the same story from several more customers. Not only had Carrot Heid muscled in on our territory, but he'd undercut us as well. This was a major problem and we had to decide what to do about it. Alex proposed taking direct, violent action. 'Carrot Heid and his cronies are tryin' tae kipper us up. We should attack them and gie them a lesson they'll never forget.'

'Aye, too right,' Chris said. 'A good doin' will sort those tubes oot.'

Rab agreed. 'Yeah, we'll smash them up and their f***in' prams.'

Albert was silent for a few moments and then said, 'No a good idea.'

'Whit ye talkin' about, no a good idea? Those guys need a kickin', the sooner the better,' Alex argued.

'Naw, as Ah say, no a good idea. Carrot Heid and his gang cannae be touched,' Albert told him, shaking his head.

'How no?' Chris asked.

'Because Carrot Heid's auld man is a polis inspector, wan o' the high heid yins. We cannae mess about wi his boy,' Albert replied.

He described Carrot Heid's father to us and I knew who he was talking about. He was a big pompous fellow who had once booked us for playing football in the street. We didn't like him, but he had enough power to be worth fearing, so perhaps it was best to give Carrot Heid a second chance. It was agreed that we would ignore the matter for the time being, until a solution presented itself.

Then it was back up and down the tenement stairs with our sticks. Rivals or no rivals, we were determined to earn a few bob. Being aware of having competition put a spring in our steps, and we found ourselves feeling a bit more enthusiastic about our little business again. There was no way that Carrot Heid – a polisman's son – was going to beat the Incredible Gorbals Diehards!

Despite the tempting offer from the other guys, most of our regulars stood by us, staying loyal and ignoring our cheaper competitors. One man told us, 'That fella wi the red hair has been here five or six times, but Ah told him tae clear aff. Ah didnae like the look o' him. And he's a polis's boy. Ye can never trust they bastards. They're always snoopin' about. F*** the polis and their boys!'

One woman said to us, 'The lad wi the ginger hair has been at the door wi his cheaper sticks, but Ah recognised him straight away as the copper's boy. His faither lifted ma man fur breach o' the peace a few months ago, and he wisnae daein' anythin' bad. The dirty polis swine! He and his daft boy can go tae hell as fur as Ah'm concerned. He can stick his sticks up his arse!'

Another loyal customer was an old Irish fellow called Patrick. He lived alone in a single-end in Thistle Street. Most mornings when we called at his door, he would open it up in his string vest and covered in shaving foam. He always invited us inside. 'It's the Diehards again with my sticks!' he'd say. 'Come away in, boys, and we'll have a blether.' Patrick was in his mid-60s, a widower whose children had grown up and moved away. His main interests in life now were the bookie's and the pub.

As he shaved himself in the mirror over the kitchen sink one morning, he told us in his thick Irish brogue, 'You know something, young Diehards? The biggest troublemaker any man will ever have to deal with watches him shaving his face in the mirror every morning. When you look in the mirror, you're looking at the face of the person who's chiefly responsible for your happiness.'

Even in the early morning, Patrick had a roaring coal fire going, and we put bundles of sticks on it so that the place would be nice and warm. Above the fireplace was a large picture of the Pope, and Patrick said, 'That's good, boys, put more sticks on. Sure, the Pope must be feeling the cold this weather!' before laughing maniacally.

'Ah'm sure even King Billy and his big horse would be freezin' their baws aff if they lived in the Gorbals,' Chris said.

Patrick had been in the area for more than 40 years. He'd come to Scotland from Donegal as a young man, thinking the streets were paved with gold. He quickly found himself a job on a building site, and he brought over his girlfriend, whom he later married. His wife had died ten years ago, and his two children rarely got in contact. 'They're a pair of snobs,' he claimed, 'who pretend they don't come from the Gorbals. The people they work with and their neighbours haven't a bloody clue that they come from here. They're glad to be away from this place. In their view, anybody that escapes from the Gorbals deserves a medal. They hate the place and won't even come back to visit their old father. Who can blame them, mind? They're both in good jobs and have nice houses. They've moved onwards and upwards from this stinking hole! Meanwhile, old men like me and young guys like you are stuck here like rats on a sinking ship. And make no mistake about it, the Gorbals is sinking every day. Good luck to my bairns – they're well out of it.'

After shaving, Patrick often pulled out a bottle of Old Bushmills Irish whiskey and poured himself a glass or two. He never got really drunk, though, as he had bets to place in the bookie's and his old Irish pals to meet for a drink in the Derry Treanor bar. After his second glass of whiskey, he seemed to buck up and get more cheery.

When we called on him on St Patrick's Day, he consumed several large glasses of the amber nectar while giving us a traditional toast:

Always remember to forget
The things that made you sad.
But never forget to remember
The things that made you glad.

Always remember to forget
The friends who proved untrue.
But never forget to remember
Those who have stuck by you.

Always forget to remember
The trouble that passed away.
But never forget to remember
The blessing that comes each day.

He seemed extremely homesick for his native land and told us, as tears welled up in his eyes, that although he had left Ireland, Ireland had never left him. Chris asked him what, after all these years, he thought of living in the Gorbals. 'Hate the place, all the stink, the hardship, the vermin and the drink. I'd rather be in Donegal. But it's too late to go back. It looks like I've missed the last ferry to the dear old Emerald Isle. Mind you, in some ways it's not so bad. I always think that living in the Gorbals is like being in a box of crayons.'

'Box o' crayons? Whit the hell are ye oan about, Patrick?' Rab asked.

'Well, you have the Irish like me, there are the Polish, the

Italians, the Jews, the Indians, the Pakistanis and the Scots – a mixed bunch of crayons, and you can learn a lot from them. Some are sharp, some are pretty, some are dull, they all have different colours, but they are all together in the same box.'

But, Rab asked, did he look forward to spending his old age in a Gorbals single-end? He thought for a moment, took another sip of whiskey and then said, 'Old age doesn't frighten me. You know, I might be 68 going on 69, but really I think of myself as 18 with 50 years' experience. People get worried about big birthdays like 40, 50 or 60. But how old would they be if they didn't know the date they were born or if there was no calendar to depress them once a year? I don't have a calendar and I never celebrate my birthday. Sometimes I just forget what age I really am, and when I look at my face in the mirror, I just think that my wrinkles are a sign of my humanity.

'Besides, you Scottish crayons say that there's many a good tune played on an old fiddle. And a Polish pal of mine said last week that they have a saying: when you're in your 40s, you've reached the old age of immaturity, and when you reach your 50s and 60s, you're in the youth of maturity.'

We bade old Patrick farewell and he shouted out a traditional blessing or two to wish us luck on our way. 'Young Diehards, may you live as long as you want and never want as long as you live. And remember, make your feet your friend, because your feet will take you where your heart is!'

Our feet were heading to other tenements to meet other characters who had their own ideas about life in the Gorbals. At least our hearts were in the right place.

CHAPTER THIRTY

✳

ACCENTUATE THE POSITIVE

When I was growing up, I always thought of the people I met as falling into two groups: the plus people and the minus folk.

The plus people were game, go-ahead sorts who were full of life, humour and character. They always made you feel happier after meeting them. Even though they lived in one of the worst areas in Glasgow, they approached their lives with an air of cheerfulness. It certainly wasn't because they had any more money than anyone else; most of them lived in poverty, scraping together enough to get by. Neither were they all particularly healthy or wise. What they had in common was that they were the sort of people who simply appreciated being alive, even in dire circumstances.

The minus folk were the ones who were always complaining and grumbling. They were never satisfied and moaned the day away. They depressed themselves and everyone they came across. The long-faced, narrow-minded, often bigoted people the boys and I came across were like encountering a dark cloud on a sunny day. We had contempt for such people and ridiculed them behind their backs, and sometimes to their faces, too.

As an example of the first type, take Wee Bert. He was an unemployed plumber in his late 50s. He had been forced to retire early after suffering three heart attacks, but he treated life as one long joke. Although he lived on a small disability pension, nothing ever seemed to get him down. When we took our sticks round to his flat in Nicholson Street, he never stopped jesting with us. 'When Ah moved tae the Gorbals ten years ago, ma pals told me it wis a violent area. But the people here are fine. The only thing that's attacked me is ma heart!' he quipped.

I was really impressed with him and one time I asked him, 'Hey, Bert, how come ye're always jokin' about when ye've got a life-threatening condition? Every day, we meet folk whose faces are as long as a horse's. Why are you different fae aw the moaners?'

'It's simple,' Bert said. 'Every mornin', Ah wake up and Ah'm jist glad tae be alive, glad tae breathe in the air, glad tae hear the birds singin' and the people talkin' and the traffic goin' by ootside in the street. And every mornin' Ah say tae maself, Bert boy, ye've got two choices today. You can either be in a good mood or you can be in a bad mood. Ah always go fur the good mood. Even if somethin' unexpected, somethin' bad, happens, Ah can choose tae be a victim or Ah can choose tae learn fae it. Three heart attacks and Ah'm still learnin' – and, mair importantly, breathin'! There's a wee woman who lives doonstairs in this close who's always moanin' and Ah try tae point oot the positive side o' life tae her. It's better tae be cheery, that's ma view, and life is aw about the choices ye make.'

He went over to a cupboard and pulled out a book, saying, 'Whenever Ah do get doon, Ah read Rabbie Burns. These words always cheer me up.' And then he read from 'A Bottle and a Friend':

> Then catch the moments as they fly,
> And use them as ye ought, man;
> Believe me, happiness is shy,
> And comes no ay when sought, man!

That day, we gave Wee Bert his bag of sticks for free. He had cheered us up and given us a new way of looking at things, and that was worth not just one and sixpence but a million dollars.

'Three heart attacks and still laughin', still takin' the piss oot o' life. Noo that's whit Ah call class,' Rab said as we went down the tenement stairs.

'Bert is definitely wan o' the plus people!' I told the others.

Just a few blocks away from Bert's place, in Bedford Street, lived a couple who definitely belonged in the minus folk category. The woman was heavily built, always in curlers with a floral headscarf over the top, and she seemed to nag night and day. Her man was a serious chain-smoker, with a cigarette perpetually hanging from his mouth. The wife was always moaning at her man, and he just accepted it.

'Ah said tae that henpecked fella the other day, "Are you a man or a mouse?"' Chris joked. 'And he goes, "Squeak! Squeak!"'

There was a story going round about the couple, that the fellow had been walking with his wife in Gorbals Street and she kept nattering on and he couldn't get a word in edgeways. She was nagging him about their forthcoming 20th wedding anniversary and said, 'Right, Charlie, it's time ye got aff yir fat arse and thought up somethin' that will mark oor anniversary in a special way!'

He was reported to have taken a deep drag on his Woodbine before replying, 'Awright, darlin' – how's about two minutes' silence?'

Perhaps part of the problem was that the couple were childless. The gossips said though it wasn't the man's fault, that the doctor had told her she was barren. Whatever the reason for her unhappiness, by all accounts she moaned day and night, and we were surprised her man put up with her.

He even managed to tell us a story that highlighted the absurdity of the marriage. 'She wis makin' the dinner the other day and it wis moan, moan, moan. So she tells me tae go oot tae Coyle's greengrocers and buy a cabbage. Ah says, "Whit size?" and she starts shoutin', "The size o' yir baw heid!" Ten minutes later, Ah came back and she says, "That's jist the right size. How did ye manage it?" And Ah said, "Simple – Ah jist tried ma hat oan aw the cabbages until Ah found wan that fitted!"'

His situation with his wife reminded me of a rhyme I had read in a comic:

> The worried cow would have lived till now
> If she had saved her breath.

But she feared her hay wouldn't last all day.
And she mooed herself to death.

For the most part, he was pretty gloomy himself, but sometimes he came over to the plus side and joked about his difficult situation. 'Ach, Ah know she moans aw the time,' he confessed to us once when we got chatting outside his close. 'That's because she cannae have any weans. But Ah still love her. Naebody's got the perfect marriage. The last couple tae have an ideal marriage was Adam and Eve, and that wis only because he didnae have tae listen tae her stories about aw the men she could have married – and she didnae have tae hear about his mother's cooking'.'

At that moment, his wife appeared, carrying a heavy shopping bag. 'Right, you!' she cried. 'Get up the stair wi this bag, useless so-and-so that ye are!' He took the bag without a murmur of complaint and headed into the close. We shook our heads in disbelief that any man could put up with such behaviour from a woman.

'That guy has the patience o' a saint!' Albert said.

'Aye, a St Bernard dug – because she treats him like wan!' Rab joked.

Pushing our pram, with one bag of sticks left, we found ourselves near Gorbals Cross and came upon Patrick, who was staggering towards us absolutely steaming drunk. He was dishevelled, with his fly open, a large wet patch on his groin, and sick down the front of his coat. As he approached, he suddenly lurched and fell over. We ran over to help him up. 'Thanks, young Diehards,' he slurred. 'I'm all right. I always fall forwards, never backwards! I seem to be pretty fond of kissing the Gorbals pavements these days.'

We walked Patrick back to his tenement and made sure he got inside safely. 'Got pished with the Cork mob,' he explained. 'It's always a mistake drinking with those fellows. I try to stay clear of them, but today I failed. Ah, well, you live and learn. I'll put it down to experience – a f***in' drunken experience!'

We wandered off and found ourselves in Nicholson Street. A

large crowd had gathered. 'What's the matter, missus?' I said to one woman.

'That fella came oot his close and fell doon oan the ground. He's deid fur sure. There's nae sign o' a pulse. We're jist waitin' fur the polis and an ambulance tae arrive. It's a shame. He wis such a nice wee fella and aw. He wis a cheery guy, full o' patter and jokes. He might have been wee, but he wis the biggest ray o' sunshine in the Gorbals.'

I already knew who she was talking about, and as I pushed to the front of the crowd my suspicions were confirmed. It was Wee Bert, and although he was dead, he appeared to have a grin on his face.

Still smiling, until the end.

CHAPTER THIRTY-ONE

✳

THE RIGHT ATTITUDE

They say that a sunbeam passes through pollution unpolluted; so it was with us. Looking back, it seems to me that, because we were happy, the boys and I passed through the grime, hardship and violence of our upbringing largely unpolluted. Somebody once said to me that there are no boring days, only boring people. Well, I can honestly say that I can't really remember spending a boring moment with the Diehards. If we weren't up to some escapade or another, we were watching the people around us and their activities, which could be very funny and thought-provoking.

It was how different people reacted to things that interested us. We would talk to anybody about anything just to see how they responded, and we usually learned something.

I remember once we approached a group of workmen labouring on the construction of the new high flats. These developments were supposed to be the future of the area, a modern replacement for the crumbling, rat-ridden tenements. They were 'streets in the sky', destined to take the inhabitants into a new age. We went up to the crowd of workmen and asked what they were doing. 'I'm a labourer, graftin' like hell mixin' mortar,' one fellow replied. We asked another guy and he said, 'I'm a hod-carrier, carryin' bricks up and doon those ladders until ma shift is ended or ma back gives in.' We then went over to a third guy, a bricklayer, and asked him the same question. The fellow pulled himself up to his full height, stuck his chest out and answered proudly, 'Ah'm busy buildin' the finest flats in Europe, perhaps the world.' Of course, it was all about perception. The third guy had the best attitude. He didn't see himself as just another cog in the machinery, but as a vital player in the creation of the new development.

It was obvious to us Diehards that it was the right attitude that got people through life. A positive attitude was worth its weight in gold. As Chris said, 'Ye've got tae be in the right state o' mind tae survive in this place, and that bricklayer has jist about got it right.'

I was always fascinated by how people developed psychological strategies to cope with life's problems. Take Archie. In his 80s, he looked after his equally elderly wife in a Rutherglen Road tenement and always had a smile.

'Hey, Archie, whit's the big secret?' Alex asked him. 'Every time we talk tae you, you're always upbeat.'

Archie laughed and replied, 'Ah've no got a bean, nae money, but the real measure o' wealth is how much ye would be worth if ye lost aw yir money! Look, boys, Ah jist think that if ye worry, ye die, and if ye don't worry, ye die. So whit's the point in worryin'? Worries are like wee babies. The mair ye nurse them, the bigger they become.

'A long time ago, Ah decided that Ah would do aw ma worryin' oan wan day – the Monday. It's the start o' the week and a good day tae get things oot the way. So every week, Ah'd write doon the things Ah wis worried about oan a piece o' paper, slip it intae a wee wooden box – Ah called it ma 'worry box' – and forget about it until the followin' Monday. The amazin' thing wis that when Ah opened the box again the next Monday, most o' the things Ah might have spent the week frettin' about had awready taken care o' themselves. Ah've still got the worry box and Ah still do the same every Monday. Worry kills people, and that wee box has saved ma life several times over.'

He went up to his flat and returned a few minutes later with the worry box. It was like a small jewellery box. He said he had made it himself during the war when he was in a German POW camp. It had the word 'Peace' carved on its lid. As we looked at it, Archie began to sing, 'Pack Up Your Troubles in Your Old Kitbag'. He glanced at the worry box and said, 'Ah didnae need a kitbag. Ma worries were always packed intae this wee box, and it's never let me doon yet.'

Archie's pal and neighbour Stuart had served in the army with him and had even been in the same POW camp, but he had a different take on life. 'Live for the moment' was his motto.

'When the Germans got me Ah often asked maself whit Ah had tae live fur. Ah asked the others in the camp and they aw said they were livin' fur the future. They were waitin' fur the day when they'd be liberated. That wis understandable, but it's the same wi some people roon here noo. They're always waitin' fur somethin' tae happen. Waitin' fur their holidays, waiting fur their children tae grow up, waitin' fur a pools win or a new job or retirement. Some people have waited so long they've forgot whit they were waitin' fur! It's good tae look tae the future, but no if it means neglectin' today. *Now* is the best time.'

Stuart was an avid pigeon fancier, and at one stage during the war he had even been part of the National Pigeon Service, which sent thousands of birds into occupied Europe. They carried messages containing vital intelligence. As a result of their deployment, a great deal of useful information came winging its way back from behind enemy lines. Stuart claimed that one of his Gorbals pigeons had braved storms, enemy fire and attacks by predators to bring back its message. He put its success down to its bravery, something he himself did not lack.

Stuart and Archie confirmed us in our belief that the most contented people were those with the best attitude. Watching the youngsters playing in the back courts, we could see the kids who were developing an optimistic approach to life. Some might have considered the Gorbals a terrible place to be a child, but a tough upbringing can give a person the strength that will carry him to success. From an early age, children like us learned to be positive even when life didn't seem to offer us much.

When we were hanging about in a back court one sunny day, Albert's younger cousin, a boy aged ten, approached us excitedly and told us that he had recently lost his front tooth. He'd put it under his pillow and found a tanner there the next morning. He put his wee pals in the picture, telling them that there was a magic fairy who paid good money for teeth. A few days later, we saw the boy and his pals midgie-raking. They knocked over one bin and out fell a pair of old false teeth. They were all running about with joy. 'When the magic fairy sees these, we're gonnae be worth a fortune!' Albert's cousin shouted excitedly to his pals. That was real positive attitude. There might be kids who had a lot more toys, but would they have got excited about an old pair of wallies?

On another occasion, we Diehards were going through the back courts between Crown Street and Thistle Street when we spotted a crowd of little boys laughing out loud. 'Hey, lads, whit's so funny?' Rab demanded.

They went a bit shy and stayed silent for a moment until one wee boy burst out, 'God must be tired o' hearin' sad stories aw the time, so we decided tae try and cheer him up.'

'Cheer God up? And how are ye gonnae manage that?' I asked.

'We were tellin' him oor best jokes,' the boy said. He looked up at the clouds and said, 'Hey, God, did ye hear about the two eggs in hot water? Wan o' them said to the other, "It's boilin' in here." And the other egg says, "That's nothin'. When ye get oot, they batter yir heid in wi a big spoon!'

It was debatable whether God was laughing at their jokes, but we certainly did. It's a well-known fact that children laugh many more times a day than adults, and it still seems to me that those wee boys had the right idea.

One person who really made me think when I was growing up was a woman called Jean, a spinster in her late 40s who always seemed to be either laughing or crying whenever we met her, and frequently both at the same time. We met her one night as she came out of the Palace bingo hall and she was smiling, but the next minute she had tears running down her cheeks.

'Hey, Jean,' Alex asked, 'how is it that you can laugh and greet at the same time?'

She shrugged her shoulders and replied, 'Even when Ah wis at primary school, Ah wis the same. Wan minute Ah wis laughin', the next greetin'. Ye see, sometimes Ah feel so happy Ah want tae cry, and sometimes Ah feel so sad Ah want tae laugh. A lot o' people cannae even shed wan tear even when they're cryin' inside. Ah like a decent laugh, and a good greet makes me feel better. Besides, the most beautiful smiles in the world are the wans that struggle through the tears.'

As she walked off, Alex said, 'A psychiatrist would have a field day wi her. She's roon the bend.'

'Yeah,' Chris laughed, 'mad as a hatter, but nice as well. There's nae harm in her. Anybody that can laugh and greet at the same time cannae be aw that bad. It's the people who don't laugh and never shed a tear that ye need tae worry about.'

It has been said that life is 10 per cent what happens to us and 90 per cent how we respond to it. We saw people who exemplified that all around in the Gorbals, and Eddie the back-court singer was an extreme example. He coped with alcoholism, homelessness and poverty by singing all day long, and although he looked like a typical tramp, he behaved like a real gentleman. He wandered all over the back courts of the Gorbals belting out the ballads, and he had a fine voice. His favourite was 'The Road and the Miles to Dundee':

> Cauld winter was howlin' o'er moor and o'er mountain,
> And wild was the surge of the dark rolling sea,
> When I met about daybreak a bonnie young lassie,
> Wha asked me the road and the miles to Dundee.
>
> Says I, 'My young lassie, I canna weel tell ye,
> The road and the distance I canna weel gie,
> But if you'll permit me tae gang a wee bittie,
> I'll show ye the road and the miles to Dundee.'

The delighted punters would throw money from their windows, shouting for more. He also liked to do 'Bonnie Wee Jeannie McColl', and he would stomp his feet and clap his hands as he sang:

> A fine wee lass, a bonnie wee lass, is bonnie wee Jeannie
> McColl.
> I gave her my mother's engagement ring and a bonnie
> wee tartan shawl.
> I met her at a weddin' in the Co-operative Hall.
> I wis the best man and she was the belle of the ball.

With songs like that, he certainly was able to strike the right chord with his audience.

Eddie, a grey-haired fellow in his late 50s, often stopped to talk to us after warbling a tune. 'The secret,' he explained, 'is tae realise that everybody has a favourite song, somethin' that gets right intae their heart. A song can remind them o' a special moment in their lives, and when Ah sing it, it takes them back. A song is jist like a friendship. If it hits the right note, it can create so much happiness. That's why they throw me money.'

As he was talking to us, a large woman threw Eddie a 'jeely piece' – a jam sandwich – from her window as thanks for him singing her favourite song.

'Thank you, ma dear!' Eddie shouted up to the woman. He might have looked grubby, but his manners were perfect. He was always polite to everyone. We asked him if he'd always been like that. 'Naw. Years ago, Ah wis a right Jack the Lad. Open the door fur anybody? Ye must be jokin'! Say thanks fur a favour? Not oan yir nelly! But then wan day Ah realised that two little words work wonders: thank you. They two words can really make a person happy. It's aw about respect. If you respect people, they'll end up respectin' you.'

When Eddie picked up the sandwich and put it into his mouth, we noticed his hands were filthy, covered in the dirt of the back courts. 'Bloody hell, Eddie,' Albert exclaimed, 'do ye no wash yir hands before eatin'?'

'Ach, Ah cannae see any point,' Eddie replied. 'When Ah saw it wis broon breid, Ah thought it didnae matter.'

Eddie was certainly an odd character with an equally odd take on life. Some people threw him fruit in the back court. One time, we saw someone throw him some grapes in a bag.

He put on a large pair of thick-lensed glasses and began eating them. But we had never seen him wear glasses before. Why was he wearing them now? 'Simple,' he said. 'If people throw me grapes or cherries, Ah put oan these specs and it makes the fruit look bigger.'

After Eddie had finished his sandwich, we walked with him down Florence Street. A funeral cortège was going by. No one paid much attention to it – except Eddie. He put his bundle down at his feet and took his hat off as a mark of respect. It wasn't until the procession had gone by that he picked up his load and continued on his way. He was a true gentleman of the road.

A few weeks later, we bumped into him while we were hanging about the Central Station. He said he was heading for a wash and brush-up in the station's toilets. Twenty minutes later, he was back, and what a transformation! He had shaved, his face was washed and his hair was brushed. He looked like a different, younger man. With his last half crown, two and sixpence, he went into the station's buffet bar and bought himself a cup of tea and a small cake. He had a shiny tanner left in his hand, and he put it into the charity box for disabled children that was on the counter. We joined him for a half an hour and noticed that although there were plenty of prosperous-looking people – or 'hawf-boiled toffs', as we called them – coming and going, Eddie was the only one to have put money in the box.

That was the way of most Gorbals people: even though they had nothing, they gave their all. While I was growing up, many of our neighbours emigrated to places like Australia, Canada and the USA, and I often heard it said that what got them to their far-flung destinations was not planes, boats and trains, it was the right attitude.

CHAPTER THIRTY-TWO

✳

A REAL LADY

One of the more unusual customers on our sticks round was Linda, who lived in Eglinton Street, not far from the local subway station. She was a glamorous type in her early 30s, with a refined Glaswegian accent. She also dressed well – fur coat, pearl necklace, high heels, all the gear. She told us she was an actress and that she had even appeared in London's West End.

We first met her one morning when we knocked on her door shouting, 'Do ye want tae buy a bag o' sticks fur wan and six, missus?' She laughed and invited us in. She had a very nice flat, with a fine inside toilet and a large Victorian fireplace. Linda purchased two bags of sticks from us and, to our delight, gave us a shilling tip as well. We surmised that she was a real toff, and it seemed we were right when she told us that she used to live in a big house in the West End. She said that she'd moved to the Gorbals because she was going through a 'messy divorce'. 'This place will do until my financial settlement comes through,' she said.

Linda was very sexy, with long blonde hair and a great figure. She had a lovely voice, too, and all in all she reminded us of the beautiful women we'd seen in the movies at the nearby Bedford Cinema.

She almost purred as she talked. 'You boys are fascinating,' she told us. 'You are so full of life and energy. You remind me of the urchins from *Oliver Twist*. And you have the cheek to call yourselves the Incredible Gorbals Diehards! How wonderful! I think it should be you guys that are on stage, not me.'

'The streets are oor stage!' Rab declared.

Albert chipped in, 'Every day we gie a show, but Ah don't think we'll be winnin' any Oscars, missus!'

'There's mair dramas and characters oot there than ye'd find oan any stage,' Chris told her.

Alex just shrugged and said, 'Everybody's an actor pretendin' tae be wan thing or another.'

She laughed again and mused, 'You young fellows are really quite articulate. The problem is, many people would find it difficult to understand your accents. They're very broad.'

After a bit more banter, Linda surprised us by offering to make us all a cup of coffee. To us, this was real class. Our families were all ardent tea drinkers; coffee was for the toffs. After drinking a large cup, I didn't feel too well. In fact, the coffee gave me a sort of strange, hyperactive feeling that I didn't like.

There was a knock at the front door and Linda went over to open it. A nervous-looking fellow was standing on the landing. He was well dressed, wearing a blue pinstriped suit, but he had a real nerdy look about him. 'Look at Baw Heid!' Chris whispered to me. 'He looks like a right Cecil.'

For her part, Linda looked slightly flustered. She said, 'Oh, it's a fellow thespian. I think you'll have to go now, boys. Thank you for your company.'

The nerd entered the flat as we left, with Alex shouting in his inimitable style, 'Thanks fur the coffee, missus, but gie me tea any time!'

Afterwards, there was much adolescent talk about how sexy the woman was. 'Ah feel like havin' a good ham shank after that,' Rab joked.

'There's a tent pole's jist slipped doon ma trousers!' Alex exclaimed.

Trundling our pram from Eglinton Street towards Gorbals Street, we came across Carrot Heid's father with another policeman. He stopped us in our tracks and asked loudly, 'And what have you bunch of degenerates been up to today? No good, I suspect.'

'No, officer, we've jist been oot playin',' I replied, in the most timid and respectful voice I could put on. The rest of the boys kept quiet.

Carrot Heid's father looked us up and down and remarked, 'You fellows are always up to mischief, and it's only a matter of time before I catch up with you. In fact, from now on, my mission will be to see that all of you end up in approved school.' He turned on his heel in an arrogant manner and strolled off with the other officer.

'Who the f*** does he think he is?' Chris said. 'That podgy polis bampot is gettin' too big fur his boots, and so is his boy.'

'Like faither, like son,' said Albert.

Before long, we bumped into Carrot Heid and his cronies at Gorbals Cross. As usual, he was polite, but we knew that he could be devious. 'Awright, boys?' he called out. 'Good day oan the sticks?'

I played it cool. 'Aye, no bad. Ten bags. How's about you?'

'Twenty bags and counting!' Carrot Heid replied, in a superior way that made me think of his father. We kept the conversation brief, not mentioning our run-in with his dad.

A few weeks later, we called at Linda's, and again we had banter and milky coffee, and just like before there was a knock on the door. A foreign-looking guy was standing there. 'Oh, do come in, Luigi. My wee pals here are just going.'

We were more or less politely ushered out, and began speculating as to whether Luigi fellow was a fellow actor or maybe a producer. 'That woman must be in demand in the actin' game,' said Albert. 'People are always knockin' at her door.'

'Next time we're up at the flat, let's ask her fur a few complimentary tickets fur her next show,' suggested Rab.

We headed for the place where we hid our two prams – a disused, run-down outside lavatory in a Thistle Street tenement – and left them there for the night. However, when we returned for our prams in the morning, we opened the door to the toilet and were horrified to find that someone had set fire to them. One was completely burnt out and unusable. The other was slightly charred but still mobile.

'Who the hell did this?' Chris shouted. 'When Ah get ma hands oan the bastards, Ah'll strangle them.'

We were all shaking with rage, and then a woman who lived up the close, and who was known as a real windae-hinger, came over to us and said, 'Ah know who set fire tae yir prams.'

'Who?' we all asked.

'It wis yir competition – the fella wi the red hair and his pals. Ah saw them.'

This information riled us up even more. Our first instinct was to seek out Carrot Heid and his gang and attack them with force. But there was still the nagging problem of his father being a police officer. Any attack could well land us all in approved school.

It was time to have a long think. Eventually, it was agreed that we would confront Carrot Heid with our information and see what his reaction was. If he was too gallus or cheeky, then we would at least 'gie him a slap' – policeman's son or not. But the other stick sellers were nowhere to be found. We thought maybe they'd decided to lie low until our anger subsided.

Of all of us, Albert had the wisest take on the matter: 'Look, Carrot Heid set fire tae oor prams. So whit? We would have done the same tae them if he wisnae a polisman's boy. Aw's fair in love and war.'

We went with our remaining functioning pram to the timber yard, loaded up and set off on our rounds, deciding to call on Linda again. She opened the door wearing a sexy negligee. 'Oh, boys, I was just thinking about you. I've had a visitor staying and the place has been rather cold. I'm running out of sticks to light the fire. Another two bags, please.' We humped the bags in, but this time she didn't offer to make us coffee and indeed she seemed to want to get rid of us as soon as possible.

Alex asked, 'Missus, can Ah use yir toilet? Ah'm dyin' fur a pee.'

'Of course you can,' she said, 'but be quick about it.' I decided to join him, and on our way to the toilet we noticed that the bedroom door was slightly ajar. We decided to have a peek inside. There, lying in Linda's bed was . . . Carrot Heid's father!

He was handcuffed to the bedpost, presumably with his own handcuffs.

I was totally stunned, but a sudden madness overcame Alex. He threw open the bedroom door and shouted, 'Hey, ya big useless polis bastard! Whit are ye doin' in here? Ya f***in' weirdo! Ye should be oot in the streets arrestin' criminals instead o' bein' a dirty pervert.'

Carrot Heid's father just lay there, too shocked to reply and unable to move. An equally mortified Linda ushered us out of the place, crying, 'Oh, no! Oh, no! Get out, boys, just go!' She must have been in complete shock, because she handed us a ten-shilling note for the sticks.

Over the next week, we knocked on her door several times but there was no answer. It all became clearer a few days later. Linda had fled from the area after a Sunday newspaper had printed an article headlined 'Gorbals Tenement Call Girl Exposed'.

The lurid report said: 'An ex-actress has been working as a high-class hooker in a crumbling Gorbals tenement. Once, she was surrounded by top stars on the West End stage, but now she has a seedy cast of professional customers who pay handsomely for regular performances . . .'

The story unfolded. Her alleged clients included lawyers, judges, businessmen and senior police officers.

We heard on the grapevine that Carrot Heid's father had been transferred to another force, taking his boy with him.

'Looks like we killed two birds wi the wan stone there,' Chris remarked.

Looking at the sensational headline, Albert shook his head and asked, 'Do ye think oor lives'll ever get a bit mair . . . normal?'

'Never! They'd have tae handcuff us first!' cried Alex, laughing the maddest laugh I'd ever heard in my life.

CHAPTER THIRTY-THREE

✳

THE MOB

There was trouble in the air and, to paraphrase Dylan, it didn't take a weatherman to tell us which way the wind was blowing. The Cumbie were congregating each night in ever increasing numbers. The leading lights in gang warfare at that time were the Young Young Cumbie, known as the YYC. They were all guys in their late teens who dressed so smartly you'd have thought that they had just stepped out of a catalogue. They dressed in hand-made shirts and Levi's trousers, and many wore garish braces, not just to hold their trousers up but to show the world that they had gallus style. They were a walking, talking, razor-slashing, fashion statement. The YYC could muster up to 200 members, all tough Gorbals guys, and their underlings the Tiny Cumbie, mostly younger teenagers, had about as many members.

The buzz around town was that the YYC were gearing up for a major battle with their Gallowgate counterparts, the Young Tongs. Like the Cumbie, the Tongs were predominantly Catholic, and they had roughly the same number of members. There was no great reason why the gangs should want to fight each other. In fact, some members of rival gangs had once been friends, having served time together in approved school, borstal or the 'big hoose'. But war is war, and these battles were staged every now and again just for the hell of it and to see who really was Glasgow's toughest gang. Sometimes the Young Tongs took a beating, sometimes the YYC were demolished. It was a wild merry-go-round.

Big Johnny was one of the main leaders of the YYC, and he definitely had style. He oozed a certain confidence that had the other members looking up to him in awe. As his troops gathered round him, he addressed them like a gallus general outlining the battle plan. 'Right, we're gonnae take oan the Tongs in the Glesga Green this weekend and we're gonnae show them who rules the roost. We are the gamest gang in Glesga and we've got a reputation tae live up tae.' The YYC listened intently. If Johnny had taken a different route, he might have been in with a chance of becoming MP for the Gorbals. But Johnny's game was not politics but the simple art of violence. The troops were encouraged to turn up for the battle 'well handed', with weapons in readiness. These battles usually took place at the halfway mark in the Green. One side of the park, the south side, belonged to the Cumbie, and the Gallowgate end was considered to be the Tongs' territory.

We Diehards watched the gang meeting in awe. Alex said, 'Ah don't know whit they're doin' it fur, but it's gonnae be a good fight aw the same.'

'It's a pity the bookies willnae take bets oan it,' Rab said.

'Ach, the odds would be too poor,' Chris told him. 'The Tongs and the Cumbie are evenly matched. It's like Rangers against Celtic – you cannae predict who's gonnae win oan the day.'

'Well, ma money would be oan the Cumbie,' Albert said loyally.

'So would mine,' I agreed.

'Naw, ye're both wrang. Look at the statistics,' Rab said. 'A lot o' the Cumbie's best fighters are in jail. And a lot o' the Tongs' best men have jist came oot. So strength-wise, Ah think the Tongs'll have the upper hand. Ah don't want the Cumbie tae get beat, Ah'm jist sayin', that's aw.'

On the day, as hundreds of the Cumbie congregated near the George Cinema in Crown Street, the windae-hingers were having a field day. 'Would ye look at that?' I heard one say to another. 'The Cumbie are up tae their old tricks again. But Ah'll tell ye whit, they're a fine-lookin' bunch o' boys!'

'Aye, ye're right,' her pal replied, 'and they're well mannered, too. Ah wis comin' back wi a heavy washin' fae the bagwash last week, and four o' they boys volunteered tae help me up the stairs wi it. Real gentlemen. And they're good-lookin', smartly turned-oot boys, as well. It's a pity a fair few o' them'll be gettin' their faces slashed this weekend. Whit a waste!'

If you wanted to hear an alternative view of the gangs, however, all you had to do was listen to the grumpy old men who hung around the street corners running everybody and everything down. I heard one tartan-bunneted pensioner say to another, 'Would ye look at that! A bloody disgrace, these so-called gang members. They'll aw come tae nae good. Ye can tell that jist by lookin' at them. When Ah wis their age, Ah wis in the army fightin' fur King and country. We were battlin' against the Germans, fightin' fur oor freedom. They fight jist fur the sake o' it. Bring back the birch, that's whit Ah say. That would clear the streets o' those hooligans.'

His pal nodded his head in agreement. 'They ruffians are no real fighters,' he said. 'We're the real fighters who got stuck right intae Hitler and his mob. Adolf wis a *real* gangster, but we managed tae beat that German hun. They should bring back National Service. That would sort the scum oot.'

Everyone in the Gorbals was entitled to their view on the gangs. But, to my mind, the opinions of these two men were invalidated by their hypocrisy. As dozens of the Cumbie swarmed in their direction – a formidable sight – the old men quickly replaced their sour expressions with smiles, shouting, 'Awright, boys?'

The way we saw it, young guys didn't join the Cumbie to batter other people's heads in; they joined to avoid having their own heads battered in. There was also an aura of glamour attached to being a member of a gang, and, like aftershave, it made young guys more attractive to pretty women. I remember one boy I knew boasting to me, 'The birds widnae even look at me before. But since Ah joined the Cumbie, they've been roon me like Ah'm a pop star.'

A lot has been written about the mindless violence of the 1960s razor gangs, but I can honestly say that I rarely saw anybody who wasn't a gang member getting slashed or being given a doing when they didn't really deserve it. Liberty-takers who took advantage of weaker folk, those who broke into working people's houses and stoat-the-baws were the culprits who were subjected to violent retribution.

Gangs like the Cumbie had their own sentencing system. A slashing was more or less mandatory for the three offences mentioned above. But a sort of appeal system was also in operation. For example, a well known 'tea leaf' called Jamie started to break into local people's houses. One elderly woman told a member of the Cumbie that he had burgled her flat. The leaders proposed that he be slashed on sight.

Hearing about the threat, Jamie lay low for a while, too scared to show his face in the Gorbals. After a few weeks, he convinced his bigger brother, who was not a gang member, to talk to the leaders of the YYC, and he pleaded for mercy on his brother's behalf. 'Ma brother's no well,' he said. 'The doctor says he's suffered some kind o' nervous breakdoon. That's whit led him tae break intae that auld dear's hoose. He's sorry he did and he's askin' fur forgiveness. He disnae want tae be slashed, and the worry is killin' ma auld maw. Can ye no show a wee bit o' mercy? He's no right in the heid. The boy needs professional treatment.'

The leaders of the YYC deliberated for a few moments at the Bank Corner. They were like High Court judges pondering the matter. Then came the verdict: 'Awright, we've heard whit ye've got tae say. Tell yir maw and yir brother he'll no be gettin' slashed. But he's got tae take a hidin' fur whit he's done tae that auld woman.'

A chastened Jamie appeared back in the Gorbals and presented himself to the gang. They took him into a back court and kicked the living daylights out of him. Result? Two black eyes and a couple of cracked ribs – but that was preferable to getting his face slashed.

Another example of a liberty-taker punished by the Cumbie was Davy, a guy in his late 20s who lived round the corner from me. He had punched a wee boy because the kid's football had bounced against his ground-floor window, almost smashing it.

The lad's mother, whose husband wasn't around, complained to the YYC that Davy had 'taken a liberty wi ma wee boy'. Because of the mitigating circumstances, the leaders of the YYC decided that the offence did not warrant a slashing. They ruled that a head-butt would suffice.

Davy was unaware of this judgement, but one night when he came out of a shop clutching a loaf of bread, he was confronted by a dozen YYC. 'Hey, Davy, fella,' one of them shouted, 'we've heard ye've been takin' liberties wi wee boys.' Davy's face drained of blood and he made to run off, but the YYC surrounded him and the biggest guy head-butted him hard in the face. The gang members walked off laughing and a bloodied Davy had got the message. He wouldn't be hitting a child again.

Those accused of being stoat-the-baws, on the other hand, had no right of appeal. They always got slashed or nearly kicked to death. One night, a boy we knew was approached at the corner of Thistle Street and Cleland Street by a man who asked him to come into a close with him and said he'd make it worth his while. The boy ran away and told his older brother, a member of the YYC. The paedophile was slashed and then kicked up and down Thistle Street. Rab saw him being carted into an ambulance and told us that he'd looked 'like somethin' ye'd see in a butcher's shop windae'.

The gang judicial system was certainly fast and effective, and arguably it did more for law and order in the Gorbals than most police officers could ever have hoped to achieve. Gorbals justice worked differently from the official Scottish system all right, but it worked nonetheless. Sometimes the razor, boot or head could be more effective than any prison sentence. Some feared the Cumbie more than they feared the police, and with good reason. There were no ifs, no buts with them. If you were out of order, you got it. It was as simple as that.

On the day of the battle against the Tongs, the Diehards joined the masked ranks of the Cumbie as they strolled over the bridge to the Glasgow Green. We were greeted by the sight of some 200 fired-up Tongs. It was like watching two rival Highland clans going into battle. Johnny and the other top guys led the way, clutching swords, and the rallying cry was 'Cumbie, ya bass!' Bricks were thrown by both sides as they charged towards each other, and then the two gangs collided. Everywhere, guys were being slashed, stabbed and kicked. Then, all of a sudden, there was the sound of gunfire, and a young Tong appeared out of the melee firing a revolver.

'He's got a gun!' one of the YYC shouted, waving his sword.

'Let's get aff oor marks!' another shouted.

The Cumbie ran from the Glasgow Green over the bridge to the comparative safety of the Gorbals as police sirens pierced the air. 'A sword cannae compete wi a gun!' one out-of-breath Cumbie guy shouted to his pals.

Afterwards, the casualty figures came in. The battle had been so brief in the end that the numbers were low: only six seriously injured on each side, with three Tongs and two Cumbie arrested for 'mobbing and rioting'.

Perhaps surprisingly, there were no reports of anyone being shot. This seemed a bit of a mystery until Johnny started telling anyone who would listen, 'Ah don't think it wis a real gun. It wis probably a starter pistol. Bastard Tongs – they've always been fly men!'

✳

CHAPTER THIRTY-FOUR

BIBLE JOHN

Me: 'Yir auld man's Bible John!'

   Chris: 'Naw, *your* auld man is Bible John!'

   Albert: 'Yir uncle is Bible John!'

   Alex: 'Yir cousin is Bible John!'

   Rab: 'Yir brother is Bible John!'

It was an absurd adolescent shouting match inspired by the topic that all Glasgow was talking about. Many people were asking if Glasgow had its very own Jack the Ripper. It was 1968, and we all fancied ourselves as budding detectives. The police were hunting all over the place for a killer whom the press had nicknamed 'Bible John'. The culprit lurked in the shadows and the dance halls, attracting women whom he then strangled. The police said they were looking for a sharply dressed man who was well spoken, polite and possibly religious. The idea soon took hold that Bible John was not only an accomplished murderer but also a good dancer who could charm the birds, especially the birds in the Barrowland Ballroom, out of the trees.

The Barrowland was a popular place to go to eye up the talent, a favourite destination for any young fellow who was searching for a romantic encounter. Hundreds of young men and women congregated there on Thursdays, Fridays and Saturdays, on the lookout for a lumber.

The Bible John story first hit the headlines after a 25-year-old nurse from Langside, who worked at the Victoria Infirmary, was found strangled in a back lane near her home. On the night of

Friday, 23 February 1968, she had been dancing quite happily in the Barras, and she left with a well-dressed man. Her body was found the following morning by a group of young boys who at first thought it was a discarded tailor's dummy. She was naked and had been strangled with her tights and raped. Her clothes and handbag were never found.

Police admitted they had very few clues as to who the killer was, and things were quiet for a while. But on Saturday, 16 August the next year, the body of a 32-year-old woman was found. She had headed off to the Barrowland, like so many other women, wearing a black dress, and, like them, she laughed, drank and danced the night away. One of her dancing partners walked her back towards her sister's house in Bridgeton, where she had arranged to stay the night. She never made it.

Her worried sister went out looking for her in the early hours of the morning and found her body in a derelict building. The murder followed the same pattern as the first. She had been strangled with her tights and raped. Her bag was missing. The police were more confident this time. They had a description of the man with whom she had been seen leaving the Barrowland, and he had also been spotted walking with her through the dark streets.

The police released an Identikit picture and it was splashed all over the papers and shown on TV. It was the first time it had been done in Scotland. The picture showed the face of a pleasant-looking young man in his 20s, clean-shaven, with dark eyes and short, brushed back, reddish fair hair. The newspapers reported that the suspect was around 6 ft tall, with a slim build, and had been wearing a good-quality blue suit with hand-stitched lapels and a white shirt.

Just about everyone in Glasgow had a theory as to who the killer might be. Even we Diehards were convinced we must have seen the man before but could not pinpoint exactly who he was.

Ten weeks passed before there was another victim. A 29-year-old brunette went dancing at the Barrowland while her husband was away serving with the army. In the dance hall, she went to a cigarette machine but found it was jammed. An apparent knight in shining armour, well dressed, offered to help, and the two struck up a conversation. They hit it off and had a drink and a dance together.

The man offered to see her home and, with the woman's sister, they got in a taxi to the Scotstoun area of Glasgow. The sister was dropped off and the taxi headed to the woman's home. The driver dropped them off near the house. He was the last person other than her killer to see her alive.

The third killing sparked a media frenzy. The police gave a more detailed description of the suspect and said that he had a well-spoken Glasgow accent and had quoted from the Bible. It was all the press needed. One evening paper nicknamed the murderer Bible John and the name caught the public imagination at once. A second photofit of the killer was released and the Gorbals, along with the rest of Glasgow, was suddenly awash with the man's image. Tens of thousands of posters were circulated throughout Scotland and to police forces all over Britain as well as to army units based abroad. Jails, hospitals and lunatic asylums were also asked to keep watch for someone fitting the description. A Bible John HQ was set up at Glasgow's Marine Police Station. The police were so determined to get their man that more than 100 detectives were assigned to the case.

As we stood looking at a poster of the suspect's image one day, Alex said, 'Ah'll bet the Diehards could find him!'

'How are we gonnae be better than 100 polis?' Chris asked.

'Don't be daft, Alex,' Albert added. 'Bible John looks like at least 20 people we know.'

'He could be anybody,' Rab pointed out.

As we were debating the matter, we realised that a crowd of women who had gathered behind us were discussing the situation. One said, 'Ah'm tellin' ye, that Bible John character is the spittin' image o' that guy who lives in the next close tae me. And, whit's mair, Ah know he likes tae go tae the Barrowland.'

'Naw, Ah don't think it's him, Maggie,' her pal replied. 'Ah think it's that young fella who delivers the coal. He's always talkin' about young birds and the dancin'.'

'Naw, ye're both wrang,' another woman announced. 'It's that guy at Paddy's Market who sells the dodgy tobacco. He's got money, he dresses up in aw the gear and he goes tae the jiggin'.'

Naturally, the men on the street corners had their theories, too. One elderly fellow who had been a bit of a hooligan in his younger days told us, 'Bible John is definitely a polis.'

'Oh, aye? How do ye work that wan oot?' asked his pal.

'Well,' the old guy replied, 'the polis cannae catch him, and ye know why? It's because he's wan o' them. He's right under their noses. As far as Ah can see, he looks like a polis and talks like a polis. Ah think it's a cover-up.'

His pal disagreed. 'The polis couldnae cover that up! Naw, Ah reckon Bible John's in the army. Jist look at the time between the murders! It's cos he's oan leave when he does them, no doubt about it.'

Another guy was convinced that the killer was a well-known football player. 'Have ye noticed that every time he's left oot the side somebody gets done in? He cannae score wi the fitba, so he tries tae score wi women, and when he fails tae do that, he goes aff his nut.'

Clearly, the theories were becoming increasingly absurd. One man we knew even told us that he was sure he had met Bible John when the murderer was working as Santa Claus in Lewis's.

Newspapers began to report that men were being attacked in the streets because they looked like the drawing on the poster. Some were even put under citizen's arrest by passers-by convinced that they had caught the notorious murderer. The latest playground insult was, 'Your da's Bible John!'

A documentary was made about the investigation, with one policeman commenting, 'We must be the best dancers in the country by now. We have been at the Barrowland at least twice a week and this has been going on for months. But people must think we are strange. We don't look at the women but the men.' The Murder Squad had even been christened the Marine Police Dancing Formation Team.

At the height of the hysteria, the boys and I took to hanging around outside the Plaza on the basis that Bible John would be too scared or too shrewd to go back to the Barrowland, as it was 'hoachin' wi polis'. As men walked past us into the Plaza, we would shout at them, 'Hey, mister, are you Bible John?' They either ignored us altogether or shook their heads and laughed.

One night, we saw a young, well-dressed guy coming out of the Plaza with a good-looking girl. He was fresh-faced, clean-shaven and wearing a smart suit. We shadowed them as they headed to a dark close just past Eglinton Toll. They went inside, presumably to get better acquainted.

'Ah'll bet ye that guy is Bible John!' Alex said.

'Aye, it does look like him, jist a bit,' I agreed.

'Ah widnae be surprised if he strangled that woman in the close,' Albert said.

We crept over and stuck our heads inside the close, and Alex shouted, 'Watch oot, missus! That's Bible John ye've got in the close wi ye!'

The woman gave out a shriek and rushed out into the street, clothes in disarray, in a nervous panic. She ran over the road and hailed a taxi before making off. As she got in, she shouted to us, 'Thanks, boys! Ye saved ma life!'

By now, the well-dressed man was standing red-faced in the close mouth. He shook his fist at us and cried, 'Ah'll Bible John you, ya wee bastards! Ah wis oan tae a good thing there before you turned up.'

He chased us well past Eglinton Toll, right up Victoria Road, before he ran out of breath and stopped. Hiding round the corner, we heard a passer-by say to him, 'Whit's the matter, pal?'

The out-of-breath guy managed to reply, 'Some stupid wee boys messed up ma lumber by callin' me f***in' Bible John. Nice girl, she wis, as well.'

The other guy replied, 'Ach, Ah widnae worry about it. He looks jist like everybody else. Ah wis called Bible John at least three times last week. Even ma missus thinks Ah'm him!'

The murders suddenly stopped and Bible John was never

caught. There were numerous theories about why this was, including that Bible John had committed suicide, that he was in jail or that he had left town in a hurry. Recent tabloid investigations have revealed that at least two convicted mass murderers hung around the Barrowland at the time of the killings. But the case of Bible John remains open, a mystery that not even the Incredible Gorbals Diehards could solve.

CHAPTER THIRTY-FIVE

✳

THE PRINTER

As we were on our way along Thistle Street one afternoon, a man pulled up in a white van and began to unload a number of cardboard boxes and what looked like a small printing press. He was obviously in need of help and Rab shouted, 'Hey, mister that's a lot o' gear ye've got tae shift. Do ye want us tae gie ye a hand?' The fellow, dressed in blue overalls, wiped the sweat from his brow and replied, 'Thanks, boys! Ah thought ye'd never ask.'

We were always on the lookout for people to help out. It was fun and, since they always gave us a few shillings in recompense, could also be quite lucrative. We lugged about 20 cardboard boxes up the close to a first-floor flat. Inside, there was nothing there except for a table and chair. There was no sign of a bed or any other comforts. Between us, we also carried the printing machine up to the flat, as well as various bottles of ink.

We all sat down for a breather and Alex, in his usual cheeky manner, said to the fellow, 'Hey, mister, Ah notice ye hivnae got a bed. When's that comin'? In the next vanload?'

The guy laughed and said, 'Naw, Ah won't be livin' here. It's jist a place fur ma new business venture.'

'Oh, aye, whit sort o' business?' Albert asked.

'Printin'', the guy said. 'Ah plan tae set up a wee printer's here. It's cheap tae rent in the Gorbals and Ah cannae afford the money they're askin' fur offices up the toon. So Ah'll build up the business fae here. If it goes well and the money comes in, then Ah'll look fur a proper place.'

The guy said he came from the West End and had had a small printing business in Partick, but it had gone bust because of the high overheads. He said he still had his flat in the West End and would go back there at night after a day's work in the Gorbals. We agreed that it was a pretty shrewd move and we often bumped into budding entrepreneurs who saw the Gorbals as an ideal launching pad for their enterprises.

A few weeks before, we had bumped into another van man who had come up with the idea of buying frozen chickens from a warehouse on the other side of Glasgow and then selling them from a little shop in Crown Street. We lugged hundreds of boxes of frozen chickens for him, but the business went bust quickly, I imagine because not a lot of folk in the Gorbals had fridges or freezers yet. Despite his experience, though, a business in the Gorbals could be a goldmine, as the many thriving local shops showed. The different ethnic groups in the area specialised in particular types of business. The Italians often had cafés and chippies, Jewish people had delicatessens and wholesalers, and Asian people often set up cash-and-carrys.

'So whit exactly are ye gonnae print?' Chris asked.

'Ach, the usual stuff, ye know. Weddin' invitations, business cards, raffle tickets, dance invites, publicity posters, leaflets,' the man replied. He pointed to the printing machine in the corner and said, 'That wee machine can do anythin' and it's cheap tae run.'

We went back down the stairs and the printer climbed into his van. He rolled the window down and said, 'Look, boys, it's aw a bit hush-hush at the moment, so if ye can keep it quiet fur a while, Ah'd be grateful. Tell naebody nothin'. Also, can ye do me favour? Keep yir eyes oan the place and make sure naebody breaks in while Ah'm away. Ah'll make it worth yir while.'

We told him that his secret was safe with us and we would be his unofficial lookouts. He seemed quite pleased to have hooked up with us and handed us a crisp ten-shilling note, which we considered a more than fair tip.

'That guy has his heid screwed oan the right way,' Albert observed. 'He's bound tae make a pile. People are always wantin' stuff printed fur aw sorts o' different reasons.'

'Aye,' Rab agreed, 'we'll have tae keep in wi that guy! If he makes a few bob, maybe we'll make a few bob as well.'

Later that day, we were walking along Cumberland Street when we saw this fellow coming towards us completely covered in coal dust. We were just about to pass him by when the coalman shouted to us, giving us a dazzling smile, 'Hey, ya crowd o' bampots! How ye doin'?' It was then we realised that it was Wullie, the former razor king. We stood and had a bit of banter for a while. We hadn't really seen him around since he'd got married and settled down. He, his wife and their baby had moved into a small flat in Crown Street. He looked somewhat miserable and disillusioned. Wullie shrugged his shoulders and said, 'Ah don't think this marriage lark is any good fur me. Ah'm no the settlin'-doon type. Aw she does is nag, nag, nag. Ah wis happier in the auld days wi ma razor and ma birds. Ach, Ah'm fed up. Ah'm away hame tae get a wash and lay ma pay poke on the table, and wi ma pocket money Ah'm gonnae go oot the night and get blootered.'

As he wandered off towards Crown Street, Alex said, 'He looks like a defeated man.'

'Aye,' Chris agreed, 'Wullie isnae the guy he wis.'

Albert added, 'It looks like she's naggin' him tae death.'

Rab nodded his head in agreement, saying, 'Nae wide boy in the Gorbals could beat Wullie, but it looks like his missus has succeeded. He's gone fae hard case tae bampot since he hitched up wi that woman o' his.'

A few hours later, we spotted Wullie again, but this time he was well scrubbed and immaculately dressed. He had obviously been drinking and he was arm in arm with a short-skirted blonde who was definitely not his wife. They entered a pub, obviously to carry on with their drinking session. 'There's gonnae be trouble if his missus finds oot he's wi another woman,' Albert said ominously. He was right. After the pubs had come out that night, we were passing by Wullie's close and his window was open. We heard his wife screaming at him, 'Ya nae-good swine, ye. Ye're oot gallivantin' wi some whore and ye've got a wife and baby in the hoose.'

Wullie shouted back, 'Ach, ye can get tae f***. Ah should never have married ye in the first place. It wis a shotgun weddin' and Ah wis forced intae it.'

His wife screamed hysterically, shouting, 'Ah'll show ye! Ah'll show ye no tae mess wi me.'

There was the sound of dishes being broken and then we heard Wullie cry out, 'Oh, ya stupid bitch, ye've done it noo.' Then there was silence. A few minutes later, Wullie staggered out of the close, swaying from side to side. We thought he was extremely drunk, but when he fell to the pavement there was a bread knife in his back. A crowd gathered round him and a woman, a retired nurse, said no one should attempt to remove the knife as only a doctor should do such a task. Wullie was still breathing when they put him in the ambulance.

Over the next few weeks, the printer was always coming and going in his van, loading and unloading boxes of paper and bottles of ink. We were true to our word and kept an eye on the place, and in return he gave us a ten-bob note every week.

However, there was something not quite right about his business affairs. We never bumped into any of his customers and he never showed us any of his work. We had expected to see posters, leaflets and invitations, but there was never any sign of his output.

As he was going past us into the close one day, Rab asked him, 'How's business?'

The printer looked a bit nervous and replied, 'Business is good, boys, very good. But it's still hush-hush at the moment. Ah'm, eh, doin' some government work, so we'll have tae keep it quiet fur the time bein'.'

Government work? What exactly did he mean? Our fevered imaginations went into overdrive and we decided that this fellow could be some sort of spy who dealt with confidential government documents. Did we have Glasgow's equivalent of 007 in our midst? A few days later, we went up the close and listened at the door to the flat, and we could hear the printing machine at work. It was very loud. We knocked on the door but there was no answer. We knocked again. Nothing. We were just about to give up when the printer opened the door looking rather sheepish. He was standing in front of the half-open door so that we couldn't really see inside.

'Eh, hello, boys,' he said. 'Ah'm graftin' away oan this secret government project, so Ah cannae let ye in. Official Secrets Act and aw that. But don't worry, aw will be revealed wan day.' He then shut the door and we went on our way, still wondering what top-secret mission he was on.

Not long after that day, we spotted two policemen going into the close and heard them batter on the printer's door. He wasn't in and his white van wasn't parked outside. When the policemen came out of the close, Albert asked them, 'Lookin' fur somebody, officers?'

'Aye,' the taller of the two policeman said. 'We've had complaints from the neighbours that a machine has been making a terrible racket in that flat over the past few weeks. Do you know who lives there?'

'Naw,' Albert said, 'but as soon as we find oot we'll tell ye!'

'Thanks, boys,' the policeman said. He wasn't to know that we never gave the police information – and besides, this was top-secret government business!

A few hours later, the printer turned up in his van. He looked ashen-faced when we told him that two policemen had been knocking on the door. 'Oh, naw! That's aw Ah need. Things were goin' so well,' he said. 'I'd better get the gear oot o' there pronto, and you guys can help me.'

When the printer opened the two mortise locks he'd put on the door 'for security' and opened up, we walked into the flat to be greeted by the sight of hundreds of ten-pound notes drying on washing lines.

'Ah cannae believe it! Ye're makin' yir ain money!' Alex exclaimed.

Chris said, 'Ah've heard o' money growin' oan trees but never oan washin' lines.'

Rab walked over and pulled one of the notes from the line. He examined it closely. 'This is almost perfect. Ye would never tell that it wisnae the real thing,' he said in amazement.

The printer had an air of panic about him. 'Right, boys,' he said, ignoring our reaction, 'let's get aw the notes doon and take the gear oot tae the van.'

Albert was placed as lookout at the mouth of the close, just in case the police turned up again, and over the next half-hour we loaded the printer, ink, paper and boxes of notes into the van. We left the flat immaculate; there was no sign that it had been used as a forged-note factory.

For our trouble, the printer gave us each a freshly made ten-pound note. 'Don't spend it in the Gorbals where people know ye,' he told us. 'Go tae the big department stores in the city centre, mingle wi the crowds and break them there. Do wan store at a time and go low-profile. Try no tae stand oot in the crowd.' Having issued this advice along with the counterfeit cash, he sped off in his van.

'This is the kind o' top-secret government work Ah like!' Albert said as we headed off to splash our cash.

CHAPTER THIRTY-SIX

✳

UP THE TOON

Wandering from department store to department store certainly opened our eyes to how prosperous Glasgow really was. Many people in the Gorbals – especially the older ones – rarely went 'up the toon', preferring to stay where they were. In fact, in some cases, people who lived in one street hardly mixed with people who lived in the next. At times, it seemed as if every street in the Gorbals was its own little world with its own shops, pubs and characters.

So this was an expedition for us, and a chance to see how the better-off people in Glasgow lived and shopped. In one store, the House of Fraser, we watched open-mouthed as a rather fat and unattractive lady tried on a fur coat priced at 300 guineas. In our area, that was enough to feed a family for at least six months, but after trying it on, the woman said to the assistant, 'This fur looks a bit cheap. Have you anything of better quality?'

The grovelling sales assistant grinned, probably thinking about his commission, and replied in an accent with a hint of (possibly put on) French about it, 'Yes, madam. We have had the pleasure of stocking a brand-new range that has been flown in from Paris. The coats are made from the best fur and start at 1,000 guineas.'

'Oh, wonderful!' the large lady replied, taking the 'cheap' coat off. As she removed it, I noticed that she had large damp patches under her armpits.

Chris laughed and said, 'That big woman disnae need a new fur coat, she needs plastic surgery!'

'Aye, she's nae stranger tae a fish supper or two,' Alex agreed.

The lady tried on the 1,000-guinea fur coat and seemed delighted with it. 'Yes, this is rather charming. And Parisian, too! I feel like Brigitte Bardot. I am going to a dinner-dance soon in the presence of the Lord and Lady Provost at the City Chambers, and only the best will do. Yes, I like it. Have it wrapped and delivered to my home.' She gave an address in the bourgeois area of Bearsden.

'Bloody hell!' Albert said. 'That woman must be oan the game or somethin'.'

'Ha!' Rab snorted. 'No wi a face like a hatchet and a body like the Michelin Man! Naw, she's probably married tae some lawyer or businessman. Too much money and nae sense.'

We left the shop somewhat shocked and bewildered that people had so much cash to squander. If people we knew wanted a fur coat, and a good one at that, they went to Paddy's Market, where they could pick up a second-hand one for a few shillings. There was silence for a while and then Albert piped up, 'Mind you, ma auld man says that if ye want tae know whit God thinks o' money, jist look at the people he gies it tae.'

We headed off to Lewis's in Argyle Street, where we marvelled at all the toys on offer. Albert decided he wanted a small toy aeroplane for ten shillings. When he handed the male sales assistant the forged tenner, he looked first at the note and then at Albert suspiciously. 'Excuse me, young man,' he said, 'but may I ask where you got all this money?'

This was it! We were rumbled! I had visions of us all being bundled out of the store and into a Black Maria. But Albert was as cool as cucumber. 'Ma mammy gave it tae me. She wanted me tae get somethin' nice fur ma birthday.' He pointed to a smartly dressed woman in a queue at the other corner of the store and said, 'That's her there.'

The assistant looked over at the woman, and said, 'Oh, sorry for the misunderstanding, but it's not often we see a young lad like you coming in with a crisp, new ten-pound note.' He wrapped up the toy plane, gave Albert his change and said, 'Many happy returns! Have a good birthday!'

I whispered to Albert, 'Let's get the hell oot o' here before that fella notices that that woman's no yir mother.' We left in a hurry; in fact, with the toy plane, you could say we flew out.

'That wis a near thing,' Chris said.

'Ach, it wisnae that close,' Rab said. 'Ye see, Albert turned oan the patter, and ye can always fool people when ye know whit tae say.'

'Albert could talk his way oot o' bein' shot by a firin' squad,' said Alex. 'Bullshit baffles brains!'

But Albert wasn't listening. He was preoccupied with his new plane, which he was pretending to fly in the air. Boys will be boys!

We headed off for another fancy department store and were hanging about outside when a woman stopped with a large Victorian-looking pram. She didn't look wealthy, but neither did she look poor. She probably had a nice flat in somewhere like Partick. She picked her baby out of the pram and it was a bonny little thing, but it was crying loudly. 'There, there, son,' she said. 'Have a wee suck on yir dummy teat and ye'll feel a lot better.' She placed the dummy in the baby's mouth but the child spat it out onto the pavement, where it landed in a puddle. Alex rushed over and picked up the dummy, wiping it on his jumper and saying, 'There ye go, missus, as good as new. A lovely baby you've got there, but he seems tae be in a bad mood the day!'

The woman laughed, clutching her baby to her breast. She said, 'He's just like his father, always grumpy about something or other. But like his pa he's a good yin at heart. Ah'm going inside tae buy him some new baby gear. Maybe that'll cheer him up.'

We all walked in together, the woman leaving the empty pram outside. In those days, you could do that. No one would have considered stealing a baby's pram, no matter how desperate they were.

The woman headed for the baby section and we went for a wander. It wasn't long before we spotted a boy we knew who was an accomplished shoplifter. He was only about our age, but he was considered something of a master of his trade. He was from sturdy criminal stock. His father was a well-known hoodlum who had once given us this advice: 'If ye get caught fur anythin', never ever plead guilty, that's fur the mugs. Always plead not guilty and then get yirself a good brief. Why make it easy fur the polis, lawyers and judges? They're the biggest crooks anyway. Not guilty gies ye a chance o' freedom. Plead guilty and you are sunk like a shipwreck.' He took his own advice and it seemed to work. He had appeared in court on a variety of charges over the years, but always pleaded not guilty and always got off.

His boy was from the same mould and had been caught shoplifting several times but the inevitable not guilty plea followed and the equally inevitable being set free followed that. The boy saw us and came over, saying, 'Hey, whit are the Diehards doin' in this neck o' the woods?'

'Jist a wee bit o' business,' Alex replied. 'How you doin'?'

'No bad,' the boy replied. 'In fact, no too bad at aw. Ah've got a new guy wi me the day and Ah'm showin' him the ropes. He's got a decent coat, as well.' Both of them were wearing fashionable-looking dark raincoats. But we knew the score. They had cut holes in the lining so that it was easy to make items such as jewellery disappear quickly. 'Right, see you later,' the boy said with the air of a busy man with plenty to be getting on with. He and his apprentice made off to another part of the store.

Alex managed to cash his tenner by purchasing an ashtray with the word 'Glasgow' etched on it. Nine shillings! But Alex thought it was worth every penny, as he had relatives who would treasure such a gift.

After the woman at the counter had wrapped Alex's ashtray and handed him the change, we heard shouting and the noise of a scuffle coming from the other end of the store. We looked over and the two shoplifting boys were grappling with two plain-clothes detectives who had spotted them sticking various items into their coats. As they were being manhandled away, the boy we had talked to was shouting, 'It's aw a mistake. Ye've got the wrang guys. Let us go.'

They were ushered into a back room, presumably to be held there until the police arrived. We decided to get out while the going was good.

We went through the doors to the street and there was a large crowd around the woman we had met, her baby and the pram. One woman was saying to her pals, 'Ah cannae believe it. Have ye ever seen such a thing? Some people are a bloody disgrace.'

Her pal nodded her head in agreement. 'The lowest o' the low. Ah mean, imagine daein' a thing like that. Whoever is behind it should be shot.'

'Aye, the bigger the gun, the faster the bullet, aw the better,' another woman commented.

We made our way through the throng to see what all the commotion was about. The woman we had talked to was standing clutching her bonny baby to her breast, but she looked shocked. 'What's the matter, missus? What's up?' I said to her.

'What's up? What's up?' she replied in an almost hysterical tone. 'Look in ma pram tae see what's up.'

We looked inside the pram and there was another baby there. Someone had abandoned it in the pram and made off. The baby was fast asleep, oblivious to the commotion around him.

A policeman and policewoman arrived on the scene and looked equally shocked. The policewoman shook her head and said, 'Who in their right mind would do such a thing? Imagine abandoning a wee baby in somebody else's pram. They can't be right in the head.' The officers began to ask members of the crowd questions and we thought it was better to make off, as we still had a few dodgy tenners in our possession.

As we walked over the bridge to the Gorbals Alex said, 'That woman wi the pram got the best bargain o' the day.'

'How's that?' Chris said.

'Well,' Alex replied, 'she started the day wi wan baby and ended up wi another – two fur the price o' wan.'

CHAPTER THIRTY-SEVEN

✳

CHARLIE

Standing on a street corner one day surrounded by crumbling tenements, Chris was in a jovial mood. 'Look at this place!' he said cheerfully. 'It's aw fallin' apart. When you live here yir standard o' livin' improves when you go campin'!'

'Wan o' these days we'll aw be oot o' here and livin' in big mansions,' Rab said. 'When Ah grow up, Ah want tae be famous, wi ma name in lights aw over the world.'

'The only way you are gonnae have yir name in lights is if ye change it tae Emergency Exit,' retorted Chris.

Round our way, if someone got too big for their boots or said something pretentious, they were always put back down to earth. In some ways it was a good thing but it must have battered many people's confidence. Dreams were made or died on the street corners.

We were still laughing when Albert appeared sporting a large black eye and bruises on his face. 'Whit happened tae you?' I said. It turned out that he had decided to 'watch the motors' outside of the Clelland Bar the night before. This meant that he'd offered to keep an eye on cars and lorries parked in the street, watching out for anyone that might be trying to break into them. When the owners returned from the pub, they usually gave the boy concerned at least a shilling for his trouble. But when Albert had asked one English lorry driver for money he was bashed in the face and given a kicking. We knew the guy in question. He was an obnoxious fellow we had nicknamed

Charlie Drake, because he resembled the 1960s comedian; he was small, stockily built, with receding fair hair. Charlie was known to park his lorry down in Hospital Street and then go into the Clelland to get drunk. Afterwards he would stagger out of the bar swearing and head for the cabin in his lorry, where he would sleep the night.

We were not great fans of Charlie Drake even before this. He never tipped us for keeping an eye on his lorry and indeed he often threatened us with violence. 'Aye,' Albert said, 'when Ah told Charlie Ah had watched his lorry and was expecting a tip, he belted me right across the face, threw me tae the pavement and laid a couple o' kicks intae me.'

This was definitely not on. Charlie Drake had assaulted a wee Gorbals street boy. And this was no ordinary boy; this was a member of the Incredible Gorbals Diehards that he'd laid his grubby hands on. Wee English bastard!

We stood on the street corner and discussed some sort of retribution. It was agreed that when Charlie arrived back from England we would smash all the windows on his lorry and let the tyres down to teach him a lesson. The plan seemed failsafe, as Charlie always parked his lorry in the darkest end of Hospital Street and there was very little chance of us being spotted.

A few days later we waited in the shadows for Charlie's return but our plans were thwarted when three guys came out of the pub. An argument developed with one fellow shouting to another, 'You've been eyein' up ma missus, tryin' tae chat her up. Do it again and Ah'll set about ye.'

'You set about me? Ha! That's a joke! You couldnae punch yir way oot a wet paper bag, ya mug, ye. Besides everybody knows yir missus is a big ride! Ah've ridden her a few times.'

The other fellow's face beamed bright red with anger. He pulled out a knife and stabbed his tormentor in the chest. The guy fell bleeding on the ground, clutching his chest. He should have kept his mouth shut instead of discussing equestrian matters. A crowd gathered and an ambulance arrived, sirens blaring, to take the injured man away. A squad of police cars also appeared on the scene. It looked like a murder, or at least an attempted murder, to us. Police cordoned off the street and as they did so we noticed Charlie's lorry pass by. Vengeance on him would have to wait for another day.

The next day the headline on the front page of the local paper was: 'Gorbals Man Stabbed After Street Argument'. A police spokesman commented, 'Surgeons fought all night to save the man's life after an extremely vicious attack took place. We are as yet unsure about the circumstances behind the attack and we are appealing for witnesses.'

The victim recovered, and the next week the police heat had cooled off. We spotted Charlie's furniture lorry parked in its usual place. Now was the time for vengeance! Only me, Alex and Albert were there. We gathered up some bricks ready to cave the lorry's windows in when suddenly Charlie Drake staggered out of the pub absolutely blootered. We had seen some states in the Gorbals but this guy was in the premier league when it came to drunkenness. He staggered, wobbled, staggered some more, wobbled again and then fell over. We walked over and Alex and Albert noticed a large wallet lying on the ground beside Charlie. Alex opened it up and there was more than £200 inside. 'Oh, ya beauty, ye!' Albert exclaimed. 'Forget smashin' his windaes. We'll take his wallet instead. Two hundred smackeroonies – that's vengeance enough!' We left Charlie Drake in his drunken stupor and disappeared into the night.

We pondered what to do with all the money. We couldn't exactly go to the bank, as they would ask too many questions about how young boys like us had acquired such a large amount of cash. Alex came up with what seemed like an ideal solution. He found a midden at the back of which was a sturdy brick wall. He managed to remove a sizeable brick, revealing a large hole – the perfect hiding place for our ill-gotten gains.

This midden wall was to be our very own safety deposit box. We already had £50 saved up from our other adventures. We stuck that in the wall, and from our recent windfall, we decided to spend £150 between us and deposit £50 in our 'midden bank'.

When we'd hidden the cash in the hole, Alex replaced the brick and we stepped out into the back court. Although it was dark and late at night, I could have sworn I saw a curtain twitch in one of the tenement windows.

'Ah think somebody's watchin' us,' I said to Alex.

'Don't be daft. You're jist bein' paranoid,' he replied. 'Besides, whose gonnae think that we'd be usin' this midden tae hide money? Nah, oor cash is safe in there.'

The next day, with £150 burning a hole in our pockets, we went on a spree. It was madness. We went to a fancy-goods shop and bought a variety of trinkets and ornaments: little dancing figurines, fancy German drinking mugs and some silver goblets. The Asian owner looked surprised at the amount of money we had spent but he asked no questions. As Alex said, if anyone did ask where we got the money, we could simply say, 'Ma maw won the bingo and gave me a few bob.' After that, we headed for a Chinese restaurant in Eglinton Street, where we had a slap-up lunch of chow mein followed by banana fritters in golden syrup. This was the life! The manager had asked to see our money before we ordered, and he seemed surprised when we showed him the cash, but he smiled, sat us down and, again, no questions were asked. We felt quite powerful having money for once.

We strolled back out onto the streets elated after a taste of the high life, but we knew we weren't absolutely in the clear yet and agreed we'd stay clear of the Clelland Bar for a few days just in case we bumped into Charlie Drake, who might just remember what had happened to him.

About a week later, we saw his lorry pulling into Hospital Street, but we were surprised to see another driver get out. We asked him where the usual guy was.

'Oh, him!' he replied. 'He got the sack. He spent the invoice money – more than two hundred quid – on drink. The company's been looking for ages for a way to get rid of him. Nobody liked him anyway. He was an obnoxious little dick, especially when he'd had a drink. You won't be seeing him again.'

As far as we were concerned, it served him right for battering Albert.

CHARLIE

'That fella Charlie wis a real joke,' Albert said, still sporting his black eye, 'and the punchline wis, he got robbed and sacked. Just deserts fur the bully.'

CHAPTER THIRTY-EIGHT

＊

A SQUARE GO

This is where things get a little bit complicated. It turned out that the guy we'd seen drunkenly stabbing the man who was insulting his wife outside the Clelland had in fact been best pals with his victim until that night. Also, the two men were distantly related, and their parents, brothers and sisters all knew each other and got on. It was a tricky situation.

The police were still searching for the stabber, but they had more chance of catching the flu. No one was about to tell them anything. Meanwhile, the injured guy's mother had been so worried she was taken into hospital with palpitations, and the assailant's mother was said to be heading for a nervous breakdown.

A family meeting was held in a local pub to discuss the matter. We heard all about it. 'Too much wine and no enough sense,' said the stabber's sister. The gist of the discussion was that the victim hadn't meant what he'd said and had been making up the allegations about the other guy's wife being a hing-oot. 'It wis the wine talkin',' his sister said. 'They two have never had a fallin'-oot before. How it aw went so far is a mystery tae me. They're jist two daft boys. Ah always said their big mooths would land them in trouble.'

It was decided by both sides that, to clear the air, the injured guy's brother, one of the Gorbals old school, a burly guy in his 40s, would challenge the stabber, a younger man, to a square go in the Rose Garden in Rutherglen Road later that week. The

Rose Garden, an old burial ground that had been transformed into a little park, was a great place to relax. Children played street games there, alkies sat on the benches and got drunk on the cheap wine, typically pasty Scots sunbathed in the hope of getting a bit of colour, lovers held hands – and the odd dispute was settled through the medium of the square go.

It was to be a fair fight, one on one, and no knives or razors would be used, just fists, heads and the odd kick. A street-corner bookmaker began to take bets on the two contenders. The odds on the older guy were 9–4. The younger guy, the perpetrator of the crime, had longer odds of 3–1, but the bookie wasn't daft. He knew the older one was the strongest contender. It was Gorbals old school against Gorbals new school.

It was predicted that the two men would use contrasting fighting techniques. The old school was all about punching and wrestling, with maybe the odd head-butt. The new school was about disabling your opponent quickly, leaping into action with head-butts and a permissible one-off 'kick in the baws'.

Fighting, or at least knowing how to fight, was part of life in the Gorbals, except for those who considered themselves fly men. To these shrewd guys, fast patter was much more effective than a punch. And, anyway, as they often said, what was the object of the fight if there was no money in it? To these guys, money was all. Fighting for dignity or honour was for those who didn't know any better. One fly man commented to us, 'Whit's the point o' those two guys beatin' the hell oot o' each other? The guy who did the deed should have apologised and offered the other guy's family money in compensation. Then they'd aw have been happy and naebody else would have got hurt.'

Another old-timer agreed. 'Apart fae the unfortunate incident, the families have always got oan well. Fightin' can only make things worse.'

The bookie taking the bets was also a bit puzzled as to why the contest was taking place. 'The young guy should jist have accepted a doin' fae the aulder brother. He's gonnae get battered anyway, so why defy the odds? Mind you, ye never know in this game. Nothin' is 100 per cent predictable. A few slip-ups by the aulder fella, and there could be a major upset.'

It was just a street fight, but the anticipation was such that some people were talking about it as if it was a world-class bout between a couple of seasoned champions. I heard two men on the corner of Crown Street speculating on the outcome, and one was saying, 'The aulder fella's gonnae beat the crap oot o' that cheeky young bastard. It'll no be a contest. He's gonnae mollicate that young guy. Experience always comes before youth. Anyway, Ah've got ten bob oan him tae win.'

But his pal was less sure. 'Nah, Ah think the young guy's in wi a chance. He'll be faster aff the mark and he looks fitter. Ah've got a pound oan him. And if he wins, we'll aw be havin' a good drink. In fact, nae matter whether it's win or lose, we'll have a damn good feed o' the booze!'

When the day came, more than 100 people turned up in the Rose Garden to witness the contest. Friends and relatives on each side were there egging their man on. 'This is Gorbals justice at its best,' a middle-aged woman said to me. 'That young fella needs the shite beat oot o' him fur aw the hurt and trouble he's caused, swine that he is. Ah've known him since he wis a wee boy and he's always been a bit o' a nuisance.'

The two men met in the centre of the park. They displayed little emotion and said nothing. The older guy had a steely, determined look in his eyes. He took off his gold rings and stripped to the waist. As the moment of truth approached, the young guy's face was a picture. A look of panic came over him. He knew in his heart that he was heading for a beating.

Suddenly, the silence was broken by the older man. 'Come oan, then, sonny boy. Any coward can use a knife. Try fightin' like a real man.'

Despite his evident nerves, the younger guy still managed to put on a gallus front. He uttered the words, 'Aye, that'll be right.'

Perhaps surprisingly, there was no exchange of curses or insults. I interpreted this as a sign that the battle was half-hearted and that underneath it all the two men secretly respected each other.

Preliminaries over, the young guy rushed towards his older counterpart and attempted to head-butt him, but the more experienced fellow elbowed him in the face and then gave him an uppercut to the chin that sent him flying. He got up again to launch another attack, but the older man punched him full in the face and his nose exploded. Another punch to the face, and two of his teeth fell out. The young man plummeted to the ground for the last time.

There was a loud cheer and the older guy raised his arms in the air in a gesture of victory, telling the crowd, 'Ah didnae really want tae beat the boy up, but he needed tae be taught a lesson. He used a knife oan ma brother and they're supposed tae be the best o' pals.'

The loser was helped back home by his sisters and the victor headed to the pub with his cronies to celebrate. One of his pals was telling him, 'Ye set about him nae bother at aw, bampot that he is. Ye showed him that he made a big mistake messin' wi you and yir brother.'

One old fly man standing beside me was less impressed with the spectacle. He shook his head, looked at us Diehards and said, 'That wis like a guy wi a bow and arrow tryin' tae fight a guy wi an atomic bomb. Mind you, unlike an atomic bomb, at least it cleared the air. Maybe it wis a good idea after aw. Pity there wis nae money in it fur the winner. It's only the bookies that have made a few bob.'

The street bookie was indeed quite happy with the outcome. He'd made well over £100 from punters who'd put last-minute bets on the younger guy, hoping that youth would triumph over experience. Counting a bundle of notes, he said to us, 'wanthing you'll learn in this life, boys, is that the bookie always wins at the end o' the day. There we had two guys tryin' tae belt the hell oot o' each other and the aulder guy thinks he's the winner, but the real winner is me. Those eejits were fightin' fur nothin'. It's a simple law o' nature: never do anythin' fur nothin'. Money cannae buy ye happiness, but it's better havin' it than bein' wi'oot it.' It was a simple lesson in economics, but we got the message, and from then on if we saw a fight and there was no money in it, we looked down our noses at the participants.

A few weeks later, we bumped into the mother of the victim. She had been sent home from hospital and had recovered enough to go down to the shops for her messages. She told us, 'That wis a terrible carry-oan. It made me sick wi worry. They two boys went tae school together and they were like brothers. Ah don't blame either o' them. Ah blame that cow they were arguin' about. She'd cause trouble in an empty hoose. The sooner she scrams, the better fur everybody concerned.'

When the victim was released from hospital, he, his older brother and his assailant met in a local pub to 'square things up'. We managed to get a good view of what was going on through the open door. They were slapping each other on the back, telling jokes and buying round after round of drinks.

'Ah'm sorry. It wis a misunderstandin',' we heard the stabber say to his victim. 'Ah don't know whit came over me. Ma heid had been done in by that bird. Ye were right enough, whit ye said about her. She is a big ride. When ye were in hospital, she ran away wi another bloke, an ugly bastard. Worst part about it is, he wis a polis investigatin' the case. He came lookin' fur particulars and ended up takin' doon hers!'

'Well, good riddance tae bad rubbish, that's whit Ah say!' the victim said cheerfully.

After a few drinks, they were definitely all pals again. They began to sing:

> I've been a wild rover for many's the year,
> and I spent all me money on whisky and beer,
> But now I'm returning with gold in great store,
> And I never will play the wild rover no more!
>
> And it's no nay never!
> No, nay never no more,
> Will I play the wild rover,
> No never, no more!

Standing outside was our pal the fly man, who said to us, 'Hey, boys, ye know the secret o' life?'

'Whit?' I replied.

'Ye need tae have a selective memory. Forget aw the bad things that happen tae ye, and life jist gets better.'

Listening to the former enemies singing quite happily together, I thought, 'Who could argue with that philosophy?'

CHAPTER THIRTY-NINE

✳

SAVING MONEY

We took the bookie's philosophy to heart. We started saving more and putting it in our midden bank. It was agreed that we wouldn't touch it until the following year, when we would all reach 15. We hoped to end up with £100 each, enough to set us up for the future. We were determined not to end up skint like most of the people we'd grown up with.

In the hope of making a bit extra, we started searching through old discarded sofas for money. As the residents of the crumbling tenements were being decanted to other areas, many of them chucked out their old couches, leaving them on the streets. We discovered that often if we dug around behind the cushions or ripped open the linings with a sharp blade, we would find some money. Sometimes it was small change, sometimes real money, like a pound note or even a fiver. We occasionally found bits of jewellery left behind in the furniture, too. 'When people see a mingin' auld couch lyin' in a back court,' Alex commented, 'they jist think it's rubbish. They don't realise they could be lookin' at a wee goldmine.'

He wasn't wrong. One time, we came across a large antique-looking sofa and decided to break it apart. We searched for ages through the springs and horsehair, and we were on the point of giving up when Chris shouted out, 'Got it! Whit a cracker!' He was holding in his hand a gold brooch. We usually took such items straight to the second-hand jewellers, the pawnbrokers or the market traders at the Barras.

Another sofa gifted us a large quantity of spare change, more than £10 in total, some of the coins dating back to the previous century. In yet another, we found a number of old banknotes totalling more than £15. We presumed that these larger amounts were the life savings of old people who'd hidden them away and died before they had a chance to spend the cash.

Some elderly people had forgotten secret caches of money under their floorboards when they'd moved out, and we searched the deserted old tenements for these. Another good way to get the cash in was to check the shilling meters. In some of the buildings earmarked for demolition, these were full to the brim. If you hit them with a hammer, the shillings tumbled out as if the meter was a fruit machine.

We also 'helped' the odd drunk to get home, making sure some money went missing from the fellow's jacket. We told ourselves we were doing these guys a favour, as they would have spent the cash on booze anyway. Watching the motors outside the Clelland Bar was always a fruitful exercise, too, and with so many families moving away, another decent way to coin it in was to help people with their flitting. We even started to speculate to accumulate, using some of our earnings to place bets with the local street-corner bookie. They were never large sums, just a few shillings at a time, and we lost as often as we won, but sometimes we had a decent win on a rank outsider and that helped boost our savings plan.

Over the years, the boys and I had become jacks of all trades, ducking and diving every day. As the Americans say, 'You've got to hustle for a buck.' Our many schemes were proving to be quite lucrative, and our savings were growing all the time. At the end of each day, we would count up what we'd made, take some each to spend, and then deposit the rest into the midden bank.

I was still unsure about this method, as I was convinced that every time we put some money in a net curtain in a nearby window moved slightly. But when I spoke to Alex about it, he would just laugh and say, 'It's jist the wind. Naebody's watchin' us. And if they were, how would they know we're usin' the midden as a bank? Naebody knows apart fae us, and naebody's gonnae find oot. He'd have tae be Sherlock Holmes. Oor money is as safe as hooses behind that brick.'

In any case, our booty had grown to such an extent that it was now certainly impossible for us to approach a real bank with it. Every time we hid more money, there would be some excited banter between us. We could hardly believe how well we were doing.

One evening, Chris laughed, 'Since Ah wis a wee boy, Ah always wanted a bank account, but Ah never thought it would be in a midden wi Alex as the manager. The Royal Bank o' Midden!'

'Ah can see the Royal Bank o' Midden gettin' as big as the Royal Bank of Scotland,' joked Albert.

'Alex can be managin' director in charge o' the accounts,' said Rab, 'and we'll be the big-shot directors smokin' fat cigars.'

'Ye never know,' I said. 'Thomas Lipton came fae the Gorbals and ended up a multimillionare wi aw those tea plantations.'

'Aye, so there's hope fur the Royal Bank o' Midden yet,' Chris laughed. 'And when the Queen turns up tae launch us, she'll have tae cut the ribbon here, cos this is oor first branch!'

'We'll aw end up wi MBEs,' said Alex. 'Midden Bank Eejits!'

It was 1969, and things really seemed to be going our way. It was an optimistic time, the year of the first manned moon landing. In a bizarre way, we Diehards identified with the first men on the moon. We saw ourselves as adventurers, embarking on a new voyage every day. Like us, the astronauts ventured into unknown territory and were unafraid of danger.

We had a pal whose mother had had a big win at the bingo and had bought a large television. He invited us back to theirs to watch the moon landing. It was certainly a night to remember. Sitting in the old tenement flat, we watched astounded as the spacecraft landed on the moon, thrilled by the words, 'Houston, Tranquility Base here. The *Eagle* has landed.' Later, we witnessed Neil Armstrong walking on the moon and uttering the line, 'That's one small step for man, one giant leap for mankind.' We all thought that the desolate surface of the moon resembled some of the back courts in the Gorbals.

Heading home in the early morning, we found that we hadn't been the only ones watching the moon landing. Two drunk guys were standing on a street corner, prolonging the party, slugging from a bottle of Four Crown. They looked as if they'd been drinking all night. One of them was singing 'Fly Me to the Moon' and the other was ranting, 'The bloody Americans! They do everythin' first.' He took a swig from his bottle, staggered, wiped his mouth with his coat sleeve and cried, 'That's wan small glug fur man, wan giant bevvy fur mankind!'

His pal laughed, spitting out a mouthful of wine, and declared, 'Houston, Glesga base here. The Four Crown wine has landed!'

More seriously, though, watching the first man walk on the moon touched a chord with us; it made us think about the fact that there was another world out there, a world miles away from the grimness we were used to, a world where adventurers like us could flourish. 'It jist shows ye,' Chris said, 'the world's movin' oan and the Gorbals is dyin' aff. When ye look at that man oan the moon, it makes ye think that we're aw stuck in the past here. Ah think we're headin' fur a new age.'

'Ah think ye're right,' Albert told him. 'The Americans have showed that if ye're game enough, ye can do anythin' wi yir life.'

'That wis a bit o' a shock fur me,' Alex joked. 'Ah thought the moon wis made o' cheese. Well, if oor Royal Bank o' Midden does well, we can build a spacecraft and go there!'

Rab laughed. 'Aye and the headlines'll say, "Gorbals Diehards on the Moon!" Stranger things have happened!'

We weren't the only ones whose thoughts were turning to the wider world. The next day, I eavesdropped on a conversation between two women who had just came out of the steamie, parked their prams full of washing on the corner and lit up their cigarettes. 'Well, Agnes,' one said to the other, 'a man oan the moon! Ah never thought Ah'd see that in ma lifetime. And jist look aroon! This place hisnae changed in 100 years. It's like livin' in a bloody history book. Ah don't really want ma weans tae grow up here any mair. Ah saw an advert up the toon offerin' assisted passages tae Australia. Me and ma man are goin' up tae the immigration office oan Monday. Whit dae ye think? Would you and yir man fancy comin' along?'

Agnes took a deep draw of her fag, thought for a moment, and replied, 'Ye know, Ina, that's no a bad idea. Ah'll talk tae ma fella. This place is finished. Ah'm fed up wi ma man bein' oot o' work and it's always bloody freezin' and rainin'. Australia might do us aw good!'

The two steamie ladies weren't the only ones. To the people of the Gorbals, with its dark, crumbling buildings and smoky chimneys, the wide open spaces of the New World exerted a magnetic pull. Many people moved their families to Australia, Canada and America. Perhaps some of them reasoned that if the USA had the drive, imagination and determination to land a man on the moon, then it could only be good for them if they landed in America.

A few days after the big event, I was standing with Albert outside the Turf Bar in Hospital Street when two drunks staggered out in the middle of an argument. It was the usual pathetic stuff, shouting and swearing, effing and blinding, and then the taller of the two pulled out a razor and slashed the other fellow. It could have been a scene from the 1930s. Albert looked at me and said, 'Aye, they've jist landed a man oan the moon, but it's still the same old pish in the Gorbals.'

CHAPTER FORTY

❋

THE BIG DO

A few weeks later, we bumped into the women from outside the steamie and asked them how they were doing. 'Smashin', boys!' said Agnes. 'We're aff tae Australia. Ma family and Ina's family have both been given the go-ahead, so in a few months we'll be in Sydney, surrounded by kangaroos and under the blazin' sun, instead o' here wi the rats and rain. Ma man's landed an engineerin' job and the weans'll be at good schools. Me an Ina are gonnae be livin' in the same area, aren't we, Ina?'

Ina smiled broadly and said, 'Aye, we're fur the aff. Ma man's got a good job as well, and ma weans'll be goin' tae the same school as Agnes's. It's worked oot perfect. The Gorbals? Ye can stick it up yir arse!'

The two women laughed loudly and Agnes continued, 'It's only costin' a tenner each oan the assisted passage lark. We've been told we'll feel homesick fur the first two years, but Ah've got Ina fur company and she's got me. The only thing is, ma man's a big Tim and Ina's is a Bluenose. They're gonnae miss no seein' their teams. But fitba's jist fitba. We're talkin' about a new life here. Bugger the fitba and bugger Glesga! We're away and we're no comin' back . . . ever! Is that no right, Ina?'

Ina took a drag of her cigarette, nodded her head and said, 'Aye, too right, Agnes. We might miss it here at first, but we'll be like the convicts who first went tae Australia – we'll get used tae it. Mind you, the people there might think we're convicts, comin' fae the Gorbals!'

Apart from emigration, there were several ways to escape the Gorbals: you died, you were decamped by the council to one of the new housing estates, you made enough money to move away or you married someone well off who lived in a better area.

Old Billy took the first mentioned route. He'd lived all his life in Florence Street when, at 86, he was sent a letter by Glasgow Corporation informing him that his tenement was to be demolished and offering him a house in one of the new council housing schemes. But he was resolute that he was going nowhere. 'Ah've been through two wars and the Jerries couldnae beat me, so Glesga Corporation has got nae chance,' he told us. The situation was becoming ridiculous, though, with the tenements all around his being pulled down until his was the only one on the block still standing. When passed by at night, there was only ever one light on in the building. Billy was the sole inhabitant left. It was a sad sight in many ways, but it bore testimony to Billy's obstinacy.

However, he was fighting a losing battle, and the stress eventually got to him. He collapsed and died of a stroke in his flat, and that was the end of him. A few days after the funeral, the Corporation knocked the tenement down and all that was a left was an empty space and a pile of rubble. Where the Germans had failed, Glasgow Corporation had succeeded.

Some residents were more ambivalent about being moved. We helped a family who lived across the road from me to pack up their things for the trip to their new home. Although they were only going a few miles up the road, they seemed a bit despondent. The man of the house said, 'It's a nice hoose, but it's no the Gorbals. We'll jist have tae get used tae it, Ah suppose. At least Ah'll be able tae have a pish indoors noo! Nae mair chanties, nae mair ootside lavvies, nae mair filth, nae mair rats. Noo that Ah think about it, we've knocked it aff, hit the jackpot!'

As I say, there were different ways out of the Gorbals, if you wanted to take them, and Margaret, a young woman in her early 20s, was going for the time-honoured method of bagging a rich husband. She was a beautiful girl who would have been considered a catch by any young man.

In her teens, she had worked in the Twomax woollen mill in Rutherglen Road, and she had got engaged to a local plumber. However, she blossomed during her engagement and she broke it off, deciding that she was 'too good' to be a Gorbals plumber's wife and work in a menial factory job. By the time she was 21, her beauty was outstanding. She had a model figure, long legs and a face that could have launched a thousand ships, or, as Alex quipped, a thousand hips. When she was all done up, she looked stunning, and she'd even appeared in a local newspaper as one of 'Glasgow's Most Beautiful Young Women'.

One night, we spotted her at Gorbals Cross in the company of two American sailors. She introduced the two of them to us. We were a bit overawed, because the guys resembled Hollywood movie stars. There was Chuck from Texas, a big, broad-shouldered fellow with thick blond hair, and Clint from Ohio, a tall, handsome African American guy. When their battleship docked in the Broomielaw they decided to hit the town, and on their travels they'd bumped into Margaret in a bar. She'd offered to give them a wee tour of the Gorbals.

Chuck said to us, 'Margaret's a beautiful broad. She'd sure as hell be a hit in the States. Pity she's stuck in goddamn Glasgow!'

Clint agreed, saying, 'I've met some beautiful gals in ma time, but Margaret beats them all.'

The sailors asked us where they could 'go to the John' and we led them into a back lane, where we joined them. When Clint undid his fly, Alex looked over and exclaimed, 'Bloody hell, Clint, yours is the size o' a baby's arm! Noo Ah know whit they tell me about black men is true. They say everythin' is big in America but that's ridiculous.'

Clint and Chuck laughed. Clint said, 'Yeah, we do everything big in America!' When they had finished peeing, the sailors handed Alex a five-dollar note for being their 'tour guide' before heading off in a taxi with Margaret.

Having packed in her factory job and her plumber, Margaret now had a fancy secretarial job in an office 'up the toon'. The fact that she couldn't type or take shorthand seemed to be immaterial. The owner of the firm had been so overcome by her beauty that he'd hired her on the spot. And, more importantly, the boss's son was also beginning to take a shine to her.

We started to spot her being driven about by the son in a big flashy Mercedes. The car pulled up beside us at Gorbals Cross one day and Margaret wound her window down and called us over. The only unattractive thing about Margaret was that, having grown up on the rough streets, she used extremely foul language, and most of the time she seemed to be completely unconscious of this drawback. 'Hello, boys!' she greeted us. 'How are you cheeky bastards doin'? Still f***in' tryin' tae make a few bob or two? Ye shower o' wee c***s, ye're always up tae some shite or other!' She then closed her mouth and looked as demure as a princess.

Margaret introduced us to her new boyfriend, Charles. To us, he looked a limp-wristed character, a bit wet behind the ears, or, as Chris put it, 'a right doughball'. Charles had a posh accent and had probably gone to a fee-paying school like Hutchesons' Grammar. 'These are ma wee pals. A right shower o' bastards!' Margaret said.

Charles smiled, nodded in our direction and said meekly, 'Nice to meet you, chaps!'

'Where are ye aff tae, Margaret?' Alex asked.

'Ach, Charles is takin' me tae some posh restaurant up the toon. They've got aw that f***in' French crap like frogs' legs and snails. Well, it'll be a change fae ma auld maw's bloody Irish stew that tastes like dug shite.' She gave us a sexy wink and the car sped off towards the town.

'What the hell does Margaret see in him?' Chris wondered, shaking his head.

'Money,' Albert replied. 'It's aw about money. Ye can be the ugliest guy in the world, but if ye've got a bit o' dosh, the birds'll be roon ye like bees aroon honey.'

'Mair like flies aroon shite!' Rab said.

'Tae tell ye the truth,' Alex reflected, 'Ah'd rather be the best-lookin' guy in the world than the richest. Because when you've got the looks, ye attract the birds and the money.'

A few weeks later, we saw Margaret coming towards us in Eglinton Street. She looked radiant, more beautiful than ever. Her sister was with her and, by comparison, she was rather dowdy and plain. Over the years, she must have got used to living in her gorgeous sister's shadow. Margaret was wearing a new fur coat, obviously courtesy of Charles, and when she approached us she waved her left hand. She was wearing a giant diamond engagement ring. 'Look at this, boys! Ah'm gettin' married! Charles proposed tae me oan bended knee in the French restaurant, bampot that he is! The weddin's gonnae be in June and the reception'll be at the Central Hotel. You boys are invited, and ye can eat and drink aw ye want. There's gonnae be nae expense spared. After that, we're aff tae Majorca oan honeymoon, and Charles's faither has bought us a new hoose in Bearsden as a weddin' present.' Margaret was certainly in a jubilant mood. She swanned off singing 'Get Me to the Church on Time', with added swearing.

Charles's parents must have been pleased that he had landed such a beautiful woman, even if she was a bit on the vulgar side. They probably trusted that she would be tamed into middle-class culture over time. Margaret's mother and father were delighted with the match. They had lived in poverty all their lives and now their daughter was marrying into a moneyed family. It was a hell of a lot better than getting a full house at the bingo.

Before the wedding, we bumped into the sister. We got chatting and she told us that the reason behind the speedy engagement was that Margaret was up the duff. We wondered whether Margaret had allowed herself to get pregnant as a means of escaping the Gorbals. But then the counter-argument was that geeky Charlie had put her in the family way because he knew he would never net such a beautiful woman again. Either way, it had worked out fine for both of them. Margaret didn't have to travel all the way to the other side of the world to make a new life. She had got where she was due to her beauty and a certain kind of feminine cunning.

The day of the wedding came and the boys and I headed for the reception at the Central Hotel. We had all managed to scrape together a black jacket and trousers that matched, a white shirt and a dark tie, and, of course, we'd made sure our shoes were highly polished. Some of our gear had come from Paddy's Market and the rest from charity shops. We gathered in the Gorbals Cross toilets to give ourselves a last preen, and when I saw us all in the large mirror, I thought that we looked like young gentlemen. I was a bit shocked by our reflection, too, because we looked so grown up, so manly. We were all approaching the age of fifteen, and we'd been roaming the streets of the Gorbals for ten years or more. In that time, we'd experienced so much and had been through thick and thin together, Gorbals born and Gorbals bred.

As we looked at our images in the mirror, we all fancied ourselves, but I secretly thought that Alex looked amazing. He had dark, Mediterranean looks and a thin build. He looked like the sort of guy you see in a James Bond film hanging about the casino in Monte Carlo. Of course, Alex knew this and, looking at himself in the mirror, he exclaimed, 'The birds at the reception'll be runnin' after me. Ye know whit, when Margaret sees me, she'll dump that idiot Charlie and elope wi me.'

There was no doubt he scrubbed up well, but he was getting too arrogant, so when he came out with stuff like this, the boys were always quick with a put-down. 'Aye,' Rab said, 'the only way the birds'll be runnin' after you is if ye become a handbag snatcher.'

We felt like a million dollars as we headed over the bridge to the town. When we arrived outside the Central Hotel, a number of limos were pulling up. These obviously belonged to Charles's relatives and friends. The Gorbals contingent, less flashy but well dressed and well scrubbed, entered the hotel on foot after alighting from a Corporation bus. We were greeted by a concierge who asked us for our invitations. We handed them over and were taken upstairs to a large Victorian function room.

A waiter, dressed to the nines, offered us glasses of Buck's fizz from a silver tray and we duly accepted. Rab whispered to me, 'Whit the hell is this?' Not long ago, I'd seen a film in which playboy types were being served the cocktail at a Manhattan party, so I was able to answer, 'Oh, it's champagne and orange juice,' in a voice that I thought made me sound like a worldly, knowledgeable guy.

We were shown to our table, with name cards for each one of us. We sat down feeling like real toffs. Chris took a sip of his cocktail and said, 'This is the life! This is whit we were made fur.'

'Aye,' Alex said, 'better than sellin' sticks or bumpin' drunks at Gorbals Cross.'

'Ah could get used tae this high-class lifestyle,' Rab said. 'Maybe when the Royal Bank o' Midden takes aff, we'll be daein' this kind o' thing aw the time.'

Alex, never backwards at coming forwards, summoned the waiter with the tray and asked for another five cocktails. Much to my surprise, the waiter didn't object and placed the cocktails before us on the table. Alex laughed and pointed out, 'If ye don't ask, ye don't get.' He proposed a toast: 'Here's tae the Incredible Gorbals Diehards!'

'The Incredible Gorbals Diehards!' we replied, clinking our glasses.

On the stage, a dance band struck up 'Here Comes the Bride'. Margaret and Charles entered. Dressed in her expensive white wedding dress, she looked more radiant, more beautiful than ever, although a small bump was visible under her dress. And Charles? He was the same as always, but standing next to his new wife he looked uglier than ever. It was a real case of beauty and the beast.

Looking around the function room, there was definitely a class divide. Margaret's people were on one side and Charles's on the other. It was the proletariat versus the patricians. But, overall, there was a happy, congenial atmosphere. The food was served and more drink was consumed, and soon the class barriers began to fall. Gorbals con men mingled with Hillhead accountants, down-to-earth labourers drank with posh teachers, fly men talked to lawyers, tenement-stair cleaners chatted with pearl-necklaced ladies. And the Diehards? Well, we mixed with everyone.

Alex was a great hit with the ladies of both social classes. One lady, who was rather overweight, in her early 20s and from

Bearsden, said to me, 'Your friend Alex is a handsome young man, but the problem is I can't understand a word he's saying.'

I found Alex and told him, 'Hey, the posh birds are aw sayin' you're a handsome bloke, but there's only wan problem.'

'Oh, aye,' Alex replied. 'Whit's that?'

'They say they cannae understand yir accent!' I said.

'Ach, they can go away and bile their heids, the bampots!' Alex retorted.

The band struck up the Gay Gordons and we took to the floor. Other dances followed, including the Dashing White Sergeant, the Eightsome Reel, the Two Step, the Waltz and the Highland Fling. I had never done country dancing before but the older ladies led the way. When some of the attractive young girls looked in my direction, however, I looked away. I wasn't being arrogant; I was secretly shy. Although I was well used to talking to fly men, crooks and drunks, a conversation with a pretty girl who might fancy me still frightened the hell out of me. The other boys felt much the same; confront us with any crazy circumstance on the streets, and we'd be gallus, but chatting up a young woman was a different matter. Alex was the only one of us who had no such problem. He'd talk to any girl, whether she understood his accent or not. Indeed, as the evening went on, the young plump lady who had complained about a communication problem was dancing with Alex and following his every move.

Albert looked over at the couple on the dance floor and said, 'Ah'll bet Alex ends up wi that big bird!'

'Ach,' Chris said, 'why no? If it's there, ye've got tae take it!'

Rab laughed and retorted, 'Ah widnae shag her wi yours!'

Seeing everyone mingling and having fun together was an eye-opener to us. We were like one big family once all the airs and graces had fallen by the wayside, and everybody in the room, rich and poor, felt Scottish. As one of Margaret's elderly relatives said to us, in a drunken state, 'Great night, great people! It jist shows ye, nae matter who ye are or whit ye do, we're aw Jock Tamson's bairns!' I didn't have a clue who Jock Tamson was, but I got the gist.

Before they left for their Spanish honeymoon, the newly married couple danced to Engelbert Humperdinck's 'The Last Waltz'. As the singer crooned, Charles looked awkward on his feet and I swear I heard Margaret say to him, 'Stop standin' oan ma f***in' toes!'

At the end of the night, the boys and I felt a bit tipsy and there was no sign of Alex. Before we left, we decided to search for him. We looked in the bar – no sign of Alex. We looked in the Gents – no sign of Alex. We looked all over, but couldn't find him anywhere. Eventually, we went into a dark room near the function hall, and we could hear grunting and groaning coming from underneath a table. Albert pulled the tablecloth back and there was Alex and the large lady, both partially undressed. Albert shouted, 'Come oan, Alex, it's time tae blow.' Alex pulled up his trousers and left the embarrassed-looking young woman lying there.

A few minutes later, we were walking over the bridge to the Gorbals. Alex laughed and said, 'That posh bird said she couldnae understand ma accent, but she had nae problem understandin' the language o' love!'

CHAPTER FORTY-ONE

✳

BOUNCING BACK

It must have been the champagne. That night, I had a very vivid dream. The other Diehards and I had escaped the Gorbals and were on a luxury yacht in the South of France. I don't know where the South of France came into it, but a few weeks before I had seen Morecambe and Wise in the film *That Riviera Touch*, so that might have been it. We were smoking large cigars and quaffing magnum bottles of champagne, and we were surrounded by a bevy of bikini-clad beauties. Alex, naturally, was the centre of attention. The beautiful women were draped all over him. Looking every inch the Mediterranean Romeo, he held his glass up and said, 'Pour me some more champagne, darling.' A blonde woman who resembled Miss World did as she was told. Chris was eating substantial quantities of caviar with brown bread. Albert showed me a large diamond ring that he had just bought, telling me, 'It cost a cool million.' Rab was waterskiing alongside the boat, and he shouted out, 'It's great being loaded!' The dream was in full Technicolor, but it was better than being at the pictures, because I was one of the stars.

Alex drained his glass and ordered the blonde to pour him another. Then he looked straight at me and said, 'Ah told ye the Royal Bank o' Midden would make us aw rich. It started wi wan midden and noo we've got thousands o' branches aw over the world.'

Suddenly, I heard loud screaming. 'Aaaarrgh!' I woke up in a sweat; it was coming from outside. I got out of bed and looked out the window; two drunk young women were fighting with each other. They were pulling each other's hair and scratching furiously at each other's faces. Behind them, a young guy looked on, somewhat shocked.

'You go near ma man again and Ah'll f***in' kill ye!' one of the women was shouting at the other.

'He's no your man, he's ma man!' the other screamed back.

The fellow who was obviously the reason behind the altercation went to break them up. 'Come oan, noo!' he shouted. 'Don't be daft. Ah'm no worth fightin' over.'

One of the women broke away, blood dripping down her cheeks, and turned on the guy. 'Ya two-timin' bastard,' she yelled. She pulled a large beer bottle from the bag containing their carry-oot and hit him over the head with it.

The guy fell to the pavement like a ton of bricks and lay there with blood dripping from a cut on his head. He was unconscious, perhaps even dead.

The other woman said, 'Ye were right tae hit him oan the nut. He is a two-timin' bastard. Let Casanova lie there in his blood and pish. He's a nae-user anyway.'

The two girls walked off, leaving the bleeding and unconscious lothario to his fate. I sighed and went back to bed. A few minutes before, I had been in the French Riviera quaffing champagne and surrounded by beautiful women. Now I was back in my bed in the Gorbals. I tried to return to my dream, but to no avail. I couldn't even get to sleep because of the sirens wailing outside.

A strange thought popped into my head: perhaps being in the Gorbals was just a dream and my existence as a playboy in the South of France was reality. But when the sunlight came in the morning, I could kid myself no longer. I wasn't a high roller, I thought gloomily, but rather a low-life scruff with a life ahead of me that was likely to comprise an ugly, nagging wife, screaming, snottery weans, poverty, violence and drunkenness.

In the morning, rather bleary-eyed, I met up with the boys, who all had a hungover look about them. It was time for the post-mortem.

'Ah had a great time last night, lapped it aw up,' Alex said.

Rab revealed, 'Ah wis so pished Ah wis tellin' people ma auld man owned Glesga Celtic, and the funny thing wis they believed me.'

Chris laughed and told us, 'Ah ended up drinkin' vodka wi this auld businessman, and by the end o' the night Ah wis speakin' fluent Russian!'

'It wis a real eye-opener, that party,' Albert said. 'It showed us how the other hawf lives. And Ah'll tell ye whit, Ah'd rather be in their hawf than this hawf!'

We had some money to stick in the midden bank, so we made our way to the back court. Alex took the bag out of the wall and announced that there was almost £1,700 in it. Our years of ducking and diving had paid off.

We decided to build up the money until December of that year, 1970, and then share it out. We talked about what we each planned do with our share. I announced that I might spend some of it on a holiday, maybe even a trip to Paris. Perhaps the French dream had influenced my thoughts. The boys teased me, saying that my head was always 'full o' daft ideas'. Rab decided, 'Ah'd like tae be a furniture removal guy wi ma ain van. This money could get me started.' Chris said that when he was old enough he would be spending some of the booty on driving lessons and would maybe try to buy a second-hand car. Albert, as cautious as ever, said he would be keeping his money for a rainy day and use it only when he needed to.

As we left the back court, I glanced up at the net-curtained window that always concerned me, and, for a brief moment, I saw a grey-haired woman peek out. Alex was right. I'd been paranoid. No old lady was about to rob the Incredible Gorbals Diehards. 'Nosy old bitch,' I thought. 'Why doesn't she mind her own business anyway?'

By December, our total had swelled to £2,000 and we were getting ready for our big pay day – £400 each, good money in those days. Apprenticeships were being advertised in the *Evening Times* at £5 to £6 a week, and a man was considered to be on a very good wage if he earned £20 a week.

We were walking along Crown Street when we saw Margaret coming towards us with her sister. Even heavily pregnant, she looked more beautiful than ever. Her skin had a lovely glow about it. As she got closer, though, we noticed that she had a worried look on her face.

'How's it goin', Margaret?' Rab called out. 'Whit are ye daein' back in the Gorbals wi us scruffs?'

For a moment, a weak smile came over her face. 'Oh, boys! Good tae see ye. Ye always make me laugh, no like some o' those snooty bastards in Bearsden. They're up they're ain arses!' Still the same old Margaret!

Her sister butted in using a more serious tone: 'Our auld maw's no well and she's been taken tae hospital. She's asked us tae go up tae her hoose and fetch her some belongin's.'

We offered to tag along and give them a hand. We headed to a close in Florence Street and we had to step over a dead, bloodied rat. I did not think this was a good omen but kept quiet and, like the rest of the boys, adopted a light-hearted tone to keep the mood jovial. Their mother's single-end was the image of extreme poverty. The room was dark and shabby and there was a little stove with an old rusty kettle on it. There was also a dilapidated table with a mouldy blue loaf on it. In the corner, there was an alcove with a soiled-looking, threadbare bed. In the other corner, there was a small battered wardrobe. *The end of the 1960s and people still lived like this!*

Margaret and her sister began to go through the wardrobe. 'That cardigan will do her – keep her warm,' Margaret's sister said.

'Aye,' Margaret replied, 'and we can take her auld woollen coat so that she'll be nice and cosy when she gets discharged.'

Suddenly, Margaret fainted. It was like watching a drunk fall. She hit the linoleum floor with a violent thud. She was out cold.

'Quick!' her sister shouted. 'Let's get her ontae the bed. That wis a bad fall. Ah jist hope the baby hisnae been affected.'

We carried Margaret over to the shabby bed and hundreds of fleas dispersed as we laid her down. She lay there for a few minutes before coming to. She gave us one of her beautiful smiles and said, 'Sorry about that, boys. The stress o' ma maw goin' intae hospital means Ah've no really been eatin' like Ah should.'

Her sister filled up the kettle and put it on the stove in order to make Margaret and us 'a wee cup o' tea'. It was a well-known fact that at stressful times like these 'a wee cup o' tea' was the answer.

Margaret sat up in the bed and took a sip of her tea, but then her face turned red and she moaned, 'Oh, naw! It's started.'

'Whit's started?' Alex asked.

'Ma contractions have started.'

'Contractions? Whit the hell are contractions?'

'It means she's ready tae have the baby!' her sister shouted in panic.

For once, we were ashen-faced with shock, as Margaret screamed in pain. 'Oooooh, naw!' she cried. 'Ah never thought it would happen here!'

Her sister held her hand and began shouting, 'Push, Margaret, push! Push harder and yir baby will come oot. Come oan, push!'

Margaret did as she was told and the next minute we saw a head appear from between her legs. It was a little black head. 'Push harder again!' the sister shouted.

Soon, a beautiful little black boy appeared. A few minutes later, Alex was holding him to his chest. He did not say anything and neither did the other Diehards; we had been shocked into silence.

As Alex held the little baby, I heard a crashing noise outside. I looked out of the window and saw a tenement come tumbling down after being hit with a demolition ball. In the sky, a little star was twinkling brightly.

> Twinkle, twinkle, little star,
> How I wonder what you are.

The Gorbals as I'd known it was in its dying days and this little boy was destined to live in an age in which the old Gorbals would be consigned to the history books.

After all the drama, we resumed our journey to the Royal Bank o' Midden for the final share-out. Four hundred pounds each, our ill-gotten gains from all our years on the streets.

When we got to the back court and headed for the midden, I glanced up at the troublesome window. The net curtain had gone. The tenement must have been cleared for demolition.

Alex pulled out the brick in the midden wall and for a moment there was silence. Then he shouted out, 'It's gone! We've been robbed!' The bag with our booty had been taken.

We sat down in the back court, disillusioned. 'Ah warned ye that somebody wis watchin' us,' I said to Alex.

'Aye, and they were fly enough tae leave it till the last minute tae rob us,' he replied, shaking his head.

'Robbin' bastards,' Rab said. 'Ah never thought we would get fleeced.'

Albert was more philosophical. 'Ach, we started wi nothin' and we ended up wi nothin'. So whit? We'll bounce back.'

Chris agreed. 'Hey, we might have nae money but we're aw millionaires in memories!'

Alex suddenly smiled, saying, 'The cash may have gone, but in the future oor adventures could be in a bestsellin' book.'

'Oh, aye, Alex?' Chris asked. 'And whit would ye call it?'

'*The Incredible Gorbals Diehards*!' Alex replied.

We all laughed, and that little star in the sky was still twinkling.

Colin MacFarlane has written for a number of national newspapers, including *Scotland on Sunday*, the *Sunday Times* and *The Sun*. He is the author of *The Real Gorbals Story* and *No Mean Glasgow*.